DATE DUE

cart			

GAYLORD 234   PRINTED IN U. S. A.

THE
ILLUSTRATED ENCYCLOPEDIA OF
MANKIND

Volume 19

Editor-in-chief
Richard Carlisle
Foreword: Professor C. von Fürer-Haimendorf
(formerly Dean of the School of Oriental and African Studies, London)

New edition edited and compiled by
Yvonne Deutch B.A. University of Exeter
M.A. University of Kansas, Lawrence, Kansas.

Consultant anthropologist: Michael Sallnow, London School of Economics
Preface: Professor Robert Canfield, University of Washington, St. Louis, Missouri.

MARSHALL CAVENDISH : NEW YORK, LONDON, TORONTO

Editorial Staff

EXECUTIVE EDITOR
Richard Carlisle

CONSULTANT ANTHROPOLOGIST
Andrew Barring

SENIOR EDITORS
Charles Fowkes
John Gaisford
Richard Widdows

ASSISTANT EDITORS
Christian Bailey
Thomas Browne
Mary Bryce
Donald Clarke
Francesca George
Stella Henvey
Maureen Lockhart
Hugh Peyman
Corine Plough
Oliver Robb
Noami Rowe
Robin Scagell
Jean Wetherburn

ART EDITORS
Sheila Buchanan
Steve Leaning
Gwyn Lewis
Barry Moscrop
Susan Williams
Jane Willis

DESIGNERS
Gillian Barlow
Angela Dunn

PICTURE EDITORS
Karin Magid
Kay McQueen

PICTURE RESEARCHERS
Antonia Gaunt
Jude Harris
Vanessa Thorpe

Revision Staff

CONSULTANT EDITOR
Michael Sallnow,
London School of Economics
EXECUTIVE EDITOR
Yvonne Deutch
DEPUTY EDITOR
Mary Lambert
EDITORIAL ADVISOR
Paul G. Davis
CONTRIBUTING EDITORS
Jeremy Coote, Wolfson College, Oxford
Jeanne de St Ouen, Sandy Carr
ART EDITOR
Pedro Pra Lopez
COVER DESIGN
Trevor Vertigan
PRODUCTION EXECUTIVE
Robert Paulley
PRODUCTION STAFF
Dennis Hovell, Steve Roberts

The publishers would particularly like to thank the
following contributors for their advice and guidance.

James Wilson (author of *Candian Indians,* Minority Rights Group)
Kenneth Duncan (Director of Oxfam for Latin America)
Dr. Steven Hugh-Jones (Kings College, Cambridge)
Dr. Peter Rivière (Institute of Social Anthropology, Oxford University)
Dr. André Singer (Disappearing World, Granada Television)
John Massey Stewart
Dr. Caroline Humphrey (Scott Polar Research Institute, Cambridge)
Professor C. von Fürer-Haimendorf (formerly Dean of the School
of Oriental and African Studies, University of London)
The late Professor Mervyn Jaspan (University of Hull)
Dr. C. R. Hallpike
Dr. David MacKnight (London School of Economics)
Dr. Jean La Fontaine (London School of Economics)
Dr. Phil Burnham (University College, London)

The Publishers wish to thank The Population Reference Bureau Inc. for
permission to reprint population data in Vol. 21 of the encyclopedia.

Reference Edition Published 1984
© Marshall Cavendish Limited
MCMLXXIV, MCMLXXV, MCMLXXVIII, MCMLXXXIV
Printed and bound in Italy
Published by Marshall Cavendish Corporation,
147 West Merrick Road,
Freeport,
Long Island,
N.Y. 11520

Distributed in India by Standard Literature

Library of Congress Cataloging in Publication Data

Main entry under title:

The Illustrated encyclopedia of mankind.

Bibliography: p
Includes index
1. Ethnology – Dictionaries 2. Man – Dictionaries.
I   Marshall Cavendish Corporation.
GN307.144   1984   306′.03′21   84-7780
ISBN 0 86307-231-3 (Set)

ISBN 0 86307 250 X (Vol 19)

Contents

Overleaf: A city graveyard
Jim Bamber

The afterlife

Throughout history we have clung to the belief that the end of our bodily life does not mean a final extinction of our consciousness and personality. The craving for another life beyond the gates of death is deeply rooted in human sentiment.

Ideas range from a hazy belief in disembodied spirits haunting the place of the living, to elaborate cosmologies of upper and underworlds where the souls of the dead find their place according to their behaviour on earth. The three-tier system of heaven, earth and hell which has dominated Christian thinking for about 2,000 years is only one of many conceived by the human spirit in the endeavour to come to terms with the indisputable fact of mortality.

It will never be known at what point we first began to believe in, or look for, a life after death. The remains of prehistoric people tell us little about our mental activities, but in many prehistoric civilisations elaborate burials indicate a provision for the needs of the departed in an afterlife. Even among the most 'primitive' of todays pre-literate peoples there is the widespread belief that a person's conscious being does not end at death, that it continues long after the body has turned to dust.

Although a belief in an afterlife may be almost universal, the attitude of the living to their departed kin is often ambivalent. On the one hand sentiments of love and reverence may persist, and the dead may become the object of a cult: offerings of food and drink may be made, and the dead are appealed to for help and support. On the other hand, the spirits of the dead may be feared, and the living make every effort to prevent their return.

At the root of the widespread belief that the departed travel to a distant land may be the wish to place a great distance between the dead and the living. The Australian Aborigines, for example, whose isolation lasted for thousands of years, believe that the souls of the deceased gather in deep caves at the borders of their tribal territories or that they travel to remote islands. The Gunai of eastern Victoria believe that the white and shining souls of the dead wander along the rays of the sinking sun to the home of the first divine ancestor.

All the different conceptions of an afterlife held by Australian Aborigines are based on the assumption that there are independent spiritual forces apart from the visible creatures of the world. Some tribes in Northern Australia believe in 'spirit-centres' inhabited since the begin-

Many people—like the ancient Egyptians—believe that the passage to the afterlife is dependent on a judgement of the soul. In this illustration from the Book of the Dead, a soul is weighed against a feather which symbolizes truth and freedom from the burden of sin.

The Buddhist concept of 'nirvana' originally meant the extinction of Self. But the finality of this doctrine led to the development of a Buddhist 'heaven'. In this painting the Bodhissattva Amitabha resides in the Western Paradise.

ning of time by spiritual beings. A child is conceived by the entry of such a spirit-being into the womb of a woman, and becomes the vital essence of the growing child. When the body dies, the spiritual essence is released and may either return to the 'spirit-centre' to await a new incarnation, or continue its life in the shape of a butterfly. Thus the frailty and impermanence of the human body is not believed to extend to the spiritual force which enlivens it.

Yet for some Australian tribes, a person's

behaviour in life plays some part in deciding their fate after death. Those who acquired merit by kindness and other acts enter a land of everlasting pleasure adorned with beautiful flowers where the dead express their joy by dancing and singing. People guilty of offences against the tribe's moral code, on the other hand, end up in a gloomy place or perish altogether. As it does among the Christian peoples, with their ideas of punishment and reward, the vision of the afterlife becomes a means of social conformity and control.

Like the Australian Aborigines, the inhabitants of the island-world of Micronesia, Polynesia and Melanesia maintain a firm belief in the afterlife. In the Micronesian cluster of Pacific islands, the people assume that the soul remains close to the corpse for a few days, but then

journeys to a distant 'Island of the Dead'.

Because the spirits of the dead abhor evil smells, the living tend to wear garlands of fragrant flowers to please the spirits of their deceased kinsmen should they return to their former homes. (The belief that the dead are sensitive to smells seems to be widespread, and the European custom of decorating graves with flowers may stem from a similar idea.)

In the traditional religion of the Polynesians, however, the conception of an afterlife was more elaborate. Spirits of common people were believed to enter a land where they led a grey and joyless shadow-life, whereas the deceased members of the nobility found their way to a paradisical, sweet-smelling island. Larger than all the islands of the Tonga group together, it was thought to possess an abundance of useful and beautiful plants bringing forth delicious fruits and fragrant blossoms which were replaced immediately they were picked.

The Island of the Dead was rich in beautiful birds and innumerable pigs. And these too were immediately replaced whenever one was slaughtered. This island, believed to lie a great distance northwest of Tonga, was considered the habitat of the gods and of all the souls of chiefs and nobles.

The notion that commoners and nobles journeyed to different realms of the dead was not connected with any idea of reward or punishment for their actions in their previous life. Their destiny was determined solely by their social rank in the world of men. The Tongans even believed that only nobles began a new and eternal life after death, whereas the spirits of ordinary mortals gradually faded and ultimately dissolved.

Widespread in much of Melanesia is the idea that the dead intervene in the affairs of the living. So is the belief that the spirits of the dead may be either benevolent or malevolent. Those who are glad to escape the cares of life think with affection of their surviving kin, and try to help in every possible way (particularly exerting an influence on the fertility of the crops). Besides these there are others which can become harmful. In order to escape their envy, surviving kin may even paint themselves white (the colour of the dead) to disguise the fact that they are still alive.

The widespread belief that the spirits of the dead may regard the living with envy is based on a pessimistic view of the Land of the Dead. Some Melanesians assume that there is nothing edible there, and that at night the dead return to the gardens they owned in life. Others believe that the Land of the Dead is similar to this world, and that the spirits cultivate gardens.

Michael Holford

Many of the tribal populations of north-eastern India and particularly the Himalayan region have a detailed image of the Land of the Dead and the tortuous path by which it is reached. This picture is derived from the visions of shamans and seers who visit the world beyond, whether through dreams or in a state of trance which releases them from all bodily ties.

The Apa Tanis, for instance, believe that the souls of all those who die a natural death go to the Neli, the place of the dead. It looks like an Apa Tani village, with the long rows of houses, and at the entrance they are questioned by a guardian spirit about the exploits of their earthly life. He asks how many enemies and wild animals they have slain, how many slaves they have bought, how much land they have owned.

As an Apa Tani lived on this earth so will he live in Neli. A rich man will be rich, a slave will serve his old master. A man will also find the cattle he sacrificed during his life-time, but those animals which have passed to his heirs are lost to him forever. Every woman returns to her first husband, but those who died ·unmarried may marry there and beget children. In Neli people cultivate and work, and ultimately they die once more and go to another Land of the Dead.

Neli is believed to be under the earth, but it is an underworld without any gloomy associations. There is another Land of the Dead situated in the sky, and all those who died an unnatural or inauspicious death go there. Men who were killed by their enemies and women who died in childbirth all go to this sky-land.

Besides the part of people that goes to a Land of the Dead, many people believe that another element remains in touch with the living, and partakes of offerings. The Konyak Nagas of Assam in India believe that when a man dies his being splits into three different spiritual entities. The first is the 'soul' (or *yaha*), to which most of the personality attaches, and which immediately sets out on a complicated journey to the Land of the Dead. The second part of the man, however, remains attached to the skull and is capable of helping his surviving kinsmen in many ways. This soul-matter is called *mio*.

When Konyaks require the magical support of the *mio*, they sacrifice a fowl near the stone-cist containing the skull of a recently deceased kinsman. They then catch the invisible soul-matter in a fishing-net, and lodge it in the house where its beneficial influence is needed. The third spiritual element, which emerges after a man meets a violent death, is called *hiba*, and can best be translated as 'ghost'.

The Nagas, like so many other peoples, firmly believe that a man's achievements on this earth affect his fate in the next world. For this reason they mark such

L. Blair

achievement by tallies placed on the grave. The Angami Nagas erect a huge stone for every enemy head he has taken, and a smaller stone for every woman he has sexually possessed.

But the idea that sexual prowess and success create merit is even more clearly pronounced among the Lushais further south. They believe that on their way to the Land of the Dead, the departed souls are shot at by the 'First Man' who guards the entrance to the underworld. Only certain men are exempt from the attacks of this guardian, and among them are men who have either possessed three virgins, or seven different women.

This idea is also widespread in South-East Asia, particularly among some of the archaic Indonesian societies. The Dayak of Borneo, for example, believe that the departed on their way to the Land of the

Paradise in many religions offers the true believer an intensification of earthly delights. This Balinese painting shows the beautiful celestial nymphs whom they believe await the souls of the dead.

Dead meet a spirit armed with a spear, who asks them whether and with whom they have made love. Those who can satisfy him about their sexual exploits are allowed to pass, but those who cannot are stabbed. Clearly virginity is regarded as a blemish, and those who have not fulfilled themselves on this earth cannot expect a fulfilled existence in the Land of the Dead.

Throughout the world, ideas about our fortunes in the afterlife are always linked with concepts of the nature of the spiritual elements in humans. The Christian

idea of a single 'immortal' soul is fundamentally different from the belief in multiple souls held by many other people.

Europeans have often misunderstood such beliefs by using the term 'soul' to describe two entirely different concepts—namely the impersonal life-substance which animates us from birth to death, and that of the dead which continues an individual existence long after the body has decomposed. The nature of these two fundamental concepts may be demonstrated by an example drawn from the Gonds, one of the largest tribal populations of India.

The Gonds share with many Middle Indian tribes the belief that a child in the mother's womb is lifeless until a life-substance or *jiv* enters the embryo. The *jiv* is sent into the child by the supreme deity who controls a pool of such life-substance. During a Gond's lifetime, however, little attention is paid to the *jiv* since it is unrelated to his consciousness or emotions. But when a Gond's life draws to its end, the supreme deity recalls the life-substance and thereby causes death.

After death, human personality lingers on in a form described in the Gond language as 'the departed'. Nearly all the rites and ceremonies of the funeral and the subsequent cult of the ancestors relate to this shade. It lingers near the corpse and follows the bier-carriers to the grave or burning-ground and hovers close by while the mourners dispose of the corpse.

While such beliefs are found among both the Hindus and tribal populations in India, the idea of reincarnation or the transmigration of souls is a specific characteristic of Hinduism and Buddhism. The Hindus of the earliest period (1200-600BC) had not yet developed the concept of reincarnation. The dead were believed to go to a heaven of eternal light, a pleasant place furnished with all the good things of life where they dwelt with Yama, the first of the mortals who found the path to the upper world, and other saintly ancestors.

There was also a belief in an underworld which—though less desirable than the celestial abode of the gods—was not thought of as a place of punishment. It is only in later Vedic scriptures that the concept of hell is found, a dark place inhabited by goblins and sorcerers, where retribution awaits murderers and other evil-doers.

It was later Hindu thinkers who developed the idea of transmigration and reincarnation. This was linked with the concept of a separable soul which could

This 16th century Persian Painting, 'The Night Flight of the Prophet', shows Mohammed's miraculous journey to paradise on his famous horse Buraq which he achieved 'in the twinkling of an eye'.

pass through an unlimited number of bodies. So people became subject to repeated birth and repeated death. A person's action in one life determined his fate after death, and the shape in which he would be reborn. The eternal cycle of birth, life and death was considered an affliction aggravated by the certainty that suffering and ageing could not be avoided.

The wish to escape from this ultimately led to the doctrine that only a conscious detachment from all earthly desires could produce a state of eternal rest. In this the individual soul lost its identity and merged with the spiritual essence of the universe.

The possibility of overcoming the attachment to earthly things and of escaping from the ordeal of rebirth also dominated the Buddhist ideology. Although its founder, the Buddha, and his immediate disciples denied the survival of a conscious personality after death, most Buddhists assume the existence of a personal 'element', shaped by their good and evil actions in their various incarnations. Such actions automatically determine the next reincarnation. There is no concept of a divine judge of the dead allocating rewards and punishments.

In Sri Lanka, the Buddhists believe a person may be reborn in human or animal shape, or even advance to a new existence as one of the celestial gods. Yet all these existences are impermanent. Even the divinities, raised to their high status by an accumulation of merit in previous lives, gradually expend this spiritual capital. And after long periods of heavenly bliss they may be reborn in lower forms of life. It is this impermanence and instability which makes Buddhists wish for an end to the chain of rebirths, and the extinction of the conscious self in the state known as Nirvana.

While both Hindus and Buddhists see the individual's life as a link in an endless chain, and both birth and death as recurring events, the people of ancient Egypt regarded death as a tragedy and made enormous efforts to alleviate its effects. No other civilization has expressed such conspicuous and lavish concern for the dead. The great tombs of the kings, furnished with all the luxuries due to a monarch, remain the most impressive monuments to our concern with the problem of death.

Innumerable inscriptions reflect the Egyptians' preoccupation with people's inevitable fate, a fate which they feared and deplored. Most descriptions of the dead in the netherworld are deeply pessimistic and the texts compare the happiness and affluence of the living with the poverty and misery of the dead. The Land of the Dead is described as oppressively dark, where the departed thirst and hunger, unable to see their parents, wives, or children. So obsessed were the Egyptians with

Many West African peoples believe that spirits can exert an influence on the living from the Land of the Dead. This mask, with its traditional white skin and slit eyes, represents a female spirit.

The medieval Christian Church emphasized that evil deeds in this life bring retribution in the next. In this detail from a stained glass window a demon carries off the soul of a woman to the torments of hell.

Michael Holford

El Greco's famous painting in the Church of St Tome in Toledo shows the death of Count Orgaz. The painter creates a powerful image showing the hierarchy of heaven and the glorious afterlife which awaits pious Christian souls.

the thought of death, that they built magnificent tombs in which kings and nobles hoped to provide for their life after death. Similarly, mummification demonstrated their desire to counteract the effects of dying as far as was humanly possible.

Only the pre-Columbian civilizations of America rival the Egyptians in their efforts to provide for their dead. In the Mexican temple town of Teotihuacan the enormous pyramids, built 1,300 years ago, match those of the Nile valley. Tombs constructed below the buildings were filled with precious burial gifts; and coloured frescos depicted a fertile para-

dise, filled with flowers and fruits, where the departed join the heavenly gods. Even more elaborate were the sepulchral chambers of the pyramids of Monte Alban in Oaxaca. Exquisite and highly realistic clay figures represented prominent dead as well as certain deities. Walls were painted with processions of divinities linked with the departed in the world beyond.

While the cosmology of the people of Teotihuacan comprised only two realms of the dead, one in the uppermost sky and one in the depths of an underworld, the Aztecs had a much more complicated image of the afterlife. They assumed the existence of thirteen upper strata, each ruled by a god, and nine underworlds, where the deceased were exposed to innumerable horrors.

To the Aztecs, the warriors and the martial sun-god assumed particular importance. Warriors who fell in battle or

Different deities, each representing a particular principle, greeted the souls of the Egyptian dead. This woman is confronted by the hippopotamus-headed goddess Taueret who assists mortals in childbirth and can help with her re-birth.

were sacrificed on their enemies' altars enjoyed a privileged fate after death. Daily they accompanied the sun as far as its position at midday, and then handed it on to women who had died in childbirth and were honoured as 'female warriors'. As soon as the dead warriors had completed their task, they floated down to earth in the shape of colourful birds and butterflies. At night and during the eclipses of the sun, the dead women who followed the sun became dangerous ghosts roaming the earth. But those who did not join the elect experienced a joyless fate in the underworld, or were turned into

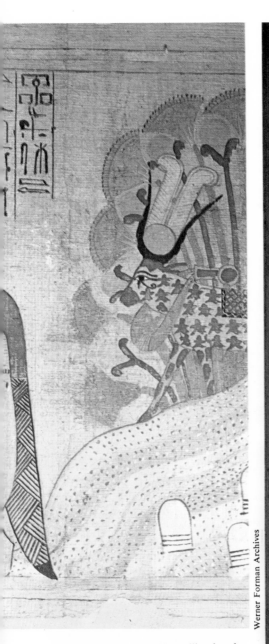

weasels, skunks and evil smelling beetles.

The Mayas of Yucatan also assumed that warriors, priest and women who died in childbirth (and also, strangely enough, people who hanged themselves) were favoured in the Land of the Dead. In the shade of a mythical tree, extending through all the celestial spheres, they enjoyed eternal pleasures while others sank into a gloomy underworld. The most sumptuous burial chamber yet discovered in the Americas lies some 24m (80ft) below the pyramid of the Mayan temple of Palenque. There the skeleton of a prince, covered in precious jade ornaments and a mask inlaid with turquoise, was found in

The Christian concept of hell which haunted the medieval imagination was never given more vivid or disturbing expression than in the nightmare creations of the Flemish painter Hieronymous Bosch.

Werner Forman Archives

Michael Holford

Andrew Baring

In much of Africa the living and the dead are mutually dependent. For the Nigerian Idoma, it means that no-one joins the ancestors until this 'mask' that speaks for them is satisfied as to the cause of death.

Mummification of the body is believed by some peoples to preserve an individual's soul after death. This Indian mummy is from the Atacoma Desert in Chile.

John Moss

a richly carved sarcophagus. The skeletons of seven men lay next to the coffin. They had been killed to provide the prince with attendants in the Land of the Dead.

The practice of sacrificing members of a ruler's household and burying them with their dead master was not confined to pre-Columbian America. It also occurred in many of the ancient oriental civilizations, and in more recent times among certain African tribes. Thus the sacred chiefs in parts of South and East Africa were buried with slaves who followed them into the realm of the dead.

Today, even where the Christian concept of a judgement and the final destiny of the soul in heaven or hell dominates official religion, there persist folk customs and tales of wandering souls and ghosts haunting their previous abodes. Although a fear of the dead may have largely dis-

appeared in the Western world, the wish to establish contact with friends and loved ones inspires many occult practices, no less than among pre-literate or archaic tribes.

The belief that the dead are not dead, and that men and women can look forward to life in a different form beyond the barrier of death still persists, and all known religions have confirmed and elaborated this sentiment in some way. Indeed the rapid spread of Christianity throughout Europe may have partly been due to the fact that Christian doctrine held out hope of eternal life. This was far more appealing than the dismal fate in the netherworld of Greek and Roman cosmology.

The Islamic concept of the afterlife, largely modelled on Jewish and Christian ideas, also promises a blissful state of unending pleasure to those who die in the

true faith. And particularly to men who perish in battle with infidels. Although an attractive prospect for Islamic men, this view of the world beyond provides scant comfort to women. Tradition and sacred scriptures are ambivalent about the chances of women entering heaven.

But in the Islamic faith there is still the clear conviction that people's virtues or sins in their earthly life determine their fate in the world beyond. One tradition tells that, at the death of a virtuous believer, angels of mercy clad in white invite the soul to rest with God, and the soul emerges with a delicious smell of musk. It is then handed on from angel to angel until it reaches the souls of the faithful gathered in the seventh heaven. The dying infidel, however, is visited by black-faced angels who violently draw out his soul and throw it upon the earth whence ultimately it is banished to hell. ☐

People and religion

In no field of activity have people expended so much time, thought, effort and even life as in the pursuit of religious goals. We have made gods out of practically everything: sticks and stones, trees and water, thunder and lightning, mountains, the sun, the moon and the stars, a wide variety of animals, and our own family and ancestors. Where our gods have been like ourselves, we have also given them every imaginable characteristic which we could fear or envy.

Our relationship with our gods has shown a similar variety: we have hated, feared, loved, worshipped, ignored, reviled, killed, resurrected imitated and pampered them. And perhaps the only thing on which students of religion are in agreement is its universal character. Saint Augustine himself remarked: 'what is now called the Christian religion, has existed among the ancients, and was not absent from the beginning of the human race, until Christ came in the flesh, from which time the true religion, which existed already, began to be called Christian.'

The study of religion, and especially the religions of other peoples, has long been a passion amongst scholars. The Greeks were certainly interested in the religions of other peoples, and Herodotus has been called the first anthropologist of religion.

But serious comparative study of other cultures and in particular their religious beliefs became widespread in Europe only during the late 17th and the 18th centuries. And much of what has been written about religion since then goes back to the lines of thought pioneered by social and religious philosophers of that period— men like Hume in England, and Montesquieu and Comte in France.

There are, however, a number of difficulties built into any attempt to find a *general* theory about religion. Not the least of these is the fact that religion itself is such an emotive subject. The majority of writers have, historically, been already committed to religion, either because of their personal feelings, or because of the intellectual and moral climate of the time. Since the end of the 17th century, on the other hand, the majority of sociological writers have been agnostic or even atheist and firmly convinced that religion, although interesting, is not 'true'.

Ancestor worship was an integral part of Chinese culture and led to the creation of art forms like this beautiful Tang ancestor figure. Ancestor worship fortified the family system and, even today in China where Communism has abolished many of the ancient traditions, one can still find forms of the ritual of ancestor worship such as incense burning and offerings of roast pig to ancestral spirits.

As a result, many have couched their theories in terms of 'How do we explain the continuance of these extraordinary ideas'? Summing this up, the historian, Edward Gibbon, remarked that: 'to the believer all religions are equally true, to the philosopher, equally false, and to the magistrate, equally useful'. Although for the magistrate's interest in keeping people in order we might now substitute the sociologist's interest in seeing how this order is maintained, this remark remains broadly true.

It is not surprising that neither the over-zealous advocates of religion, not their over-passionate opponents should have failed to produce convincing general theories. We may have greater hopes for sociologists, but they also may be inhibited by an attitude of mind which pretends to impartiality but is actually hostile to religion. If this is the case they may be like deaf people trying to understand music—studying something which always remains beyond their experience.

However, religious beliefs are sociological facts. And our task is to compare them with each other and with other sociological facts.

The 19th century was a period in which the individual was thought capable of commanding his own destiny. It was a period of rationalism in which our scientific and intellectual accomplishments were regarded as evidence of our supremacy. And consequently, in this period, theories about the origins of religion started from the standpoint of the individual—his or her thoughts, emotions, experience and attitudes.

Several writers suggested that religious beliefs were inspired by natural phenomena like the sun, the moon and the dawn, or even the great rivers or memorable floods. Max Muller, one of the most famous writers on religious matters, suggested that it was distant and untouchable things like the sun and moon which gave us our idea of 'the infinite' and provided us with symbols for it.

Gradually these symbols of the infinite became gods in their own right, and their original symbolism can be revealed by linguistic research. The Greek legend of Apollo chasing Daphne, for example, becomes comprehensible when Apollo is translated as the Sun, chasing Daphne who is the Dawn.

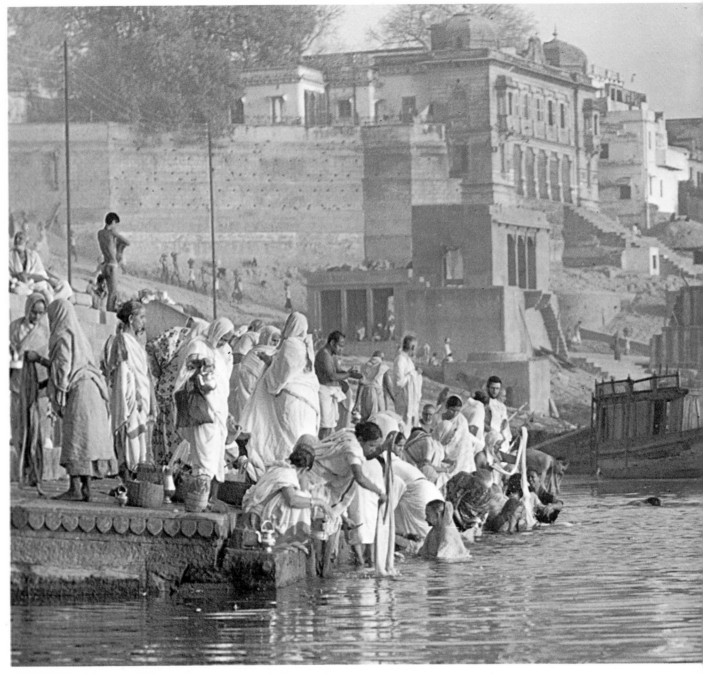

No river on earth has such religious significance as the Ganges: these pilgrims at Benares are among the many Hindus to whom it is sacred.

Heliopolis was the centre of the Sun Cult of ancient Egypt. The chief gods of other places were combined with the Sun as Egypt became politically unified. When Thebes became the capital her god, Amun, joined the Sun to become the famous Amun-Ra. The Sun was also worshipped in South Arabia; and Stonehenge in England was probably connected with Sun worship.

Similarly the way in which people contrasted parts of the body, the material against the immaterial, was suggested as the origin of the idea of a soul. Breath, for instance, was immaterial yet had a clear connection with life. And so it could be used to suggest the soul, the principle of life. Both the Egyptians and the Greeks, and even later the Arabs followed this idea.

Herbert Spencer, the 19th century social philosopher, suggested a similar origin for religion but by a mechanism of 'ghosts'. Primitive people saw the sun and the moon, the clouds and the stars perpetually coming and going. This suggested the idea of a duality of visible and invisible conditions, and thus a real and a shadow part to humans. Temporary states of insensibility like sleep furthered this idea. And with the appearance of the dead in dreams, ghosts became established as the earliest form of supernatural being. Ghosts became gods—and so, in this fashion, ancestor worship could be described as the root of every religion.

Some South American peoples still consider the 'spirit' world more important than the material one. And many peoples of West Africa think of the spirits of their ancestors as having an important effect on the lives of the living.

Other theories substituted the idea of the soul for that of a ghost. Early people's reaction to trances, death, disease, visions and dreams was regarded as leading to the idea of an immaterial entity, the soul. This could be detached from its material base, the body, and could ultimately be a separate being altogether—a god, superior to living people and controlling them.

Sir James Frazer, the famous anthro-

pologist and author of *The Golden Bough*, suggested that 'religion' was a stage between magic and science as civilization evolved. Both magic and science shared a belief in, and used, physical laws; religion was distinguished by wishing to control the material world by the intervention of spiritual beings.

Thoth, the god of wisdom, was one of many Egyptian gods subservient to Ra—the embodiment of the sun.

An unquestioning faith draws three million pilgrims to the healing shrine at Lourdes each year, and the Vatican has recognized 62 miracles since St. Bernadette's original vision.

Su Gooders/Ardea

Lloyd Phillips

Spectrum

2428

John Moss

The spirits of his ancestors and his gods are an intimate reality to this African Voodoo priest who believes he becomes a god himself during the drama of the possession ritual.

However, the idea of these three stages is not now accepted. More lasting were some of Frazer's observations which anticipated the more sociological theories of the 20th century. For example, the observation that many rulers are also magicians or priests. This was true of many ancient kingdoms of the Middle East, Bablylon, Persia and Egypt. Similar ideas are found all over Africa and a distant memory of 'Divine Kingship' may still be seen in the fact that the Queen is still head of the Church of England.

Another well-known anthropologist, the late Sir Edward Evans-Pritchard, has rightly condemned all these intellectualist theories. Not, however, because they are untrue, but because they are unprovable. Even where they are logically attractive, there is no way in which we could possibly know if they are true or not: we just do not have the historical information. Out of them all, the best idea that we can retain is that we are rational in our religion: we do things, and believe them, for reasons which it is the anthropologist's task, in part, to explain.

Explanations of religion based on concepts of the soul and ghosts have also been criticized on the grounds that these ideas were too sophisticated for prehistoric people to handle. Something more basic was required, and one suggestion was the theory of *Mana*—a stage in which religion was dominated by the idea of luck, and so by the use of spells and charms. Variations of this idea were widespread.

Others disagreed with the idea that goods developed from ghosts, and suggested that people would think it

essential to their security that the world should be designed and ordered. This necessity would lead to the idea of a creative, moral father-god. This theory is at odds with many others in suggesting that one-god (monotheistic) religions came before a diversification into many-god (polytheistic) systems.

Another theory disputed the idea that religions were 'thought out' at all. An anthropologist, Marett, suggested that they were 'danced out'. "Primitive" people's feeling that mysterious powers lay in certain people or in certain objects divided what was sacred from what was profane. The sacred sphere was characterized by feelings of fear, awe, admiration, interest, astonishment and finally love. And whatever generated these emotions was sacred and 'religious'. Magic resulted from similar feelings: and both magic and religion were seen as outlets of superfluous energy.

Yet, still other theories took an almost opposite view—regarding religion as the result of people's fear, lack of initiative, self-doubt, inexperience and ignorance—emotions particularly characteristic, it was suggested, of the "primitive". An American, R. H. Lowie, in his book on *Primitive Religion*, regarded it as a reaction to a sense of 'the Extraordinary, the Mysterious, the Weird, the Sacred and the Holy'. Religion was a matter of feelings rather than behaviour.

Once again criticisms have been levelled that such ideas are too speculative, difficult or impossible to prove—and actually say less about religion than they do about their authors. There are also many ways in which later ethnographic evidence makes them suspect. What we know about sacrifice, for example, suggests that it is less an activity to release stress in a crisis, than a routine, a precaution, and a regular duty. This was true of early Semitic sacrifices and is still true of the Christian Communion.

It was pointed out by the French sociologist, Emile Durkheim, that psychological interpretations of social facts are usually wrong—and of course religion is a social fact. Religious practices, beliefs as well as rites, are better seen as creations of society. Neither the thoughts nor the emotions of individuals are a sufficient explanation of the universality of religion, or of its varied forms. And just as the late 19th and 20th centuries saw an increased awareness of the degree to which we are all largely controlled by our social circumstances, similarly, it is in relation to societies rather than to individuals that we should seek to explain religion. ☐

'Dancing out' their religion, the Dervishes of Kurdistan attain 'oneness with God' in a state of self-induced ecstatic trance.

Victor Englebert/Transworld

Religion in society

The effects of the Industrial Revolution meant that for most Western countries the 19th century was a period when the numbers and concentration of their populations increased dramatically. One result of this unprecedented increase was a shift in the emphasis of social and political thinking. The 18th century concept of people as essentially rational beings, master of their destiny and capable of unlimited progress, gave way to a view in which the individual was far less important. The idea of the mob, the faceless power of 'society' as an irresistible force acting on its own laws, came to predominate. And this impersonal view of people saw them as being acted upon rather than acting.

It is no coincidence that the mindless idiocy of the trench warfare of the First World War should happen at the same

time as the publication of a book called 'The Instincts of the Herd in Peace and War'. Sociologists' views of religion underwent a similar change: it was no longer possible to think of it as a private business, with individuals working out their own reactions to life and its problems helped by a benovolent God. Religion became one social process among many.

But at the same time there was a growing interest in the political aspect of religion. And although Sir J. G. Frazer was not the first person to formulate the idea, he was the first to collect a vast body of evidence to prove the important link between religion and politics.

Greek writers like Plato and Aristotle well understood the inter-dependence of the political and religious 'establishments'. And the advantages in political terms of a belief that the king was also a god are so

clear that it is impossible to believe that many ancient rulers like the Pharoahs of Egypt and the god-kings of other Middle Eastern monarchies were not fully aware of them. The elaboration of ritual and mystery, adding fear and worship to a relationship of legal and social obedience, was bound to strengthen a ruler's hold over his subjects. In effect, people defer to the will of such a leader because he controls not only their social but also their

Katsina in Nigeria is one of the Hausa states still ruled by a Fulani Prince whose traditional authority derives from the Jihad, or Holy War of Uthman dan Fodio the 18th century Islamic reformer. The Emir of Katsina is both the religious and the political head of his people.

Alan Hutchinson

Ian Berry/Magnum

spiritual welfare.

The efficiency of the practice is shown in its wide distribution. The person of the king was sacred, for example, among the Polynesians—and the idea that his body could not therefore be touched has given us the word 'tabu'. When European explorers first reached parts of Africa, they found similar customs: the ruler of Bornu in Nigeria spoke to his subjects from behind a curtain; the Oba of Benin was surrounded by rituals of great complexity; and the idea that the king was too holy to speak directly to mere mortals underlay the use of 'spokesmen' at many royal courts—as, for example, among the Asanti and in Ethiopia.

But to point out that religion has political uses is only to a very small degree an 'explanation' of religion. It is true, however, that there are parallels between the type of religion in a particular society and its type of government, as the Baron de Mostesquieu (the 18th century French political philosopher) pointed out. The Englishman Robertson Smith also showed that, in particular, there was a parallel between the single-god, monotheistic religions of Asia and monarchic rulers, and he contrasted this with Classical antiquity. The Greeks and later the Romans both believed in many gods, and in both cases monarchy was superseded by other forms of government—aristocracy or oligarchy.

Yet to say that the political system explains its religious counterpart is to start on a 'chicken and egg' type of argument. There is no way of determining, historically, which came first. There are, indeed, a significant number of cases which appear to argue against the universal association of monotheism with strong central government. A number of hunting and gathering peoples, living in small bands with little connection with each other and no central government, are strongly monotheistic. The Nuer of the Sudan, whose political system is highly de-centralized, still believe in a single High God.

It might seem therefore, that the idea of seeking an explanation of religion in terms of other social institutions, is no more likely to succeed than the 'individualist' explanations. In fact the mistake lies not in the 'social' approach, but in seeking to provide only a single level of explanation: religion, like most social 'facts', is a very complex matter.

Each of the 'explanations' of religion holds some part of the truth. We have already seen that there is something to be retained from the individualist explanations of the 19th century. Even if it is hopeless to try and establish how religion originated, it has become apparent that people do act with some logic in religion as in other matters. And the emotionalist view also has something to be said for it. Religion does lessen the fear, despair and

anxiety which reduce people's capacity for action. And by increasing confidence, religion can help Man to act: it is psychologically 'useful'. This idea, combined with part of the 'political usefulness' theory, underlies much of modern sociological thinking about religion: it is valuable in that it makes for social cohesion.

Fustel de Coulanges, the 19th century historian, suggested that the centre of religion was the family, held together by an ancestor cult in which the head of the family acted as priest. The idea was not new: what was significant was that Fustel de Coulanges came to this conclusion as part of a wide-ranging study of social action—the development of social life in the ancient city.

Robertson Smith's study of the religion of the Semites also drew conclusions about religion from other social facts. He saw ancient Arabian society as consisting of matrilineal clans, each with a sacred relationship to a species of animal, the totem. God was therefore the clan itself deified, and its unity was expressed by killing and eating the totemic animal in a 'communion' ritual. Although there was actually very little evidence to support this view of religion, and it is almost certainly a misinterpretation of totemism, it is important for the influence it had on the most famous of the 'sociological' writers about religion—the French author Emile

Many oriental religions exalt the idea of detachment from this world. This Hindu holy man worships at Benares on the sacred river Ganges.

In Buddhist society the status of holy man has been institutionalized. These young novices eat their frugal meal in a monastery on the Mekong Delta.

Durkheim.

For Durkheim religion was a social, and therefore an objective, fact. Subjective views, and explanations of it in psychological terms were excluded. He pointed out many problems which other theories had overlooked or avoided: if religion is a mistake, an illusion, they why is it so universal and enduring? If its origin lies in some form of animism (the worship of nature spirits) or totemism, then why are the least significant natural objects chosen as symbols for gods as often as the most impressive? The sun and the moon might be understandable, but why wichety-grubs?

Durkheim's approach was based on several principles which are worth looking at in detail. He accepted that religion was the product of people's, therefore of individuals', minds, but he maintained that as a social phenomenon it is independent of them. Like language, religion is transmitted through generations; it is general (at least in simple or 'closed' societies); and it is obligatory in that assent to it is automatic. As a social fact, religion is bound-up with other social facts such as the law, economics and art, but it later acquires a dynamic of its own. In other words, once started, it continues to generate its own rules, and to develop and change on its own terms.

It was unfortunate that four of Durkheim's basic ideas derived from Robertson Smith, because there is actually very little evidence for them. He accepted firstly that primitive religion is essentially a clan cult, and secondly that the clan was totemic. His two conclusions were that the god was therefore the clan deified, and that totemism was the most elementary form of religion. Because totemism is found in connection with the simplest social structures, Durkheim believed it could be explained without reference to previous religions. And so, he did not believe that it was a religion in itself. However, within the very broad definition that we have used, it must be accepted as a religion. But there is no reason to accept it as 'basic' any more than the other

Stones were worshipped as gods in many early Arabian religions. After the rise of Islam, the stone of the Kaaba in Mecca was retained as a focus for pilgrims—as it had been since the time of Abraham.

Mary Fisher/Colorific!

Pete Saunders

Robert Cundy

can be no religion without a society to create it, and it is bound therefore to have a relation to the economic, political and other spheres of social action. But in saying this, what we have actually developed is not a theory about religion but about society. All social activities interact, and each sphere of action affects other spheres.

It is more satisfactory to view religion in this light than to search for its origins which are now forever lost in the distant past. We must try to find out how religion works, what it does, in society. This is not a total, nor is it the only possible 'explanation', but it is perhaps the most useful of the partial explanations.

One of Durkheim's most exciting ideas was the parallel he drew between religion and language. The similarities are remarkable, and just as views on language have developed, so we can use these to help us to understand religion. There is now widespread acceptance of the view that language itself creates mental capacity: in a crude sense, the existence of a word is a necessary precondition for the existence of the concept. In a similar way, religion has advanced far beyond nature worship, the family, political structure or simple emotive responses. As Durkheim said, it has a dynamic of its own, it creates its own rules.

Religion offers a view of the physical world, combined with a view of society in such a way that the two form a conceptual whole. It is essentially a map, a guide to human experience. As with all maps and diagrams, religions are coded: that is, they are specific to each culture. If you do not understand the particular code, the religion will mean nothing to you at all. If you do understand the code, then the religion can offer insights and may explain the whole of your experience.

It is this, of course, which makes each religion meaningful only to those people in whose society it evolved. Religions can only with difficulty be transferred from one culture to another. When they are, they are either only partly understood or they have effects which are so radical that they change or destroy the receiving culture. Each religion is thus explained best, not in relation to other religions, but in relation to the other institutions of the society of which it is part. This is the essential task of the anthropologist, and it is the main reason for the detailed study of other cultures. It is, in fact, the process by which we gain more insight into the different aspects of the world. ☐

origins we have discussed: it might be, but there is no way we can prove it.

Durkheim defined religious beliefs as collective representations, 'which express the nature of sacred things'. He called rites 'the rules of conduct which prescribe how a man should comfort himself in the presence of sacred objects', and pointed out that religion was essentially a collective, group affair: their is no religion without a church of some kind. Durkheim saw a person as possessing a body which obeys natural law, and a spirit which obeys the social imperative: 'Society establishes itself within us'. Rites which people conduct together are therefore not to be explained by their stated purpose, but their real, social functions: they draw clan members together, and renew

feelings of solidarity between society's members. They do not so much *release* as *create* higher emotional states: the psychological effects are the result, not the cause of the social events. The essence of Durkheim's theories is simple—God is society.

The idea is neat, but however elegantly it is formulated, it must be admitted that it has great weaknesses. The detailed arguments he presents in relation to totemism were based on a very limited amount of material relating to the Australian Aborigines, and it is extremely doubtful if it was sufficiently accurate or correctly interpreted. There is actually no evidence that totemism developed as Durkheim suggested.

However, one basic idea remains: there

Forms of religion

Brian Culley

Although India is the original home of Buddhism, many monasteries have been built outside to encourage the contemplative life.

All societies must have some means of organizing their beliefs about the physical world, and a method of relating social behaviour to these beliefs. This is a function of religion. And the task of the anthropologist or the sociologist is to explain, not why a society has a religion, but why its religion should take a particular form.

The world still has, despite the progress of 'westernization', an enormous number of different societies. Each of these societies needs a 'map' to symbolize and organize its 'universe', and to provide a guide as to how its members should act in relation to it. We do not expect all societies to be the same, and we should not expect their religions to be either. However, it is reasonable to ask if there are any generalizations to be made about types of religion.

The most comprehensive attempt to do this was made by a German writer, Max Weber. He took as his main area of study the five great world religions: Hinduism, Buddhism, Confucianism, Christianity and Islam, and also included Judaism as the historical ancestor of the last two. All these religions have existed for many hundreds or even thousands of years, and all have written texts which have given them continuity. But even the 'written' religions change. And it was the differences between them, as well as the changes that took place within them in the course of time, that chiefly occupied Weber.

Weber was particularly interested in the connection between religious and economic activities, and among his major achievements was his demonstration of the relationship between European capitalism and the Protestant Christianity. He realized, however, that religious belief was only one among many influences on economic activity. Economics in its turn had a similar effect on the development of religious practice. In particular he sought to show how the form of a religion was deeply influenced by the status and aspirations of a particular social class.

To prove his point, Weber contrasted situations where groups who had most influence on the evolution of a religion

੧੦੦੦ ਗੁਰੂ ਮਹਾਰਾਜ ਜੀ ਨੇ ਅਪਾਰ ਕ੍ਰਿਪਾ ਕਰਕੇ ਇਹ ਸੇਵਾ ਅਵਤਾਰ ਸਿੰਘ ਰੰਗ -
ਵਾਲਾ ਪੁੱਤਰ ਸ੍ਰ ਗਵਾਨ ਸਿੰਘ ਅੰਮ੍ਰਿਤਸਰ ਨਿਵਾਸੀ ਪਾਸੋਂ ਕਰਵਾਈ ਅਗਸਤ ੧੯੬੯

Dennis McGilvray

John Moss

St. George's victory over the serpent symbolizes the Christian Church Militant's victory over the forces of evil and makes him an ideal symbol of national identity.

templation offered them entrance into the profound and blissful tranquility of the All-One.' He singled out three groups of people within this general category of 'genteel intellectuals', and showed the influence they had on three of the religions with which he was particularly concerned: Confucianism, Hinduism and Buddhism.

Confucianism he saw as the status ethic of paid officials who had achieved their status as a result of education. Their cultured, literary background gave them an overall rational and secular outlook which deeply influenced Chinese society, and spread well beyond the confines of their own 'class'.

In the earliest period of Hinduism a 'hereditary caste of cultured literati' was the group most crucial to the development of the religion. They functioned as ritual and spiritual specialists whose duty was to give advice to both communities and individuals. Although they did not hold controlling offices themselves, they were the focus of status differentiation and the social order was arranged in relation to them. Initially only high-caste Brahmans held this desirable status, and it was only later that other groups began to compete. The lower strata of society were then able to share in their 'holiness' through the influence of lower-status preachers.

Among the Buddhists, it was the monk who possessed nothing and who travelled from place to place, rejecting all ties to home and the structured world of normal mankind: the monks alone could achieve the detachment essential to Buddhism. The rest of mankind remained forever at a disadvantage.

All three of these classes were detached from immediate worldly pursuits, and this is clearly both a cause and an effect of the 'contemplative' quality of the religions.

The situation was very different in the case of societies where the class which most influenced the development of religious ideas, was also concerned with other spheres of social activity.

Islam, for example, was initially the religion of a group of warriors, intent upon conquering the world: an aim in which they achieved considerable success. They were a body of men to whom discipline was essential for military as well as for religious reasons. Such men were not prone to thinking too greatly about other worlds and other states of being. Their religion is detailed in relation to this life, and sees the afterlife as a glorified version of it.

Christianity, however, has shown the greatest amount of change in the course

(Left) Jerusalem has been successively a centre of faith for Jews, Christians, and Moslems. The Wailing Wall is the last remnant of the Great Temple of King Solomon.

were either 'active' or 'inactive' in practical life. Where 'religions and religious ethics . . . have been quite strongly determined by genteel strata of intellectuals as was the case with Asiatic and above all, with Indian world religions . . . contemplation became the supreme and ultimate religious value accessible to Man. Con-

(Far Left) The Golden Temple at Amritsar is the sanctuary of the Sikh faith, a religion which has formed an ethnic group of distinct cultural heritage and national sentiment.

The origins of Islam, the religion of a nomadic warrior people who successfully conquered all of the Middle East and North Africa, accounts for its militaristic ethos.

of time. It started as the religion of a group of wandering craftsmen—carpenters and fishermen—but it became something very different. As long as the people to whom it was of interest remained at this social level, it remained a rather simple faith with a tendency to turn away from this world and the success in it which its members knew they could not command: 'Blessed are the poor . . . the meek . . . the humble'. But once its membership had spread beyond this class it changed dramatically: the Popes at the time of the Italian Renaissance were neither poor nor weak, and the periods of greatest change and development have

always been urban. It is in relation to a class of economically *active*, urban citizens that we must study its later forms, and in particular Protestantism.

It is also noticeable in the development of Christianity that the different objectives of particular dominant groups have given it a different emphasis at various times. The politically powerful have preferred to use religion as a means of social control, and bureaucracy has led to ritualism in religion. Military achievement, on the other hand, is reflected in religions of struggle and war: the Church Militant of the Crusades and Victorian England. Peasants, within Christianity as well as outside it, have been more inclined to magic, the mechanical control of the processes of nature with which they are in such close contact. This is why, for example, Roman Catholic missionaries from a peasant background in Ireland

have generally been more sympathetic to the religions they found in West Africa than the urbanities from the English Protestant Churches.

Weber's ideas are not totally accepted today. It is also, of course, much easier to make generalizations about religion in a situation where the society in question is 'closed', and where there are few choices available to the individual. This has ceased to be the case with the majority of Western societies and a different set of considerations must be employed.

In the West today, no religion, and no form of any one religion, has a monopoly. In fact any number of alternatives is available, and any organized body seeking to propagate its own brand of belief must compete in what has been described as a 'market' situation. Ironically this is why recent research into the sociology of religion has been largely undertaken with

the patronage of existing Churches. In America, particularly, many Churches have access to considerable funds sustained by tax-relief donations as well as hopes for celestial credit: it makes sense to use part of them for market research.

As the economico-political machine of Western (and particularly American) capitalism has become more 'monolithic', acquiring greater and greater power over people's lives, it has produced corresponding effects in the intellectual and religious spheres. It has led its adherents to try and intensify 'loyalty' to the system and repress dissent; but the intensification of efforts by the organized churches to recruit members also reflects this process. The activity of any pressure group, or the intensification of effort in any one social direction, is bound to produce a reaction in an 'open' or diversified society.

In America, recent years have seen a marked intensification of dissent, just as the success of the mainstream establishment of Victorian England produced a similar crop of 'non-conformist' opinions. But the process is a complex one, and it is misleading to think of it as proceeding in one direction only: dissent itself acquires 'establishment' values and at times becomes a new kind of conformity, the badge of the intellectual.

This is the situation of religion in the Western world today. No one church is any longer accepted by all, and even where Christianity is still accepted by many, as it is in America, its forms are varied and no single one has the smallest monopoly. The capacity, therefore, of religion to offer the sort of map and guide that it once did, is reduced. In the search for new maps, new religions are offered. Some of these masquerade as science—sociology is a clear example. It pretends to provide facts when it is only providing opinions and beliefs. Only in so far as its facts are generally accepted, do they become 'collective representations' and thus social facts. But such general acceptance is a long way off.

Political creeds like Communism and extreme Republicanism are also 'maps' in this sense. Smoking 'pot' and dropping-out are also, in a perverse manner, attempts to control a world which has become almost too complex for any map. It is the absence of real success on the part of any of the new map-makers which accounts for the alienation which so many people feel today—an absence of purpose, and an absence of hope.

Many attempts to explain the reasons for this situation have been made. Those who are attached already to a particular faith or a particular church, naturally explain it in their own terms: as a going away from God, for example, such as was so often the cry of the Old Testament Prophets. Many, as did the primitive Christians, attribute it to an insufficiency of love.

Whatever the answer, it is a situation which we have to face. We have devoted a lot of time and thought over the last 500 years to 'opening' our society. We have succeeded in that we no longer live in the closed world of our own past: our choices are freer, our opportunities greater, the variety of our lives considerable, constraints are fewer and the alternatives innumerable. If we are pleased with these results it is inconsistent to complain at the same time that we do not know where we are, what to do or how to behave. It is in the nature of religions, as of all maps, that they constrain as well as guide: they offer psychological help, but at the expense of discipline. We cannot refuse the discipline and still expect the comfort.

In one way the dilemma becomes particularly clear. We have seen that there is a connection between the form of a religion and the type of person who developed it. We have aimed at, and partly achieved, democratic societies in which no class is dominant. In such a situation the beliefs of no one group will predominate and no form of religion will achieve general acceptance. Nor is it possible that we can again achieve the classless consensus of belief characteristic of very small-scale homogeneous societies, like bands of hunters and gatherers. Our society has already become too large-scale, too complex and too diversified. The only way consensus can be achieved would seem to be by dictatorship: the re-creation of a dominant class like the Communist Party apparatus. And even that seems to be only partially successful.

The choice is finally up to the individual. Anyone to whom an organized religion, its comfort and its control, is necessary, must join a 'church' of some kind. They will thereby accept a particular set of views and beliefs, and will be sustained in them by the community and by its rituals: they will have a map. For the rest, a partial acceptance of several maps may lead to an eventual synthesis. Until it does individuals will have to make a choice of maps to guide them in each situation: it is bound to lead to conflict in standards of behaviour, of morality, of aim in life and indeed to disagreement in every sphere of social activity. Competition may thus be good for the society, but it may also tear it apart. It may have advanced the West, but it may yet destroy it. Many take pride in living in a 'post-religious' age: we may yet change our minds. □

The world view of a religion dominated by 'genteel intellectuals' is likely to be detached from mundane considerations. This devotee of Vishnu follows the Brahman ideal of study and contemplation.

Andrew Baring

Dennis McGilvray

Gods of the earth and sky

If a male Martian visitor found himself in central London on Armistice Sunday, he would probably view with interest the large crowds of people converging on Whitehall. Skimming silently over their heads, he would observe the considerable interest they all showed in him, many shading their eyes as they looked, while others cast themselves on the ground with gestures of awe and fear. He might well conclude from this that they thought him

The Hindu god Vishnu appears in different forms or avatars. As a fish he warned of a Flood, and when the earth was captured by demons, he tracked it, as a boar, by sense of smell.

a god. Unable to bear the brightness of the vision they covered their eyes, in fear and adoration they prostrated themselves before him. Many sought to hide from his possible anger in doorways, perhaps thinking that his presence presaged the end of their world.

If, however, our Martian visitor followed the crowd down Whitehall and stayed passed midday, he would see that he was mistaken. Obviously their real god, or at least their most important one, was a large rectangular column of white stone in the middle of the road. Around this column assembled the most important people, priests and soldiers. A female leader of this society led her people in worship. And if our Martian understood

a little English he would hear the Cenotaph (for that is its name) addressed as Our Lord. He would hear the people ask for mercy on behalf of the dead, particularly the (holy) dead who died in war.

At other stone buildings where crowds were also assembled, he would see the leaders of each crowd offered similar words to smaller stones rather like tables, on which rested metal objects. Everywhere he would see that people wore a particular red flower. And his interpretation of what he saw might reasonably run as follows: this particular tribe of Earthmen had a big annual ceremony attended by almost everyone in honour of a High God called Cenotaph, whose sacred flower was the poppy. There were also a number of lesser

Michael Holford

stone or metal gods who each had a smaller number of followers. These were, local spirits, or 'children' of Cenotaph.

This account of the events of Remembrance Sunday is so inaccurate that it would be considered insulting if it could be taken seriously. And yet the actual 'method' by which our hypothetical Martian 'studied' this particular religious ceremony is very similar to methods which have been applied to religions of other times and other peoples.

Our Martian was inhibited by his lack of knowledge of English, and the little time he was able to spend on his study. But many travellers who have written about religions in various parts of the world have suffered just such limitations. Where studies have been made of ancient religions, limitations of textual material, or its total absence, have imposed a similar limit on understanding—there are still many archaeological studies which describe material objects as gods merely because they appear to have been placed in 'worshipping' positions. Inevitably the results have been odd, and people reading these descriptions have been prepared to believe that men from other places and other times have worshipped the most bizarre of objects. But they are easily offended if similarly misinformed suggestions are made about their own religious practices.

Even within Christianity, disagreements based on this sort of misinterpretation have been common. The Iconoclasts of the early Greek church thought that people had gone too far in substituting images of the divine for the Divine itself. For example, pictures of the Virgin Mary, originally intended as reminders to recall her person (or events connected with Our Lord) to the minds of the faithful, began to be taken by the ignorant as holy in themselves.

Russian peasants, whom we are told were emotional and prone to mysticism, used to see in particular icons such holiness as to demand virtual worship. Their holiness and healing power, or perhaps their power over enemies, were sufficient to attract worship for themselves. And so icons became Gods. It was to prevent this 'pagan' atavism that the Iconoclasts rushed about destroying such images, casting down statues, burning icons and painting out the murals in Churches with whitewash. At times, English Puritans have thought the same, accusing the Catholics and even the High Church of England of actually worshipping 'Graven Images' in direct disobedience of the Ten Commandments.

It is important to bear this in mind when reading accounts of other forms of worship. And while we briefly examine those objects which have been called gods, it may be as well to put aside any definition (particularly when derived from our own

beliefs) of what constitutes a god or what makes worship. For the time being we will include anything towards which human societies have shown any special reverence, directed particular forms of behaviour, or to which they have attributed natures or powers of an abnormal kind—particularly those objects which societies have seen as vehicles for the power which controls the world and the destinies of the people who inhabit it.

The first class of such gods must, by virtue of numbers, be animals. Almost every animal one can think of has apparently been deified—from obvious ones like bulls, cows and lions, to the least significant like the wichety grubs deified by some Australian Aborigines, or the dung-beetle, the *Scarab* of the Ancient Egyptians.

Bulls, cows and oxen are the most

The Maori of New Zealand represent gods, spirits and heroes in carvings. The marks of tattooing, which the Maori, like many Polynesians, applied to their own bodies and faces, are a sign of maturity.

common choice. *Abudad* was the sacred bull of the ancient Persians, and *Osiris* of the Egyptians was also often represented as a bull. In Egypt also (as well as in Greece and Syria where Egyptian beliefs spread) the cow was worshipped as *Isis* and as *Hathor*, whom we shall also encounter as the moon. Many other gods had a bovine form: for example, *Audhumbla* (the cosmogenic earth) of the Scandinavian Edda-literature, *Moloch* of the Ammonites and the Phoenicians, *Brahma*, the Hindu creator, the *Minotaur* of Crete.

The Romans had a goddess, *Bubona*,

Bury Peerless

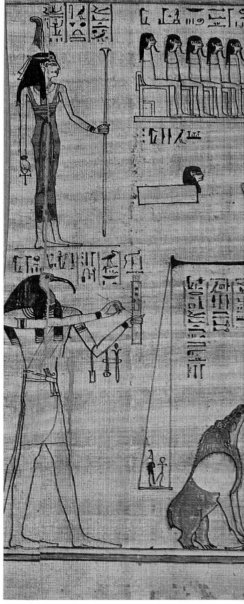

(Above) This statue from Chitor in India is of Ganesh, the son of Shiva and Parvati. He is the god of prudence and wisdom.

(Right) The Egyptian goddess Tauret is represented as a pregnant hippopotamus. She is the goddess of childbirth, suckling and maternity.

who protected cows, and both the Gauls and the Israelites worshipped bronze calves or bulls. In Sicily *Hebon* had a bull's body, and in Greece and Rome *Juno* was sometimes represented with cow's eyes. *Taurus* the bull is the second sign of the zodiac, *Shiva* of the Hindu triad rides on and sometimes appears as a bull, and at Miaco in Japan there is a bull shrine. Bulls' horns were a symbol of divine power in Judaea, Persia and China; and similarly the bull has been used to represent the creative powers of the earth the sun and the moon.

This random list could be prolonged indefinitely, but enough has been said to prove the point: cows and bulls are often sacred, and not only to the Hindus. The

obvious usefulness of the animal only explains its wide distribution and thus its availability as a symbol of divinity: it does not really explain why it should be chosen in preference to other possible symbols. This can only be discovered by detailed analysis of the actual role played by the animal in the thoughts and rituals of each people.

Only by comparing beliefs associated with cattle with other social and economic facts can each case be satisfactorily explained. Where this has been done among the Dinka and the Nuer of the Southern Sudan, the lesson is clearly that the animals are not worshipped in any real sense at all—at least, certainly not for themselves.

Michael Holford

Michael Holford

Dr. Dennis McGilvray

(Left) Bulls and cows are the animals most commonly associated with gods. This image from Mysore in India is of Nandi, on whom rode the Hindu god Shiva, the Lord and Master.

(Above) The Egyptian god Horus, with the head of a falcon, presents Anhai for judgement. Her heart is weighed against truth and if unsuccessful she will be cast to the Amemait and devoured.

The lion has occasionally been deified, but not as frequently as cattle. It is well known as the symbol of the tribes of Judah and, following this, of the Ethiopian throne. It was also used in sacred images by the Persians and the Assyrians; by the Egyptians as a symbol of the Sun God, *Ra*, on the Lion Gate at Mycaenae, perhaps with sacred connotations; and by the Greeks to whom the animal was sacred to the Goddess *Rhea*. The late Shah of Persia gave the Order of the Lion, and many African Chiefs treat the lion as a symbol of royal power. One of the most attractive forms of a lion-god is *Apademak* of ancient Meroe

in the Sudan, whose images can still be seen in the desert north of Khartoum.

Dogs are among the many other animals used in sacred contexts—in Egypt and Greece, and among North American Indians like the Chippewyan group. Some Eskimos believed the dog was the father of the human family. The Japanese revered the Dog Constellation because of its astrological connection with royalty, and the Spartans sacrificed dogs to Enyalius.

Elephants have also been sacred—the Hindu *Ganesh*, for example, and in Siam where they were part of the Royal Regalia. So too have wolves—Scandinavian myth-

The totemic cults of pre-Inca Peru persisted after the Inca Sun Cult had become predominant. The puma continued to be represented, often in gold ornaments, like this with a human face on the tongue.

ology tells of *Skoll* pursuing the sun, and *Hati* the moon; and the male and female Roman gods *Lupercus* and *Luperca* took the form of wolves. Monkeys were sometimes sacred in Egypt, Japan, Africa, Babylon and India; leopards, particularly in Africa; bears, among the Ainu of Japan, several northern Siberian peoples, and among the Dakota Indians and the Finns. Crocodiles were sacred in ancient Egypt and Africa; flies were sacred to *Baal-zebub* who was, perhaps, a god of the dead.

The list is endless and includes bees and butterflies, rams and sheep, goats and foxes, fish, asses, cats, tigers, hares and rabbits, shrew mice (sacred to *Buto* in Ancient Egypt) sharks, dragons (in the west as well as in China), boars, deer, and a wide variety of reptiles, usually snakes, which are sometimes good but often bad. Nor is any generalization possible about the animals' usefulness, colour, edibility, importance to the economy, danger strength or even 'usefulness to think with'.

Similarly with birds: the most common is the eagle or other birds of prey. He was *Horus* to the Egyptians, sacred to *Jupiter* among the Romans, and to *Ashur* among the Assyrians. The Dayaks of Borneo treat *Antang* as the heavenly appearance of a popular hero. The Aztecs' supreme god was represented by an eagle, and the condor also represents a Peruvian god. The Scandinavian god *Odin* is represented as an eagle sitting in the top of a sacred tree. Other birds have also had sacred roles; sparrows, swans, swallows, doves, owls, parrots, vultures, cuckoos, wild ducks, ravens and even a quail. Storks were sacred in Egypt and still are in parts of Africa.

Natural objects, like the sun and the moon, belong to the next most popular category of sacred images. It used to be said that the awe inspired by these heavenly bodies, along with the fear of associated phenomena like thunder and lightning, were the emotions which first led us to think in supernatural terms. Although this is unlikely to be true, there is no doubt that they were important in the evolution of religion. The most popular image is some form of personalization of the earth, but the sun and the moon run a close second. The stars and the sky have also been used to represent gods—as have the seasons and time, fire, volcanoes and earthquakes, mountains (sometimes connected with volcanos, sometimes merely as high and therefore nearer to a heavenly god), rivers (like the Ganges

Michael Holford

Dr. Dennis McGilvray

Snakes feature in the religions of many peoples, sometimes evil and sometimes good as in many creation myths in Africa and India. The sacred Nagas are propitiated all over southern India.

Andrew Baring

Lions sometimes represent the Sun-God, as in ancient Persia and Egypt. At Meroe in the Sudan the Sun was the principal god, and the lion-god, Apademak, was worshipped at Wad ben Naga.

which is holy to the Hindus), water and the sea, winds, stones, rainbows, the night and the dawn.

Trees are also very often used in religious contexts. The very extensive variety of tree-types, and their distribution throughout the world, make them a useful image. Sometimes they appear to have been worshipped for themselves; but they frequently serve as symbols of other gods, as altars, as churches, and they often house gods or spirits. They provide wood for sacred and sacrificial fires, and gum for incense.

Although the oak is the most popular, others include the ivy, the laurel, the olive, the fir, the linden, the ash, the bo-tree (under which Buddha sat), the bamboo, and the persea of Ancient Egyptian Heliopolis, which like many Indonesian trees was a symbol of the whole universe, an earthly proxy of the tree of heaven.

Abstract qualities also have been deified —justice and law, peace and war, happiness and luck, truth, love and things like dreams and visions. The body, particularly the phallus and the vagina, have attracted worshippers in many parts of

the world: the sacred lingam of India and the huge stone phalluses of Southern Ethiopia are as well known as the Egyptian god *Min* (represented with an erect penis) and the Roman *Priapus*. Breath, representing life and the soul, has sacred connotations, and even speech has been deified, as by the Roman god Fabulinus. Among other things Mercury was the god of eloquence.

Finally, we may mention a variety of man-made objects, which have either been deified, or dedicated to gods, or had gods dedicated to them or their protection. Houses are commonly seen in this context, as are money and iron, and occasionally wine and honey. Arks used to carry sacred scriptures, as well as the scriptures themselves, may also be regarded as holy— among the ancient Israelites, for example, an unauthorized person touching the Ark of the Covenant was struck dead.

With this immense variety of things which people have worshipped or to which they have attached sacred associations, is any generalization possible? About the objects chosen, the answer is probably no. There are too many, treated in too many ways, attracting too many beliefs, generating too many different relationships, for any really meaningful explanation to be offered as to why they are chosen.

Some generalization does seem possible, however, as to how these things function. There will always be exceptions, of course, but to consider all these objects as 'gods' is too simple. Most should not be regarded as gods at all. They are more often symbols of other gods than they are worshipped for themselves. Just as with images of the virgin, the ignorant may transfer attitudes of fear and love from the god to its representation but this does not mean that the object can be explained as a god. It is only understandable if the original belief and the matrix of beliefs of which it forms a part is also understood.

Once again we return to the prescription that understanding comes more from comparing institutions and beliefs within one culture than between them. In general it seems that these objects have been chosen as representatives of qualities, not as sacred in themselves. The qualities are various, and although strength, fertility, power, goodness, beauty and

Ronan Picture Library

Malcolm Kirk

In the Comore Islands off the coast of East Africa, the lake in the centre of one island contained sacred ducks to which the people gave sacrifices of food, and prayed for assistance and protection.

This yam has been decorated to represent a woman by the Abelam of New Guinea. They depend on the yam for their subsistence, and the fertility and strength of the community is reflected in the yam-cult rituals.

creativity are frequent components, it serves no real purpose to try to pin down one of them or one group as more basic than others. It is more important to recognize that they are all human qualities.

These emotions, capacities, talents and forces are qualities of which we are aware by being aware of ourselves. They are extrapolations or extensions of the only thing of which we are intimately aware—our own nature. It is therefore not surprising that our gods should have most frequently taken a human form. Nor is it difficult to see why the objects which we choose as symbolically valuable, even if they do not take human form, actually represent human qualities.

Religion provides us with a guide to the universe, the world, society and to ourselves. It lays down what is morally and ethically desirable, and it buttresses the whole with stories and beliefs as to how everything came to be and how it is maintained. The technique common to all religions is to do this by personalizing everything.

Because Westerners no longer believe in a personal universe, but in a system of impersonal, scientific 'laws', to such explanations as religions have given no longer attract us. It is difficult to worship the atom or electricity. □

Family gods

It is difficult for people brought up in a modern and largely secular society to realize how large a part religion has played in all historical societies and the importance it still has in many today.

This becomes easier to understand when we consider that in societies less complex and less differentiated than those of the West, magic and religion include what are for us quite separate realms of thought and activity: philosophy, cosmology, medicine, natural science, ideas of causation, ethics and the means of controlling the visible and invisible environment. All these form part of what anthropologists call the magico-religious or ritual life of a people.

It is convenient to distinguish between magic and religion. Both deal with, and try to influence, what are regarded as invisible, but powerful, forces in the universe. But, in general, religion tends to think of such forces as a 'thou'—to be addressed in prayer and perhaps propitiated by offerings. Magic, on the other hand, sees them as an 'it' to be manipulated and compelled by rites and spells. In theory, the difference is easy enough to understand; in practice, it can be very difficult to distinguish a spell from a prayer.

Let us take it, however, that religion presupposes one or more forces addressed as 'thou' by a congregation of worshippers, who thus enter into a kind of social relationship with them. The relationship is usually an unequal one: the congregation—or the priest or priests acting on their behalf—address the deity humbly, with praise and supplications, and make offerings of whatever that particular divinity is supposed to like best: food, flowers, human hair, or sometimes blood sacrifices. Yet the relationship is not one-sided. In return for offerings, the congregation expect the divinity to shower down blessings—or at any rate to withhold curses. And in some sense the divinity is in turn dependent on the worship received: many peoples believe that the existence of the gods is quite literally sustained by offerings. Sociologically, this is true.

The Toradja bury their dead in caves in limestone cliffs. Their wooden effigies, tau-tau, look down on the living who believe them to have both good and evil powers.

Divinities come in various orders of magnitude, from the great universal God of the world religions to the intensely localized deity inhabiting a particular rock or tree, or the dead and deified father of a particular group of brothers. On one level, religion mirrors society; and the size of a divinity is usually in proportion to that of the congregation worshipping it.

The potential congregation may well be larger than the actual one, as in the case of the Supreme Deities of Christianity and Islam, each conceived by his worshippers as the God of all mankind. Peoples more hemmed in by geography tend to be less inclined to convert others: their gods are entirely their own and foreigners are naturally expected to have different gods. But whatever the size of the congregation, the divinity worshipped will tend to reflect whatever holds that congregation together: common interests and common ideals.

The small congregation worshipping a small god may simply be one of near neighbours. In such cases the god will probably be thought of as inhabiting some prominent geographical feature, which also functions as his, or her, shrine. Alternatively the congregation may be recruited by descent: people who are all related to each other, either in the male or in the female line. In this case the divinity will be the deified ancestor of the group.

The two-way relationship between divinity and priest or congregation is easiest to understand in the case of ancestor worship. The most important ancestor for religious purposes is usually the most recently dead: it is through him that more remote ancestors are approached. The priest is often his eldest surviving son, who is also his heir and successor in authority. Such an ancestor is, in a sense, still very much a part of the family: he can easily be supposed to take an interest in his children's and grandchildren's welfare, to protect them against harm, to want them to be on friendly terms with each other and to punish them for any breach of custom or morals.

Being so recently dead, this ancestor is supposed to require food and drink, and thus to be genuinely dependent on offerings. The Manus fisher people of the Admiralty Islands in the Pacific will only worship a dead father, never a dead grandfather. They say that a father deserves to become anonymous and dishonoured when he fails to protect his own son from death. And so when a man dies, he may become a *Moen Palit*, a 'Sir Ghost' or honoured ancestor; but the father whom he himself worshipped as 'Sir Ghost' is cast out to become a mere *palit*—an undifferentiated ghost of the middle seas, destined for oblivion.

Robert Harding Associates

The Manus case is exceptional only in its stark simplicity, in the promptness of the ritual response to the replacement of one generation by another. More usually, the most recently dead ancestor (even if it is he who receives most of the attention) is thought of as a link with his own father and grandfather, and so on back into time. But 'back into time' does imply a loss of distinction. Among peoples who have no writing, it is a very exceptional ancestor who is remembered for more than a generation or two.

The Chinese developed an ancestor cult more elaborate than any other in the world. Tombs were equipped with pottery figures representing the guards and entertainers whose services the ancestors would require in the afterlife.

This man from the Sepik River area of New Guinea holds a figure representing the spirit of an ancestor whose continuing good-will is sought by his descendants.

Even where written records exist, it is clearly not possible to overburden a purely domestic shrine with too many generations of honoured forebears. Thus in the sophisticated society of traditional China, where the ancestors were enshrined in inscribed wooden tablets, the tablets were removed after the third (or sometimes the fifth) generation to ancestral temples some distance away. There, they still received invocations and offerings, but more formally at festivals twice a year. The temples naturally served several family households whose common ancestors they enshrined. They thus became rallying points for lineages of varying size, whose male members met there at the festivals. Sometimes an impoverished member of the lineage acted as the temple priest.

The Manus example is particularly interesting in the distinction they make between 'Sir Ghosts' and ordinary homeless ghosts. A 'Sir Ghost' is a recently dead ancestor whose skull hangs in a place of honour, in a carved wooden bowl in the house-front rafters. It is frequently and respectfully addressed by the householder who is his son and regarded as the moral and material guardian of the home. A mere ghost, by contrast, is nameless, forgotten, disregarded, homeless, 'washed by all rains, burned by all suns'. At first it haunts the edges of the island, later the open sea and finally it dwindles into a sea-slug.

Most people who practise ancestor worship make similar distinctions. The Romans differentiated between *lares*, regularly worshipped ancestors acting as protective household deities, and *larvae*, sad and spiteful wandering ghosts who revenged themselves on mankind for its neglect by causing illness and other

misfortune. To turn a hostile *larva* into a beneficient spirit, the Romans only thought a resumption of offerings by descendants was needed—for the happiness of the soul after death depended entirely on such offerings.

Roman *larvae* seem to have been more malignant than the poor outcast ghosts of the Admiralty Islands; but the basic distinction—between the socially recognized, responsible ancestor and the nameless unincorporated ghost—is exactly the same. Not everyone who dies can become an ancestor, let alone remain one.

Who, then, is an ancestor? In life he or she need not have been a good, wise or brave person: ancestorhood is conferred indiscriminately on the just and the unjust. All acquire the same stern, though potentially benevolent, personality. But the essential condition for ancestorhood is to have the right descendants—usually at least one son—who can perform the right funerary ceremonies and make appropriate offerings thereafter. This is one reason why it is considered so important to have sons in the non-Western world: nobody, understandably, wants to become a nameless ghost.

In matrilineal societies the 'right descendant' is commonly a man's sister's son rather than his own. But the principle is the same: a man's successor and heir is expected to perform the rites that transform him into an ancestor. A daughter cannot perform such rites.

By the same token, although a dead mother may well be honoured, female ancestors are in general less important. But in exceptional circumstances a daughter's son, a daughter's husband or even sometimes an unrelated male may take a son's place. At best, however, this is regarded as a third-rate expedient.

In any case the general rule still holds: The care of the sacrifices shall always devolve upon the one who receives the inheritance. A man who dies childless will leave all he owns to the man who undertakes his funerary rites.

The importance of such rites is obvious. For one thing, they transform what was potentially a spiteful wandering ghost into an honoured ancestor—one who may still send misfortune, but is trusted to do so in a responsible way. The Edo of Benin in West Africa speak of funerary rites as 'planting' an ancestor. In many societies such 'planting' takes a long time and may involve a good deal of expense. It is not merely a question of ceremonial burial, accompanied by music and perhaps feasting.

Often, one or more shrines have to be set up in the dead man's former home or elsewhere. Here communication with the new ancestor can be established; and there may be processions, funerary effigies and further music and feasting. Because of the expense, the final rites may not be completed for several years. In Africa these final rites are sometimes spoken of as 'second burial'. The Chinese, however, traditionally practised a literal second burial. In this the bones of the deceased, placed in an urn, were consigned to a site carefully chosen by divination. This was intended to offer the dead, by its topographical features, the maximum of ease and well-being, thus ensuring the welfare of their descendants.

Not until all these rites are completed is the dead man fully established as an ancestor. At the same time the man responsible for the rites becomes his full successor and the priest of his cult. The 'planting' of the father as ancestor and the attainment by his son of full status as a senior person, in charge of a potentially powerful shrine, are in fact aspects of a single indivisible process. A two-way relationship is established between the recently dead and the representative of what is now the senior living generation. The newly enshrined ancestor represents all the ancestors, stretching back into time; his son, successor and priest stands for all the living descendants who implore the ancestors' protection.

Naturally, the lineage priest's position can be one of great power—especially where, as among most African ancestor-worshippers, ancestors have the power to curse as well as to bless. African ancestors are often more aggressive and

Malcolm Kirk

Andrew Baring

Many West Africans believe that the spirits of ancestors can cause illness if their descendants neglect the proper sacrifices. At the shrine at Upu in Nigeria sacrifices are made regularly and particularly when there is any reason to think that the spirits are feeling neglected.

Agence Hoa-Qui

This haunting mask, carved by the Dan people of the Ivory Coast, is used in the traditional rituals of their ancestor cult. The Dan are famous for their carved masks, decorated with plumes and shells.

Among the Idoma in Nigeria a funeral can only take place when the body has been purified. Evil is 'captured' in these small vessels which are thrown away in the uninhabited forest.

Andrew Baring

demanding than Roman or Chinese ancestors, and most misfortunes are attributed to their anger. That anger may be caused by neglect, insufficient offerings, or by breaches of either general social morality or what is sometimes called kinship morality: disobedience to elders, or quarrelling among members of the group.

The significant fact is that it is the lineage priest who determines what has caused ancestral anger. Not surprisingly, it is often a disregard for what he considers his own legitimate authority. This means he will jealously guard his privilege of serving the shrine and speaking for the dead. It also means that others, especially his disgruntled younger brothers, will try by devious means to take it from him.

Among the Lugbara of Uganda, elders assert their authority by claiming the power to curse—that is, to invoke ancestral power against the disobedient.

Therefore when misfortune strikes the tribe a curious situation arises: ambitious men vie with one another in claiming responsibility for successfully invoking the ancestors. A successful claim means an established right to speak for the ancestors independently, and usually leads to the founding of a new lineage. In this case ancestor worship is clearly a means through which conflicts and shifts of power are given expression.

It is clear also that ancestor worship generally follows the established lines of descent in any society, whether through men or through women. Properly 'planted' ancestors are, by definition, those who have provided links in a genealogy; the expense of 'planting' may also, in more stratified societies, confine them to the upper strata. Thus, not all Chinese ancestors get as far as a well-chosen permanent grave, but only those whose descendants can afford the fees of a

reputable specialist in site selection. The others remain above ground in their urns, and, in the end, they are forgotten. It is the rich, too, who can afford to set up lineage temples to provide a permanent focus for continuity and unity.

Ancestor worship, for obvious reasons, is a religious expression of societies based on descent. And the very wide distribution of this form of social organization accounts for the recurrence of similar forms of ancestor worship in the most widely different societies. But it is dangerous to assume a direct correlation between ancestor worship and the descent principle: the Nuer of the Sudan and the Tiv of Nigeria are both organized in lineages. But neither worship their ancestors. For although religious beliefs and practices inevitably tell us something about a people's social structure, it must never be forgotten that religion is more than a mirror image of society. □

Priests

Priests are religious specialists. There are a number of different types of specialist: *shamans* 'specialize' in religious ecstasy, prophets are concerned with moral leadership, and diviners with consulting the oracle. But in this article we shall take the term priest to refer to those religious specialists who are appointed to the task of maintaining the correct relationship between the gods and the members of their community, and to restore that relationship whenever it is disturbed—the priest as an intermediary.

Priests are appointed to their task by the community or its leaders. They are different from prophets who are motivated by moral indignation or by a sense of responsibility for the well-being of their fellow men, and establish themselves as moral or religious leaders, as the 'conscience of the nation', usually at a time of crisis.

The priesthood is frequently attached to membership of a particular group, so that everyone who is born or becomes a member of the group is eligible for priestly functions, or automatically becomes a priest. The Levitical priesthood of ancient Israel were drawn exclusively from the tribe of Levi; only they were eligible for priesthood. There is even evidence that any non-Levite who performed priestly functions at one of the local shrines was recruited into the tribe of Levi and made a Levite.

Priesthood is often attached to chieftaincy. Among the Lugbara of Uganda the elder of a lineage is also the priest of the ancestor shrines of that lineage. In fact he has to prove his influence with the ancestors before he will be permitted to form an independent lineage with himself as the elder. Among the Krachi of northern Ghana the chief of the Dentewiae clan is also the priest of the local deity, *Dente*. When he is installed as chief of the clan he automatically receives the power and the authority to perform the *Dente* ritual on behalf of the whole Krachi tribe.

Judaism has no sacraments, only symbols and ceremonies; rabbis are teachers rather than priests. But the rabbi officiating at this Barmitzvah fulfills many of the functions traditionally associated with the Levitical priesthood.

Ted Spiegel/John Hillelson Agency

In Japan the great Shinto shrines support large numbers of priests who intercede between worshippers and 'the eight hundred myriads of deities' who make up the Shinto pantheon.

The priesthood, then, is an established office. It carries with it responsibilities which are entrusted to an individual by the community or by those in authority over the community. It is definitely not a function undertaken spontaneously and performed only as long as the need is felt.

The task to which a priest is appoin-ted is to maintain, to celebrate or to restore the right relationship between the community and the deity, and he has to use an established ritual in performing this task. The Levitical priest of ancient Israel was expected to celebrate the coven-ant which Yahweh had made with His people. Various forms of sacrifice were prescribed to restore the covenant relationship if a person had broken the law, and the form of sacrifice differed accord-ing to the nature of the transgression. Today, the liturgy by which the Catholic priest celebrates the new covenant estab-lished by the death of Jesus Christ is fixed in all its details, some of which are considered essential for its validity.

In many parts of the world, com-munities express homage and gratitude to their deity, or implore it to come to their rescue, through traditional rituals. Performed either at regular intervals or in times of crisis, these have remained un-changed since the earliest times.

Because of their task of maintaining the right relationshaip between people and the deity, priests are spoken of as media-tors or intermediaries. R. B. Kibongi describes the Nganga of Kinshasha, for example, as a mediator, not between

have pointed out that it is the act which the priest performs and the object which he sacrifices, rather than the personality of the priest, which mediates between god and humans, and maintains or restores the right relationship between them. But, in fact, it is impossible to separate the priest and his ritual function, because the act may only be performed by the priest if it is to be valid and therefore successful.

Priests usually form a separate group within a community. The Catholic clergy in most countries forms a class apart. The same is true of the Buddhist clergy in Ceylon. They live in considerable comfort in their residences in the temple grounds, a life which is in marked contrast to that of the Bhikkus or mendicant monks who are not priests and perform no special ritual tasks. The Bhikkus are ascetic monks who strive to lead the pure unwordly life of Buddha's teaching. They deny the validity of the formal organization of the established clergy, and claim that 'the charisma of the Buddha

A Roman Catholic priest hears confession. In this and his other priestly functions he is acting as the instrument of God, a role for which the priest prepares himself by vows of poverty and chastity.

Nzambi, the 'all-powerful, eternal and unconfined Creator' and people, but between people and the other superhuman agents of evil. The famous anthropologist, Professor Evans-Pritchard, described the Nuer Priest of the earth as 'being essentially a person who sacrifices on behalf of Man below to God above' and who 'acts as intermediary between Man and God.'

The Epistle to the Hebrews, a late 1st century Christian document, describes the Levitical High Priest as follows: 'taken from among men he is appointed to act on behalf of men in relation to God.' Hubert and Mauss, in their essay on sacrifice

Ian Berry/Magnum

Burt Glinn/Magnum

Dr. Dennis McGilvray

Priesthood often depends upon membership of a particular class or caste. Brahmans are the dominant caste in the Hindu community, and this man from Ceylon, his head half-shaved in the Brahmanical style, is eligible to supervise the rites and sacrifices.

has been lost in the formal edifice of the Church'. Moreover, the recent growth of interest in their life and the subsequent increase in their numbers may be interpreted as a reaction against the life of comfort and luxury of the established clergy.

The creation of a clerical class, precisely for the purpose of safeguarding the sacred character of the priesthood exposes it to the danger of losing its charisma. Formalism and legalism will always tend to develop where the exclusive powers and prerogatives of the group remain unchallenged from outside. The prophetic movement in ancient Israel was a reaction against the formalism of the Levitical priesthood; and underground movements within the established Churches today are a similar reaction against varying degrees of formalism and legalism.

For the Nuer, however, it is also socially important for the priests to belong to a special group. They choose the Priests of the Earth from lineages which do not own the tribal territory and who will live as strangers among them. It is important that their priests should not be identified with political groups because they have to act as peacemakers between such groups.

But frequently there is religious rather than social significance in the fact that priests are placed in a group separate from the other members of the community. The underlying idea remains the same: if their task is that of intermediary between the community and the deity, they should not be identified with the rest of the community, just as the Nuer priest should not be identified with the local political groups between whom he is the intermediary.

Restrictions on the private and social lives of priests are widespread. Levitical priests were only permitted to marry virgins or the widows of other priests. Roman Catholic priests are expected to be life-long celibates. The priest of the *Yentumi* cult in West Africa is not permitted to have sexual intercourse with his wife except on Thursdays, and in many African cults no priest is allowed to enter the shrine unless he has abstained from intercourse the night before. It is not difficult to find similar restrictions on the sex life of priests in other parts of the world. But are these restrictions as similar as they appear? And is the obligatory celibacy of the Roman Catholic priest really the same thing as the prohibition which prevents an Akan priest from entering the shrine for 24 hours after having sexual intercourse?

In the Greek and Coptic Rites of the Catholic Church the law of celibacy has been relaxed to the extent that married men may be ordained to the priesthood, but are required to abstain from sexual intercourse during the night before they celebrate the Eucharist. This seems to place the celibacy of the Catholic priest within the Greek and Coptic rites in very much the same light as the abstention of the African priest. But for these Catholic priests the stress is on personal asceticism, not on ritual purity. If one of them breaks the law concerning his sex life he may not officially perform the liturgy of the Eucharist. Yet if he does insist on celebrating the Eucharist, the validity and efficacy of the rite is not in question. The same is to be said of Buddhist priests: their celibacy is a standard of asceticism imposed on them by their Church. Its observance or non-observance in no way affects their ritual performance.

Ritual impurity is a different matter. It renders the ritual performance null and void, and makes it a dangerous undertaking. The priest of the *Yentumi* cult will not attempt to perform the rites if he has broken the prohibition. The ritual could only have an ill effect.

A woman in ancient Israel who had had sexual relations with a non-Levite be-

A procession of Greek Orthodox priests on Corfu. The Orthodox priesthood has sometimes been criticized for its involvement in politics, an accusation levelled at priests of all times and cultures.

Jon Gardey/Robert Harding Associates

longed to the non-sacred category of the ordinary people from which the Levites were rigorously distinguished. If a Levite married such a woman he placed himself outside the sacred category and was therefore disqualified from performing priestly functions. From this it is evident that it is impossible to impose a uniform interpretation on all prohibitions and restrictions which the various systems of priesthood impose on their members. It is necessary to consider each restriction, each prohibition and every rule in relation to the priestly functions of the system.

The authority of a priest derives entirely from his ritual task. A prophet's authority, on the other hand, comes from his personal charisma. Professor Evans-Pritchard's description of the Nuer Priest of the Earth illustrates this point. Only the Priest of the Earth can perform the rites which are essential in a homicide case: to give sanctuary to the killer, to negotiate a settlement, to make a sacrifice to enable normal social relations to be resumed and to rehabilitate the killer. The priest is important only because he alone can perform these services. He is

(Above) Lamaistic priests dressed for the sacred Tsam dance in Ulan Bator, Mongolia.

(Left) This 'rainmaker' from the Congo is a specialist in asking the help of gods. He remains separate from the rest of the community in order to preserve his identity.

(Right) A Buddhist High Priest officiates at the New Year ceremony. In Tibet, Mahayana or 'Greater Vehicle' Buddhism has evolved a modified form in which the priesthood is strictly hierarchical. A priestly hierarchy often leads to formalism and the loss of the more charismatic elements of a religion.

Popperfoto

taken from a lineage that owns no land and has no political influence precisely because this enables him to perform the mediating services without bias. Sometimes they appoint a member of a Dinka lineage (whom the Nuer despise) to be Priest of the Earth. The priest has no personal authority or importance: his only authority derives from the performance of these services.

It is important to distinguish this priestly power and authority from whatever power and authority he may obtain from his social status. In many European countries the local parish priest has long been regarded as an authority on everything from agriculture to questions of health and education. This was simply because he was the only member of the community known to have received higher education. With the spreading of education his image changed, but for the believer his power and authority as a priest remained unchanged.

The distinction between sacred and secular power becomes still more indistinct when 'priest passes into King'. Among the Mapuche Indians in Chile the chief who presides at the *nillatun* or fertility rite is by that same fact the *nullatufe* or ritual priest. It follows that these ritual powers are part of his powers as a lineage head. If he is trained in the ritual he can perform it. Among the Lugbara a lineage elder who has proved that he is the trustee of the ancestors can split off his lineage from the rest of the family. He becomes an elder in his own right and owner and priest of the ancestral shrines. In Mapuche society, then, priestly power is the prerogative of the chief. But among the Lugbara a man's political power and the independence of his lineage depend on his performance as a priest.

The reaction of the Buddhist monks in Ceylon against the life of luxury and comfort of the established clergy shows that the former did not confuse the latters' prestige as landowners and incumbents of temples with the sacred character of their priesthood. Among the Krachi of Northern Ghana, although the priest of the local deity, *Dente*, is also the chief of his own clan, there is no evidence that he has more authority in his clan than the other chiefs have in theirs.

The process of becoming a priest is interesting. Where priestly functions form part of the task of a chief it is evident that a man becomes a priest on his election to office and subsequent installation. The candidature may be influenced by the fact that important priestly functions have to be entrusted to the successor. Where no such situation exists, becoming a priest is a matter of personal vocation. The candidate expresses the wish to become a priest, or the belief that the deity has claimed him as his priest.

Leimbach/Robert Harding Associates

Besakih temple in Bali is built on the side of an active volcano which has claimed many lives. A woman priest sprinkles holy water on Hindu devotees in a ceremony designed to attract the protection of the gods.

Among the established Christian Churches, a candidate must not only want to be a priest but also show himself fit for his priestly tasks during a lengthy theological training. This is also regarded as sufficient evidence of the will of God. Among many traditional cults in Africa the gods claim or call their future priests by taking possession of them in their infancy. If a child is seized by a fit and this is interpreted as possession by one particular god, the child will be earmarked and in due course trained to be a priest.

The often lengthy theological and ritual training which a candidate for the priesthood has to undergo makes him into a ritual specialist. But to suppose that every priest during his training obtains a store of secret information which is kept from the layman is an oversimplification. A priest knows more about his religion and its ritual than the ordinary layman, but the theology of the Christian Churches is being taught in theological faculties around the world.

Priests of many local cults in West Africa in the course of their training do receive items of information which are never divulged to the layman. But by its very nature, it is impossible to estimate the extent or the importance of the knowledge—which includes personal insights into the meaning of the ritual and the teaching of the religion—imparted in this way.

As has been seen, the priesthood in the vast majority of world religions consists of men only. Women more usually perform tasks concerned with caring or education (like nuns) but few, if any, ritual functions. They also have little say in formulating theological ideas. In the West, though, more women in both the Roman Catholic and Protestant faiths have been seeking recognition for their rights to be priests. Their success has been very limited to date, with the Catholic Church in particular, firmly refusing to accept them in this role. □

Shamans

The term shaman has come into English usage from Russian, but was originally derived from the dialect of the Tungus people of Siberia. Although it is in Siberia that shamanism is found in its classic form, it occurs throughout the world mainly among nomads and hunters and gatherers in the Americas, Asia, the Arctic, India, Indonesia and on the islands of the South Pacific.

Although the shamanistic tradition has now declined, it once extended even over most of Europe: Stone-Age cave people probably possessed shamanistic beliefs. And survivals of these beliefs can be seen in a variety of fairy stories and superstitions: the hobby horse, for example, is probably a survival of the shamanistic ritual of sacrificing a horse to the divine protectors: the eating of the horse's flesh facilitated the shaman's ascent to heaven. In the ritual that followed, the shaman danced around, mounted on the remaining head and spinal column of the horse, until he or she (for not all shamans are men), attained a state of ecstacy.

A remarkable feature of shamanism is the way in which the main elements involved are found in so many different parts of the world. There are two essential traits which distinguish shamans from other magico-religious practitioners like witchdoctors, medicine men and magicians.

These are, firstly, the intimate relationships between the shaman and one or more tutelary spirits, and secondly, the shaman's ability to undertake ecstatic journeys to other worlds.

It is the shaman's relationship with spirit helpers that distinguishes him or her from the spirit medium—a passive participant through whom the spirit speaks—and from the individual who suffers from involuntary spirit possession. The shaman is on at least an equal footing with the spirit-helpers and is often regarded as their master, with the power to control and command them. Thus many South American shamans refer to their spirit-helpers as their pets.

The monotonous beating of his drum aids this Nepalese shaman from Charicot, known as a Thami, to enter a trance state and summon the assistance of his spirit helpers in healing his patients.

The shaman is able to call on the spirit-helpers for a variety of purposes. Healing is perhaps the most common function of the shaman, especially in those societies where sickness is thought to be the workings of a supernatural agency. The shaman contacts the spirit-helpers and with their aid is able to diagnose the patient's complaint—that is, determining the sort of spirit attack the patient is suffering, and effecting a cure. The latter may involve a desperate and lengthy battle with the spirits responsible for the illness.

The ecstatic journeys, another fundamental part of the shaman's activity, are closely connected with the shaman's

Prof. C. von Fürer-Haimendorf

relation to the spirit-helpers. The shaman, in order to contact the spirit-helpers and to obtain supernatural assistance for ordinary men, enters a trance. In the past, these trances were regarded as self-induced, or thought to be the result of hysteria, epilepsy or some other neurotic or psycho-pathological condition. However, recent evidence suggests that this is not the case. In many societies, shamanic trances are induced artificially by the consumption of narcotic or hallucinogenic substances.

It is also clear that many shamans, far from being merely eccentric characters or social outcasts, are the most intelligent, far-sighted and ambitious members of the society. Even in cases where there may be a connection between neurosis and shamanism, learning shamanic techniques seems to provide a cure for the original condition by channelling it into socially acceptable and useful avenues. Indeed the psychiatrist Julian Silverman, has drawn an interesting parallel between the shaman and what we term a schizophrenic. In Western society, however, the schizophrenic is isolated and subjected to 're-education', whereas in the shaman's society, there is acceptance.

However shamans achieve their trances, the important thing is that they enable them to invoke the spirit helpers. They discuss the problem with them, and send them to the spirit world to summon or obtain information from other spirits. When the shamans are in trance they are also able to travel to the spirit world. They either ascend to the heavens or descend to the underworld in order to obtain divine or supernatural assistance for human affairs, and especially to obtain information regarding their patients' maladies.

During these journeys the shaman's spirit is in great peril since it is highly vulnerable to attack. These passages to the other world are often symbolized by a ladder which the shaman gradually mounts. This also symbolizes the spirit's journey to the sky. Drums and rattles are often used as an accompaniment to the shaman's trance during a séance or as a way of inducing the trance.

Shamanic séances, the sessions when the shaman goes into a trance to talk to the spirit helpers or visit another world, take many different forms. In some cases they involve what amounts to a private consultation between shaman and patient, and the shaman has often been compared with the psychoanalyst in our own society. Séances may also be very dramatic public affairs and, as in voodoo, they have a strong theatrical component. Shamans may perform in full sight of everyone or out of sight so that only their voices and the imitated voices of their spirit helpers can be heard. During the séance, when the shamans try to cure the patient by diagnosing what supernatural force has caused the

sickness and to remove its malignant effects, their actions depend on the socially accepted notion that sickness results from supernatural agencies, whether it be malevolent spirits acting of their own volition or those directed to attack the victim by another person—usually in the form of a sorcerer.

The techniques employed by the shaman vary enormously. In the case of soul-loss, where the patient is thought to have had his soul 'eaten' or stolen by spirits, the shaman may have to visit the underworld to argue or fight with the spirits in order to recapture the lost soul. Another method of treatment is for the shaman to blow clouds of tobacco or other smoke over the patient in order to drive out the offending spirit. But perhaps the best known and most controversial form of treatment is by sucking out the evil from the patient.

The shaman, having diagnosed the nature and exact location of the illness, sucks out from the patient an object which has been 'shot' into the patient by a spirit. This spirit weapon may be seen to take the form of a piece of wood, a dead beetle or a small pebble, which the shaman has previously concealed in the mouth. This form of cure has given rise to the observations that shamans cannot be regarded simply as fraudulent, since both they and their patients act out the deception.

In fact, it is not as straightforward as this. It would be extremely hard to demonstrate that either party, even when fully aware of the technique, had any sense of deception. Even if one of the parties did entertain doubts—and there are well attested cases of sceptical shamans—the self-confirming nature of the system, and perhaps the whole society's

These Amerindian shamans from Xingu Park in Brazil, are smoking an hallucinogen. They attribute the effect of the substance to the spirit associated with the plant from which it is extracted.

(Above) In Siberia, the Evenki shamans wear carved wooden masks. These masks are designed to make them unrecognisable to hostile spirits during their journeys through the spirit world.

notions about causation, tends to prevent radical criticism: the object concealed in the shaman's mouth is not only the recipient of the evil responsible for the patient's sickness but is the very symbol of the shaman's mastery over nature. While it may be possible to show that an individual shaman is occasionally a fraud, this does not undermine the acceptance of shamanism which is an integral part of the society's beliefs.

The duties of shamans are by no means limited to the curing of the sick. They often use their powers to obtain information about which direction it would be best to hunt in, whether there are enemies about, or if a war party will be successful. The shaman also plays a political or legal role. In a situation where shamans diagnose sickness resulting from sorcery, for example, they are able to publicly expose the tensions and ill-feelings that underly

sorcery by revealing them through the spirit helpers during a trance. By bringing unexpressed discontent into the open the shaman clears the air and restores harmony in the community.

Although both male and female shamans—the latter are sometimes referred to as shamanesses—are found, it is rare for both to exist within the same society. Women are usually deeply involved in a peripheral cult, which is subsidiary to a male-dominated belief system. One example of this is found among the Mapuche Indians of southern Chile, where historical evidence indicates that, as a result of the growth of a male, priest-controlled cult and of other social and economic changes, shamanism passed into the hands of women. This is not to suggest that priest and shamans are mutually exclusive roles: the Huichol Indians of Mexico have priests who are

also shamans.

While on the subject of the shaman's sex, we may also consider the frequently reported fact that shamans are homosexuals or transvestites. It is certainly true that in many societies the shaman exhibits attributes of the opposite sex. This is especially the case among the Chukchee of Arctic Siberia where some male shamans take husbands, although it should be noted that these shamans are also believed to have spirit wives. However, these characteristics are not an essential ingredient of shamanism. In many cases it can be understood as a symbolic expression of the shaman's ambiguous role (in relation to the structure of the society) compared with those men who do not have shamanistic powers.

The shamans' ability to move between cosmological layers—ascending to heaven and descending to the bowels of the earth —is paralleled by their failure to conform to an expected mode of behaviour. In most societies shamans, in their everyday behaviour are indistinguishable from their fellows. Indeed, in some societies, all adult people are expected to have some knowledge of shamanic techniques and to communicate with spirits while in a trance. In such societies, certain individuals are recognized as having greater skill than others, and it is on them that the task of

(Above) Shamanism originated among the Siberians, who were mostly nomads and hunters. The drum belonging to this Yurak shaman is marked with the symbols of his tutelary or helper spirits.

curing devolves.

It has been noted earlier that shamans are not necessarily neurotics, or social misfits, nor, as we have just seen, homosexuals. On the contrary, they are often the most ambitious members of the society, and shamanism, in those societies where it represents the only form of specialization, is the only avenue open to them. There are numerous examples of societies in which the shamans, because of their accumulated wealth, form a distinct class. It should, however, be added that in cases where this is found there is often evidence to suggest that it has occurred as a result of the disruption of the traditional system by the introduction of materialism.

Traditionally, an individual becomes a shaman by firstly recovering from a serious illness by means of a shamanic cure. Again there is a parallel between psychoanalysis and shamanism: any would-be psychoanalysts are themselves expected to undergo analysis as part of their training. This is a particular form of what might be called 'vocational shamanism', and its other modes include experiences in dreams, the visitation by a spirit, or even the discovery of some spirit object such as an oddly-shaped pebble.

The other main way of becoming a shaman is by hereditary transmission. This can be regarded as a weaker form since it may not involve much more than the child inheriting and subsequently caring for the shamanic equipment of the parent.

The decision to become a shaman, however motivated, is only the first step: a universal feature of shamanism is the long and arduous apprenticeship that it entails. Individuals may accomplish this by apprenticing themselves directly to a spirit—frequently the one who 'called' them—or to an experienced and practising shaman. This involves learning not only the traditional knowledge of the society, but also new knowledge collected on journeys among neighbouring peoples.

The apprentice shaman also has to undergo ordeals which include the initial journeys to the underworld and to heaven. These journeys are fraught with danger and the shaman is conceived of as being torn limb from limb while sitting 'outside himself' watching it happen. The shaman is then reassembled: the whole experience symbolizing the process of death and rebirth as a new person.

The apprenticeship also includes meditation, fasting, sexual abstinence and lengthy periods of solitary isolation. During this time they are expected, with the aid of masters, to learn healing techniques and to induce trances. Where, the trance state is achieved with an artificial aid, as it is in most places, the would-be shaman must learn to conduct the seance under the influence of the halucinogenic or toxic substances, while maintaining control of the senses. The South American Akawayo shamans for example, consume greater and greater quantities of toxic, herbal preparations during their apprenticeship with the aim of finally accustoming themselves to drinking an enormous amount. of tobacco juice, following a severe fast.

Even when fully qualified and able to conduct their own séances the young shamans may have to practise for many years before they become fully skilled in various shamanic techniques and are recognized as fully competent practitioners. Many apprentices never make the grade but remain ordinary individuals with some shamanic knowledge and experience.

While there are other rewards in being a shaman, there are also attendant dangers. It can be appreciated that an individual who is in touch with supernatural agents and has spirit helpers has the ability to use the power for good or bad ends. Shamans can curse just as easily as they can cure. Accordingly, in the event of numerous deaths or other misfortunes, the shamans may find themselves the scapegoats and be killed or driven out of the community. □

Societies which attribute sickness to supernatural forces, such as the Jah Hut of Western Malaysia, depend on the shaman's skill in persuading the possessing spirits to withdraw from the patient's body.

Anti-Gods

A permanent difficulty in many religions is the problem of evil. Where there is believed to be a Divine Creator, a being who is the essence and the total of goodness and benevolence, it is not easy to explain the existence in the world of evil and the prevalence of pain, suffering and waste. It is a paradox. How can a being who is ultimate goodness create evil?

In many of the world's religions the problem is overcome by the concept of an Adversary—a being of divine, or semi-divine status, who is antagonistic to the Creator-God. While the Creator-God is benign, always working for the welfare of people and the source of all goodness; the Adversary is malicious, intent on bringing about our downfall and the source of all evil. In the Judaeo-Christian tradition this Anti-God is called Satan, which means 'adversary'. But the concept is to be found in varying forms in other religions: Ahi and Shiva in Hinduism, Ahriman in Zoroastrianism, Mara in Buddhism, Hel and Loki in Teutonic mythology, the dragon Tiamat in Babylonia, Set and the serpent Apap in Egypt, and the Titans and Prometheus in ancient Greece.

The way in which the Anti-God exerts his influence, and the extent of his power varies enormously. Mara is seen as a tempter, he tries to attract the Buddha from his right path with his beautiful and lascivious daughters. In Africa, evil is often portrayed as a mischievous force. The spider Anansi of the Asanti, and the god Eshu of the Yoruba are 'tricksters', and having little power in themselves have to employ cunning to achieve their ends. The Teutonic Loki is a seducer, he relies upon his handsomeness and charm to bring about the pain and suffering he longs to create.

The attractiveness and charismatic quality which is attributed to many Anti-Gods is significant. Firstly, of course, evil is very often attractive to Mankind. The laws of a righteous and moral Creator-God, like the Yahweh of the Jews, may not always be easy to follow. In this case the evil principle is naturally endowed with attractive qualities. John Milton in his epic poem 'Paradise Lost' —written to 'justify the ways of God to men'—finds that the charismatic quality of the Anti-God creates an insoluble dilemma. As the poem progresses the

magnificent figure of Satan ('he above the rest in shape and gesture proudly eminent, stood like a tower') becomes an increasing embarrassment. Ironically, and significantly, Satan comes near to being the 'hero' of one of the greatest religious poems in the English language.

Apart from the obvious artistic necessity which they saw, Milton's contemporaries argued that God's adversary had to be portrayed as a being of stature and quality, a 'worthy' opponent. Intellectually this brought them to a tacit acceptance of a doctrine which had been heresy in the Christian Church since the 3rd century—dualism.

In all dualistic systems (and the concept runs through many religions) good and evil are seen as having a separate existence. Although the good principle is, almost without exception, expected to triumph ultimately, the evil principle rivals the good in power and strength. Apart from a pleasing logic in the system, which may have led to its appearance in many different religions at different times, dualism has one great advantage. If the evil principle, the Adversary, is not the

Satan appears as the hideous Goat of Mendes in Goya's masterpiece 'Aquelarre'—The Witches' Sabbath. Anti-Gods of many religions were believed to assume different shapes in order to achieve their purpose of creating destruction and despair.

creation of God but a separate power with a separate origin, then evil is outside divine control. The problem of reconciling the existence of evil with the Divine attributes of perfect goodness, omniscience, and infinite power is thus solved. John Stuart Mill in his 'Essay on Religion' said that he 'preferred to disbelieve the omnipotence of God, rather than relinquish a belief in His goodness.'

Both the Syrian Gnostics and the Manichaens attempted some reconciliation of the doctrine of dualism with Christian principles. Both were in their time condemned by the Catholic Church as heretical, and both offered a synthesis of ideas from other religions apart from Christianity, in particular Buddhism and Zoroastrianism. Manichaeism superseded

Known as the red god and identified with the desert, Set is the personification of evil in Egyptian mythology. This bronze statuette is very rare: with the rise of the cult of Osiris, Set's brother and counterpart, the images of his twin and murderer were destroyed.

Gnosticism, taking many of its former adherents, and was more significant both numerically and in the coherence of its dualistic doctrine.

Mani, the founder of Manichaeism, was born in about 215 AD in Persia. Like Abraham before him and Mohammed after him, he travelled extensively, until the age of 30 when he proclaimed his new religion at the court of Shapur I, King of Kings. New religions are very often, perhaps always, syntheses of important principles from older bodies of belief.

From contemporary oriental sources it is certain that he travelled into Transoxiana, China, and south as far as India.

Manichaeism is uncompromisingly dualistic. The opposing principles of Good and Evil are co-existent and co-eternal. Mani associates Good with Light and Evil with Darkness, but not as a metaphor—Good is actually Light, and Darkness is Evil. The Kingdom of Light is God, from it radiates love, faith, wisdom, meekness, knowledge and understanding. The five tokens of the Kingdom of Light are the mild zephyr, the cooling breeze, bright light, fire and clear water.

In Manichaeism the Kingdom of Darkness is the source of confusion, disorder, ignorance, pride, and destruction. This also possesses five tokens: mist, heat, the sirocco, darkness and vapour. The two kingdoms have stood in opposition for all eternity, with God at the head of the Kingdom of Light and Satan 'born out of the darkness' as the dominant being within the Kingdom of Darkness. The two kingdoms remained unmingled until Satan entered the Light. It was to correct the imbalance and fight against Satan that God created Man. But the tokens of Light had become intermingled with the tokens of Darkness, Satan proved a powerful adversary, and the battle still continues.

By the middle of the 4th century Manichaeism had spread widely throughout the Roman Empire. It drew its adherents from the old Gnostic sects on the one hand and from a cultured élite on the other. To this body of people it gave a simple and 'rational' explanation of the existence of evil which the subtle and difficult theories of the Catholic Church could not rival. The attraction which Manichaeism had for the best contemporary minds is shown by the fact that before finally rejecting the doctrine St. Augustine himself was an adherent.

It is significant that Manichaeism was nowhere more successful than in the country of its origin, Persia. The similarities between the doctrines of Mani and the far older Persian religion of Zoroastrianism are obvious. In Zoroastrianism there are the two principles: Good, Ahura Mazda, the Prince of Light; and Evil, Ahriman, the Prince of Darkness. But the doctrine of Zoroaster, who seems to have existed historically, possibly as early as 1000 BC, is not strictly speaking dualistic. Ahura Mazda and Ahriman are seen as the twin sons of Zervana Akarana —'Limitless Time', into which they will both ultimately be re-absorbed. An eternal unity is both the origin of the two warring principles, and is conceived as transcending them. This makes Zoroastrianism the world's first great monotheistic religion, except for the short-lived solar monotheism of the ill-fated 14th century BC Egyptian, Amenhotep IV—Akhenaton.

As Zoroastrianism developed it became increasingly dualistic. The unity represented by Time, the first principle, tended to be forgotten and emphasis was placed on the warring brothers: Ahura Mazda and Ahriman. Both spirits possessed creative power, but one manifested itself positively, the other negatively. Ahura Mazda was light and life—the creator of law, order, truth and all that is good in the world. His twin brother and his antithesis, Ahriman, was darkness and the creator of filth, death, ignorance and all that is evil.

Whatever the reasons for the tendency towards dualism in Zoroastrianism, it did not stem from any difficulty in explaining the creation of an evil being by one that was totally good. This problem was dealt with in the earliest books of the Avesta—the ancient records of the Zoroastrian doctrines. With startling logic and simplicity the Avesta explains that the origin of evil cannot be attributed to God, since it was not his intention to create Ahriman, but only Ahura Mazda. But just as the darkness of night follows the light of day, and everything that has substance also has its shadow, so the creation of a good being automatically resulted in the creation of an evil one.

The theme of the two brothers is not restricted to Persia. In Phoenician mythology the cuneiform tablets of Ras Shamrah tell of the struggle between Aleyin and Mot—a tradition already old when the tablets were written in the 14th century BC. The brother Aleyin 'he who rode on the clouds' is victorious, and Mot is banished to the underworld. In Egyptian mythology the brothers were Osiris and Set. Osiris is 'the Good One': as a vegetation god he dies and is ceaselessly reborn, he is the crops upon which life depends. Osiris is also the Nile which rises and falls with the procession of the seasons, and the rays of the sun which die with the sunset and live again with the dawn.

Set is the evil brother who murders Osiris. The son of Geb and Nut he finally becomes the incarnation of evil, in eternal opposition to the spirit of good personified by his brother Osiris. Set is associated with the arid desert, infertility, drought and darkness. The struggle between Osiris and Set is the battle between the Nile and the barren desert, between the green vegetation and the scorching wind, between fruitfulness and barrenness, and between light and darkness.

A bronze image of Kali 'The Black One' in the Old Royal Palace at Kathmandu in Nepal. Kali is the most terrible of all the aspects of the Mother Goddess. Her devotees are known to have practised human sacrifice during the Indian Middle Ages.

We have seen that the good principle is very often represented by light, and the evil principle by darkness. It is a concept which runs through many of the world's religions. In the Hindu pantheon Vishnu and Varuna are associated with light and the heavens, while Kali 'The Black One' and Shiva lurk in dark places and battle-fields. In the Hindu trinity or Trimurti, Brahma is 'the Creator', Vishnu 'the Preserver' and Shiva 'the Destroyer'. But unlike Vishnu, Shiva—who evolved from the fierce Vedic god Rudra—is ambivalent. As well as being the god of mystical stillness and asceticism, he is Lord of The Dance: it will be the wild rhythm of one of Shiva's dances that will destroy the world. He wears a necklace of skulls, he is death and time, which consumes all things.

The theme of opposing light and darkness was important in the religions of the great Assyro-Babylonian empires. It is interesting that many of their Anti-Gods —transmitted through the Chaldaeans, the Babylonians, and the Jewish Kabbala to medieval scholars and magicians— have become accepted embodiments of the evil principle in the popular Christian tradition. The Mephistopheles of the Faust legend, for example, was originally the antithesis of Marduk, 'The Lord of Light', in the religion of ancient Mesopotamia. 'Mephistopheles' means, literally, 'he who loves not light.' The widespread identification of the forces of evil with

The Yin-Yang concept is fundamental to Chinese Taoist philosophy. This red lacquer panel depicts the two principles of the universe—the Yin which is female, negative and passive; and the Yang which is male, positive and active. Together they make up the whole, which is Tao.

things. Although Tao is impersonal, it is omnipresent and works towards order and goodness. Out of Tao were born the Yin and the Yang, the opposing but complementary halves of the whole, which is Tao. The Yin is negative, female, dark, concave, receiving and passive. The Yang is positive, male, light, convex, giving and active. Heaven and earth and everything in them are the product of the interaction between the Yin and the Yang. Where this interaction is imperfect, where the opposing principles are not in harmony, evil, pain and suffering are the result.

The parallels between the concept of the Yin-Yang and the dualist religions are obvious. There are also similarities between Tao and the Buddhist Nirvana and the Hindu Brahma. In many ways the Yin-Yang concept in Chinese Taoist philosophy contains the essence of the many 'religious' explanations of the problem of evil and pain—but in a human context.

The Yin-Yang draws the strands together; but even more exciting are the parallels with the Anima-Animus concept of the Swiss psychologist Carl Jung, and with German Romanticism with its insistence that the denial of the male principle in woman and the female principle in man is the cause of the world's evils. The message is clear: evil has its existence and its origin within the human mind. □

A stained glass window in Gloucestershire, England showing the Devil. In the Christian mythology of medieval Europe the Devil fulfilled an ambivalent role. He acted both as tempter and as the instrument of Divine retribution by torturing the souls of sinners.

darkness places many of Christ's utterances in an interesting perspective, notably 'I am the Light of the world'.

In China the concept of opposites took a unique form. Until the Communist revolution three 'religions' existed side-by-side: Buddhism, Taoism and Confucianism. From Buddhism and Taoism a uniquely Chinese pantheon developed which resembled a government or civil service in its construction. The evil principle was represented by various Anti-Gods, including the Yama-Kings who presided over hell. It is, however, in the philosophical system of Taoism that we find the most interesting Chinese contribution to the question of good and evil. This is the Yin and the Yang.

The term 'Tao' originally meant the apparent revolution of the heavens about the earth, but it came to mean the universal cosmic energy, the unity behind all

A wooden mask representing Eshu, the Anti-God of the Yoruba of Nigeria. Eshu is the opposite principle of Ifa, who is good. Like the evil principle in many African religions, Eshu is a 'trickster'—once he persuaded the sun and the moon to change places in the heavens.

Sin

In our modern permissive society the concept of sin has become unfashionable. It would be pertinent to ask, therefore, whether a sense of sin should be regarded as an inherent trait of human nature or whether it is a phenomenon peculiar only to certain periods of history or types of civilization. Throughout the two millenia of the Christian era, the problem of sin has played a crucial role in Western philosophical thinking.

Heaven and hell symbolized the division of the world into contrasting realms and few Christians doubted that our ultimate destiny is determined by our virtuous or sinful actions on this earth. The doctrine of original sin also attempted to explain the existence of evil and suffering in a world believed to be the creation of a benevolent God.

The paradisical state destined for humanity was supposed to have been ruined by the transgression of the first parents, Adam and Eve. Moreover, the original sin was believed to have caused an 'evil inclination' inherited by all of Adam's descendants. However, recent discoveries regarding the early stages in human development have suggested to many theologians that the myth of paradise requires reconsideration and in doing so they are abandoning the doctrine of the fall of man as an historical event.

Yet, the debate on the nature of original sin could not have continued for close on 2,000 years if the awareness of sin as a blemish oin human nature had not been deeply ingrained in a large part of humanity. Since there is no European language which does not contain the word 'sin', Western people were long convinced that this phenomenon was common to the whole of humanity. However, during the age of discovery, Christian missionaries found that there were languages which did not contain the word sin, which suggested that the people who spoke these languages had no concept of a form of conduct which brings people into conflict with supernatural powers who are guardians of morality.

An investigation of a cross-section of societies on different levels of economic and social development demonstrates a great variety of attitudes of behaviour which do not conform to accepted Western moral ideas, and indeed to the whole problem of the origin and nature of evil.

At that time men and women did not indulge in sexual intercourse and hence no children were born. When a man became very old he was placed into a lake and he arose from the water fully rejuvenated. In this way no one died and there was no need to replenish the population by sexual procreation. This idyllic existence ended, however, when the Creator's adversary persuaded men that a life in which they had nothing to do but to eat and sleep was dull and unsatisfactory. He advocated a world in which men and women would experience the joys of love, women would bear children, and at the end of their life-span people would die and be replaced by their sons and daughters. Men were tempted by this prospect—by abandoning the life laid down by the Creator, they gained the pleasures of sex but also brought upon themselves the evils of pain, illness and death.

The idea that sinful actions on the part of men can bring about disaster prevails among many peoples. The Semang, a Pygmy tribe of Malaya, believe that thunder and lightning are caused by the transgression of certain moral rules, and that the danger inherent in these phenomena can be averted by the act of expiation. This is executed by the offering of a person's own blood. The blood is drawn from a small incision in the leg, mixed with water and thrown into the air. The Semang interpret thunder, for example, as a sign of the anger of a powerful deity, placatable by a blood offering.

An offender of the moral code is obliged to offer some of his blood, for the omission of this act of expiation would cause hurricanes and floods. This is an irksome duty, not necessarily a sign of contrition, but it does indicate that the Semang have a sense of sin, the consequences of which must be counteracted by shedding blood.

The most serious sin is incest. If not expiated this attracts the punishment of death by lightning. The taboo applies not only to the act but even to conduct which may potentially lead to it: lack of reserve, for example, between son-in-law and mother-in-law is condemned and subject to supernatural punishment. More surprisingly, equally stringent rules cover behaviour towards animals: it is taboo to tease dogs, cats and monkeys. Nothing,

however, suggests that the Semang believe in retribution in a world beyond. Punishments incurred by men on account of their sinful actions relate only to their fate on earth. All men, good and bad, are thought to enter the same Land of the Dead, where they lead a carefree existence.

The Semang's reaction to breaches of taboos, and their beliefs in supernatural sanctions of moral lapses, is by no means general among tribes of foodgatherers. Among the Chenchu, a tribe of Indian jungle-dwellers, for instance, supernatural punishments play hardly any part in promoting conformity to moral standards. Although the Chenchu believe in several deities and pray to them for success in the chase and for protection in hazardous enterprises, there is no evidence that fear of divine anger acts as a deterrent against breaches of the moral code. Indeed, the gods of the Chenchu are not thought to concern themselves with such actions as adultery, violence or murder. There is no concept of sin nor is there a need to expiate offences against the accepted ethical standards.

Among the more advanced agricultural groups of India, a variety of views on the effects of offences against accepted moral standards exist. Despite the widespread belief in the automatic ill-effects of unlawful acts, sin, retribution and contrition are concepts foreign to most tribal ideologies. In many tribal languages where there was originally no word for 'sin', the term, and with it the concept, has since been introduced from other languages. While 'sin' in the conventional sense of the term generally affects only the spiritual status of the offender, some tribes, such as the Gond of Central India, believe that certain unlawful acts affect other members of the household, and possibly the whole village community, as well as the offenders. Thus if a wife commits adultery when her husband is out hunting her act will defile the earth and the hunt will be ruined for the participants.

There is an African parallel to the idea that a husband is placed in physical danger by his wife's adultery. The Nuer of the Sudan believe that a wife's adultery pollutes her husband, and that if sickness results from adultery it falls on the husband rather than on the woman.

The belief that a wife's infidelity affects

The Thakali of Nepal subscribe to the Buddhist system of Karma, in which sins—natural events in the chain of 'cause and effect'—can be atoned for by acts of virtue.

the strength and well-being of her husband occurs also in ancient Hindu scriptures. Indeed, the seduction of a wife is described as the surest means of breaking an opponent's power, for a man's power depends not only on his own virtue but upon his wife's chastity. This notion that the evil consequences of a wife's unfaithfulness affect her husband rather than herself is certainly very different from the Christian concept of the wages of sin.

In Western thought the concept of sin, which clearly depends on Man's ability to choose between 'right' and 'wrong' behaviour, has often been linked with a sinister force antagonistic to human welfare. This force leads men to

choose 'wrong' conduct, and thus become enmeshed in sin.

North American Indians personify evil in the form of a trickster, who appears in myths as the opponent of a benevolent creator-god and the enemy of human well-being. The tribal people of India, on the other hand, do not believe in such a concentration of evil forces. Even the blood-thirsty and menacing deities of disease and epidemics are not agents of evil in the sense that they lead people into sin.

Examples of societies which do not have the concept of sin are found among

In spite of their comparatively recent conversion to Christianity, the Nagas of India have no concept of sin. Offences are considered social rather than moral and do not affect their afterlife in the Land of the Dead.

the Tibeto-Burman tribes of the Eastern Himalayas. Not only are these tribes devoid of any sense of 'sin', but they also lack the desire to acquire 'merit' in a system of supernatural rewards. Apa Tani men, for instance, endeavour to achieve, by fair means or foul, a favourable place within the social and economic framework of their own tribal group. They do not distinguish between meritorious or sinful actions within a universal system of supernatural values.

The fate that awaits them after death is regarded as a reflection of life on earth. Happiness in the world beyond is not gained by acts of charity but by success and prosperity in this life—achievements which are perpetuated automatically in the Land of the Dead. Gratification, both immediate and in another life is thus not opposed. The very idea of self-denial, austerity or renunciation in pursuit of lofty moral ends is foreign and presumed to be contrary to a universal ethical code.

We are justified therefore in assuming that the concept of sin and the belief in an innate tendency of human nature to evil is not only unknown to some hunters and foodgatherers such as the Chenchu, but also to such materially advanced and socially complex communities as the tribal populations of Northeast India.

In Hindu mythology, however, the problem of evil and sin looms large, and there are various attempts to explain their existence. They are seen as a corruption of a happier state, a kind of golden age, when people were pure and godlike. They were immortal and free of want as well as of evil desires. A common theme of the ancient epics is that in which people originally lived without fear of death. Neither were there sexual relations between men and women: as people did not die there was no need to replace them. Sexual intercourse arose only in later ages and with it passion which is regarded as one of the roots of evil and sin. The parallel to the myths of the North American Indian is striking, but in Hindu thought the link between sex and evil is more prominent. Women are seen as the cause of many sins, and they appear in numerous myths as temptresses of sages and ascetics.

In Buddhist ideology, the whole universe, people as well as gods, are subject to a reign of law. Every action, good or bad, has an inevitable and automatic effect in a long chain of 'cause and effect' which is independent of the will of any

(Right) In the Judaeo-Christian tradition the 'fall from grace' of Adam and Eve in the Garden of Eden is responsible for the 'evil inclination' inherited by their descendants and is the source of suffering.

Prof. C. von Fürer-Haimendorf

Prof. C. von Fürer-Haimendorf

Prof. C. von Fürer-Haimendorf

The execution pole is a central feature of Apa Tani villages, reminding would-be offenders of the consequences of such crimes as theft and adultery. Like many Indian tribes, the Apa Tani see such actions as offences against the community's property rather than sins against their gods.

deity. Even though this may leave no room for the concept of 'sin' as an act of defiance against the authority of a personal god, Buddhists speak of 'sin' when referring to transgressions against the universal moral code.

Central to Buddhist thinking is the principle of the balance between merit and demerit. This is evident among the people professing the Tibetan type of Mahayana Buddhism, such as the Sherpas of Nepal. Their moral system is based on the belief that every act of virtue adds to an individual's store of merit; whereas every morally negative action or sin diminishes this valuable store. Sherpas conceive of sin only in respect of interpersonal relations and the relations between people and other animate beings. They discount the possibility of committing 'sin' by offending any of the divinities of the Buddhist pantheon.

A typical feature of Sherpa morality is the idea that certain sins cannot be avoided, and that those who commit them must make up for the loss of merit by undertaking meritorious works to redress the balance. Trees have to be felled, for example, in spite of the knowledge that it is sinful to destroy plant life. Similarly, yak-breeders will castrate bulls knowing that they are inflicting pain on animals.

The Sherpa overcome the discrepancy between the desirable and the practicable with the comforting thought that good works can outweigh sins. This emphasis

on the possibility of offsetting evil actions by meritorious deeds may also take the sting out of the distaste for such an avoidable sin as adultery. For if all sins are capable of being cancelled out—and a layman cannot lead the normal life of a farmer or herdsman without committing a number of inevitable sins—there is no overwhelming incentive to avoid the more pleasurable sins: these will simply be added to the sum of sins which can be outweighed by good works. The idea of a store of merit on which a man can draw in order to balance any sin he may be tempted to commit is totally different from the concept of the state of grace in contrast to mortal sin.

A survey of the ideologies of various societies suggests that whatever the origin of the concept of sin, it is by no means common to all societies. We have seen that not only societies of hunters and foodgatherers, but some relatively complex tribal societies do not embrace the idea that a person's actions can affect their spiritual status so adversely as to jeopardise their relations with powerful supernatural forces and bring them into conflict with divine law. Even though such societies may judge human conduct as either meritorious or reprehensible in social terms, they do not link offences against the social order with a change in the relations between men and gods.

The ideology prevailing in Christian and Buddhist societies—that a sinful action inevitably attracts supernatural retribution quite distinct from any secular punishment human justice may inflict— is entirely different from this view. It would be misleading, however, to attribute the sense of guilt and sin only to sophisticated, literate civilizations. Sin was clearly a dominant concept in the early books of the Old Testament. We have also seen that it was relevant to a relatively primitive society of pastoral nomads

like the foodgathering Semang who expiate sins by offering their own blood. Moreover, the feeling that people were intended for a fate better than their present condition is found among populations of all economic levels.

The decline of humanity from a primeval idealized state is often attributed to a sinful act, or at least a misjudgement of people's real interests on the part of mythical ancestors. But it is only in relatively advanced societies that the messianic idea of a saviour conquering sin and spiritual death has arisen: the individual's attitude to sin has assumed a central role in religious thinking. It is believed that salvation can only be attained by eschewing sin, or at least by wiping out the stain of sin through penance and meritorious works.

In societies taking this view, the emphasis on evil effect of any transgression of moral rules—even if escaping public detection—has undoubtedly resulted in a strenthening of the social order: feelings of guilt and the fear of punishment in the world beyond deters people from ciminal acts even if they have every expectation of evading human justice.

While it is simple to point to such practical effects of a strongly developed sense of sin in the Christian or Buddhist sense, it is as yet impossible to establish a universally valid correlation between concepts of sin and economic levels or political systems. Indeed, it would appear that like other religious beliefs the sense of sin is a phenomenon in its own right which intertwines with social and economic factors. However, it is neither determined not explained by secular social conditions.

An eminent theologian recently suggested that 'Man is haunted by two spectres: the sense of individual guilt and the awareness that the whole race suffered a fall.' Anthropological evidence demonstrates that although both these sentiments occur in societies of very different types, they are by no means universal. There exist today, as there existed in the past, societies whose members, though no different from men and women of other societies, are unaware of any sense of individual sin or guilt. Neither do they have a tradition of a fall which corrupted the whole of humanity.

While anthropological studies can illuminate the diversity of moral convictions and record the various interpretations of human imperfection, it must be left to philosophers to speculate on why some societies regard themselves and the condition of humanity with profound dissatisfaction, while others view people as part of a world in equilibrium: neither on a downward path to greater corruption, nor on the way to salvation and a better future. □

Cargo cults

The earliest European visitor to the northern coast of New Guinea, a Russian scientist called Baron Mikloukho-Maclay, reported in 1871 that the indigenous people of that area believed that a figurehead from a European ship found washed up on the beach had actually come from the Land of the Dead.

Since those early days of contact with White people similar beliefs, and organized cults based on them, have been widely reported throughout the islands of Melanesia. These notions about the Land of the Dead which are possibly quiet ancient, and other traditional themes concerning, the return of ancestral spirits from that Land, have been given a new, anti-European twist by the Melanesians. Now they say that the material goods possessed in such abundance by Europeans—known as 'cargo' in Pidgin English, or 'Neo-Melanesian'—not only come from the Land of the Dead but are also made there by the ancestral spirits of the islanders themselves. Hence, the islanders believe that the Cargo really belongs to them.

When White people first arrived, they were often thought to be the returning ancestors—white because they were dead. But the Melanesians soon found that the newcomers kept power and wealth for themselves. Cult movements have evolved from the basic belief that the Cargo would arrive and be delivered to the islanders by other agents—usually the returning spirits of the islanders' ancestors. Such movements have often been widespread. They tend to suddenly gather momentum, to rise and fall away, and are prone to periodic, dramatic revival, and also to a simmering underground persistence over long periods. To the foreigner they seem bizarre and have often been considered by White people to be expressions of collective delusions.

The arrival of material goods is often envisaged in association with a wider change of the whole cosmos. Birds are expected to live in water, fish will fly, mountains will be levelled and valleys raised. The members of some movements envisage that White people will become Black, or vice-versa. In others, a new, common human identity is expected: everyone will become either Black or White.

Sometimes it is thought that the cult followers themselves must carry out certain acts in order to help bring about the coming of the Cargo and this may involve disruption of many basic social institutions. Thus, marriage is replaced either by the denial of sexuality altogether, with men and women sleeping in separate dormitories, or the normal rules of incest and exogamy regulating relations between the sexes are abolished.

Two features of Cargo cults normally stand out: there is the Cargo belief itself, and secondly, the implicit or explicit criticism of Europeans. In the light of the history of Black-White relations over the whole of the Melanesian region, the latter is understandable. The indigenous society of the area was severely disrupted by colonial rule in the late 19th century. The disruption continues today especially in the remoter areas of the New Guinea Highlands where control by central government is still being established, while neo-colonialism causes disruption everywhere else in Melanesia.

The White men began by appropriating land for cultivation and recruiting men to work in hard conditions often by force or trickery. The many hundreds of small tribal societies across the islands were unable to put up any effective political or military resistance to this colonization. Usually lacking permanent, hereditary chiefs or any form of centralized State

Pigs slaughtered as part of a ritual exchange on Tanna in Vanatua. On occasions, members of Cargo Cults throughout Melanesia have abandoned their farms and thown their possessions into the sea in the belief that the coming of the 'cargo' of the white people was imminent.

Kal Muller/Susan Griggs Agency

Kal Muller/Susan Griggs Agency

Public displays of singing and dancing may sometimes express the frustration felt by the islanders at the White man's behaviour. Cargo cults, however, are an attempt to understand why the White man has such wealth and power.

institutions, they were easily deprived of their automony, and were artificially welded together to form new political entities—such as Papua, the Solomon Islands Protectorate and the condominium of the New Hebrides—under a variety of European powers.

There followed years of economic ups and downs, as the fickle prices of copra, oil, gold and other local products on the world market resulted in boom and slump for the islands. In 1941 came the devastating Japanese invasion, followed by the restoration of the pre-war colonial régimes. Then there were further post-war transformations as Papua-New Guinea moved towards independence, and Dutch New Guinea became Irian, a part of Indonesia.

Hundreds of thousands of villages lost their able-bodied men to the plantations and mines, or had them conscripted as porters. The villagers had to pay taxes to new White governments and came to experience the direct and indirect effects of invasion and very bitter fighting as the Japanese were pushed back in the Second World War. They came into contact for the first time with American soldiers, some of whom were Black and well-

equipped with all the cargo usually reserved for Whites.

It was a strange, unpredictable world and it confused the Melanesians. They felt that if such enormous changes had already occurred, it was not beyond the bounds of possibility that even vaster and stranger things might come about.

Cargo cults are only one way which evolved to help the Melanesians come to terms with the experience of colonialism. In other parts of the world, and even within the islands themselves, there were other responses such as nationalism and the hardening of traditionalism as a way of resistance.

Amongst these diverse responses to colonial rule, the emergence of Cargo cults in Melanesia has been a common and widespread phenomenon. To understand why these apparently strange movements emerged rather than some Melanesian equivalent of Gandhi's 'Civil Disobedience,' for example, it is essential to understand more about the Melanesians' world view.

Melanesians often do not make an absolute distinction between the world of the living and that of the dead. To them the ancestors of the dead are all around, and actively interested in what their descendants do. While recognizing the physical effort which must be put into growing good crops, the islanders believe that the approval of the ancestors and magical spells are also needed; what a Westerner distinguishes as 'practical farming' and what he would call ritual or magic both form part of a whole set of

(Above) Christian has played a significant part in the development of Cargo cults in Melanesia since the islands were taught that the key to the White people's culture lay in their religion.

(Below) Painted with the letters USA, an islander parades with a bamboo rifle. Most Cargo cults in Melanesia require members to make preparations for the coming of the 'cargo'.

Kal Muller/Susan Griggs Agency

Kal Muller/Susan Griggs Agency

seen, perhaps, as profoundly materialistic: they are pre-occupied with ensuring the production and reproduction of the things in life which are most important to the islanders. They are concerned above all, with producing crops and children, and with avoiding sickness and the failure of the reproductive cycle of animal and plant life.

Melanesians naturally tended to try to understand White people's world in terms of these ideas. In the past such ideas had always been effective in enabling them to cope with the world as they knew it. But the world had been greatly changed with the arrival of White people. The islanders were prepared to accept that perhaps new ideas were needed in order to understand this new world, and that the White person's own ideas were worthy of serious attention. For the old ways of thought were not necessarily contradicted by the ideas that the Melanesians received from the Whites. The form of education they received in mission schools, for example—and the missions virtually controlled whatever education there was—told them that the key to the White people's culture, and to their obvious power, lay in what they called their 'religion'. The heart of European culture was the worship of Christ, and the repository of the ultimate in knowledge was the book called the Bible.

Parts of the Bible were translated into various Melanesian languages and in the early days there were mass conversions to Christianity. People flocked to the missions, many of them because they believed that they would thereby be fully accepted into the White man's world and allowed to share in the 'Secret of the Cargo'. They were somewhat mystical when they did come to read the Bible, for they could find nothing about Cargo in it at all. Nor did their new church membership seem to make any practical difference in everyday social life. Black people still received poor wages for very hard work, and White people who did no physical labour at all, still kept the Cargo. The Whites, even the missionaries amongst them, continued to mix socially only with each other, and to treat their Black fellow-Christians as inferiors.

The islanders had an explanation for this continuing White superiority: the Whites were deliberately hiding the crucial portions of the Bible. The Melanesians knew that the entire Bible had not been translated and that there were rival schools of Christianity, each with its own interpretation. In the extreme, mission-

equally necessary and interrelated activities. Melanesians often use one word, usually translated as 'work', for these activities.

To the islanders the source of all human knowledge lies in the Creation, when the gods or the creator-spirits brought the world into being. They created plants, animals, geographical features and the knowledge of how to make fire and stone axes. They also created the social order of the world—the tribes and clans, cultural activities and social laws

such as the rules of marriage and the principles of good conduct. These things brought into existence at the dawn of time have always been the basis of their earthly human existence, but to keep them going and to ensure harmony in social life, Melanesians believe they must perform rituals and lead proper moral lives. If they do not, the ancestors will be displeased and exert their power to punish the living.

These beliefs are a powerful response to the 'other world'. But they can also be

Kal Muller/Susan Griggs Agency

The Cargo cult on Tanna, led by the mythical John Frum, gained popularity in the 1930s. These islanders make offerings to a red John Frum Cross hoping to hasten the coming of their 'messiah' who will bring all the things they desire.

aries were believed to have purposely omitted, or torn out, the pages on which the 'secret' was written. The ritual actions needed to make Cargo accessible were also kept secret: they were plainly something to do with making marks on pieces of paper or with messages sent by Whites back to the Land of the Dead. For this was the only 'work' White people did, and in return they received shiploads and planeloads of goods.

The reasoning developed by the Melanesian is perfectly logical and consistent, and they tested their hypotheses by carrying out a set of successive experiments. Firstly, they tried joining the missions. Then a period of disillusioned return to traditional beliefs occurred. But, inevitably, the older beliefs had become intermixed with newer ideas taken from the White people's world and incorporated within a basically Melanesian context. Given an anti-White and pro-Black bias, these beliefs became the ideological basis for new kinds of Cargo movements that were neither traditional nor entirely new.

These beliefs about Cargo may seem irrational to Europeans because of different basic assumptions in the world view between the Melanesian and Western cultures. Western people largely explain what happens in the world, nowadays at least, in secular terms, rather than in terms of divine intervention. Secondly, they have accumulated a much more extensive body of information about the natural world through the development of empirical science. They know, for instance, that 'cargo' is made in factories and are aware of the principles of mechanics, chemistry and physics involved in its manufacture, the machinery and technology used and the way labour is organized. But, more precisely, most Westerners do not individually understand all this process at all. What they do know is that there are specialists who can invent and operate machines, and accept their knowledge of this 'science' on trust.

'You believe that diseases are caused by things called germs', one islander once said, 'yet you say they're invisible and you've never seen one!' Conversely, Melanesians rely purely on their senses: they see ships arrive and planes land, and observe the White people signing bills of landing and form their theories on that evidence.

None of this is illogical when seen from a Melanesian viewpoint. The well-known zoologist, David Attenborough, was arguing with Islanders from Vanatua about why they continued to believe in their messiah, John Frum, even though he had not brought the Cargo they had been expecting for 19 years. One man replied that the Christians had been waiting for the return of *their* Messiah for nearly 2,000 years and yet they still believed in Him.

The difference in the amount and nature of factual information about the world available to Westerners and the Melanesians thus helps to explain the different ways in which we make sense of the world. But Melanesians are also members of societies in which kings and classes based on private property are unknown, and in which exchanges leading to the redistribution and dispersal of accumulated property are commonplace. Goods are not communally owned, nor are distinctions of rank and status unimportant to them. Indeed, Melanesians avidly seek to raise their standing in the eyes of their fellows. There are 'big men' such as political leaders and successful trading entrepreneurs. But these roles tend to be the result of individual achievement rather than inheritance. Moreover, a person acquires high social status by giving away property. By holding enormous feasts, they convert wealth into prestige, both their own prestige and that of their clan or lineage.

Hence Melansians place a high value on generosity and the sharing of goods, whereas Westerners encourage individual accumulation and competition almost as ends in themselves. The anthropologist, KOL Burridge, who studied a Cargo movement in New Guinea, has emphasized how these movements express the loss of this highly-valued mutuality in the modern world, and how they seek to restore it again. It has been lost partly because of the emergence of the 'spirit of capitalism' within Melanesian society, but more importantly because the crucial division in society is the gap between the few wealthy Whites and the Black population who are poor. To the islanders, the Whites are immorally monopolizing wealthy and refusing to treat them as equals in social terms.

The Cargo cult thus contains a profound moral criticism of Western society. It is not necessarily antagonistic to Whites; many Melanesians imagine that the new world associated with the coming of Cargo is a world in which both White and Black people become equals and brothers. But sometimes the Whites are envisaged as occupying the lowly status that was formerly the islanders' lot.

Not surprisingly, frustration and irritation at the White people's behaviour has at times shown itself explicitly—particularly in the form of public displays of collective emotion such as passionate singing and dancing, 'speaking in tongues' and ecstatic possession. Large-scale turbulence of this kind has involved symbolic imitations of White styles of life and preparations for the arrival of the Cargo such as the wearing of 'military' uniforms, sending messages by 'wirelesses' made of bamboo and creepers and the clearing of landing-strips for the Cargo aeroplanes. This has so frightened governments,

planters and missionaries that they have tried to repress the movements in one way or another, even though outbreaks of violence have been rare.

More often, the cults die of their own accord, since the Cargo does not come, no matter how much ritual is performed. But the underlying inequalities and unsatisfied hopes do not disappear. Some enthusiasts keep the cult beliefs alive, and, periodically, a set of events will spark off a revival. The cults have also successfully adapted themselves to changing technological conditions; whereas the Cargo was once expected to come by canoe, then by European ships, now it is by aeroplane. There have even been cases of space-age Cargo cults, based on reports of American attempts to land spaceships on the moon, in which satellites figure as the new means of transport. One United States Presidential election resulted in the 'President Johnson cult', where the islanders first tried to vote for President Johnson, then to buy him. The Americans particularly have retained the symbolic importance which they acquired during the Second World War. They were then believed to be the eagerly-awaited harbingers or bringers of the Cargo, because of their sudden arrival from nowhere, the abundance of their resources, their relatively egalitarian attitudes towards the islanders and the liberation from Japanese rule they achieved.

It is likely that the Cargo cults will continue to appear and disappear, though they will probably be transformed into more conventional political movements, by business enterprise or co-operative developments in the economic sphere and by Western religions. This has been the trend in the increasingly secularized Western culture, where similar movements anticipated the imminent end of the world.

Ultimately all such movements are expressions of deep hopes and aspirations for the future, inspired by the loss of security often created by the clash of two cultures. To this degree at least, Christian conceptions of heaven, or socialist dreams of a classless society, can be seen as variations on this same theme.

Cargo cults, then, are not just about achieving access to more property; they also involve the attempt to rationalize the changing world. Within the limits of available knowledge and ideas, their adherents act in a 'rational' way. They are not 'mad' or incapable of coherent and systematic thought. The Cargo cult beliefs involve making moral and intellectual sense of an apparently unjust world in which evil people flourish and the good often suffer. Hence the movements are likely to persist, even if on a reduced scale, just as Western sects which believe that the end of the world is imminent still exist alongside secular movements. □

Peyote cult

Kal Muller/John Hillelson Agency

In the deserts of northern Mexico and southern Texas grows a small cactus called peyote which has been used for centuries for religious and medicinal purposes by the Indian tribes of that area. This cactus, with its strange power to produce visions, has formed the basis of a cult which has now become the most widely practised religion of the Indians of North America.

How and when the Indians first discovered the hallucinogenic properties of peyote is not certain. But they themselves explain that it was revealed to a woman in a dream. One version of the story explains that this woman had somehow become separated from her group as they roamed over the desert—the men hunting desert animals, the women gathering roots for food.

Alone and lost in the desert, the woman gave birth to a child. She lay with the child under a small bush, in the little shade it offered from the burning sun. Weak and ill, she knew she would not have long to live. She lay down to sleep

and, while she slept, dreamed she heard a voice which told her that she must eat the plant which was growing beside her and that it would be a great blessing for all her people. She woke up and looked around; it was near dawn. Beside her grew a small cactus. She reached down, pulled up the cactus and ate the small lobed head.

Immediately she felt strong and well, and when she had fed the child she gathered as many cactus plants as she could carry and set off in search of her people. By some miraculous chance she was able to find them. The woman then took the plant to her uncle, one of the elders of the tribe. Hearing the story he knew that the plant was a great gift and blessing sent by God for all his people.

Peyote is known to have been in use in Mexico in pre-Columbian times. It was one of the offerings made to the gods in Aztec temples, and was ritually eaten by the priests. The name itself comes from the Aztec word for cactus, *peyotl*. In various Indian tribes it was eaten at

Huichol Indians gather at the start of a pilgrimage to the area where the peyote cactus grows. Before their departure, members of the party prepare themselves by undergoing purification rites and abstaining from sexual intercourse.

religious ceremonies and probably also used by individuals in a non-ritual way. And tribes such as the Comanches and Shawnees carried peyote in their 'war bundles'—collections of objects believed to have magical power.

In some tribes rival *shamans* used peyote in their witchcraft practices as they continue to do today. However, no cult seems to have been associated with it until the mid-19th century when its use gradually began to extend north from Mexico into the Great Plains. By the 1870s the Mescalero Apaches were using peyote, and by the end of the 1890s it was in common use among all the Indian tribes of the Great Plains as far north as Canada.

2474

A cluster of peyote cacti is found growing amongst some rocks. Before the cactus is picked, arrows are shot around it to prevent the spirit inside from escaping.

At this time peyote began to develop into a distinct religion, a transition which probably began among the Kiowa and Comanche Indians of Oklahoma. The new religion combined elements of Christianity with traditional beliefs and rituals, and centred on religious ceremonies at which peyote was eaten, and which also included prayer, ritual chanting and contemplation. The peyote was seen as a symbol of the spirits being worshipped and was eaten as a sacrament to give 'power' to the worshippers.

Peyote itself is a small, spineless cactus with the botanical name of *Lophora Williamsi*. It has a long carrot-shaped root, and only a small tuft above ground, in the centre of which is the white button which is the flowering part of the plant. When the button is cut and dried for eating it is rather like a small mushroom.

Peyote contains various substances which have a sedative or intoxicating effect on the body. The most important of these is mescalin, a hallucinogenic drug which has effects like those produced by LSD. During a ceremony each person will probably eat between 12 and 20 buttons.

The actual physical effects of taking peyote are to heighten and distort perception, particularly the sense of colour, but also of sound and touch. Most users also experience dreams and visions. Taking the drug is not always a pleasant experience; it often causes violent nausea. To most people, however, it also gives a feeling of great mental well-being and a sensation of being in spiritual contact with the surrounding people and the natural environment. To Indians it is a religious experience, allowing them to communicate directly with the supernatural. Describing the difference between Western-style Christianity and peyote Christianity, a Shawnee saying states that the White people go into their church and talk *about* Jesus, whereas the Indians go into their tipis and talk *to* Jesus.

The visions which the Indians experience are often of God, Jesus or a spirit who gives them a personal revelation—the peyote user's own culture and personality inevitably affecting the images seen. The Mexican Indians, for

example, refer to the coloured birds which occur in their mythology and the Plains Indians' visions recall the prairies and buffaloes of their traditions.

Peyote fitted easily into Indian religious beliefs, but probably the major reason for the conversion of the Indians to peyotism was their social and historical situation. Their traditions, culture and way of life had been totally destroyed by military defeat. The buffalo herds on which they depended for food, and which had been of fundamental economic and religious importance to them, were gone. Huddled on reservations, they lived in desperate poverty, decimated by malnutrition and disease, and with a consequent loss of pride and identity. They were a people socially and culturally isolated between two worlds. The old world based on the traditional prairie existence had gone except in memory and ritual. The White person's world was a

A Huichol Indian packs a year's supply of the peyote cactus to take back to the settlement. During the four or five days spent collecting peyote, the men eat nothing but the cactus itself.

hostile environment based on values that the Indian found totally incomprehensible.

Peyote came after other spiritual outlets had been tried. In the 1890s the cult of the Ghost Dance swept the reservations. Wovoka, an Indian messiah, had prophesied the return of the ancestors and the old way of life if Indians would dance for several successive nights particular steps that had been revealed to him in a vision. The Ghost Dance was carried from tribe to tribe as the Indians eagerly seized the message of hope it offered. The fervour with which the Dance was performed led to trances and visions

(Below) These Indians are preparing the peyote cactus for consumption. Only the top of the plant is eaten; when cut and dried it resembles a small mushroom; hence its name 'the sacred mushroom'.

concerning the destruction of the Whites. The message was a call to action for thousands of hopeless and dispirited tribesmen. Out of their common condition emerged a new sense of what it meant to be not merely a tribesman, but an Indian.

However, when the ancestors failed to return and the Whites did not leave, despair and disillusion returned. The way was then open for a less ecstatic cult that could build on the new inter-tribal sense of identity of the Indian people.

Peyotism spread rapidly in the 1890s to more than 50 Indian tribes north of the Rio Grande. It soon met the opposition of Church groups and the Department of Indian Affairs, and the use of peyote was made illegal in several states. Groups practising peyotism formed themselves into the Native American Church in 1918, as much for legal protection as for promoting a coherent set of institutionalized beliefs. In the 1960s this Church claimed to have 200,000 adherents.

It is hardly surprising that peyotism has remained so strong. Not only did White people create the socio-psychological need for a peyote-type experience, but the American Indian continues to see peyote as a protection against further cultural invasion by the Whites. Peyote, with its all-enveloping psychological and spiritual power is seen by Indians as protecting them from the White people's laws, customs, prejudices and alcohol. The strong mystical experience of peyote was and is attractive to a people denied material, cultural and political expression.

The way peyotism is practised differs from tribe to tribe, even from meeting to meeting, and combines Indian and Christian elements in varying degrees. Most peyotists consider themselves to be Christians, defending peyotism as an Indian form of Christianity. Christianity and the traditional beliefs have much in common, especially their ethical teachings. The Great Spirit is equated with God, the supreme being who created the world and controls the destinies of all its creatures. Then there are various intermediaries: Jesus Christ and the Holy Spirit find their place in the Indian pantheon, like all spirits, considered to be immaterial manifestations of supernatural forces. Peyote is sometimes personified as the Peyote Spirit, considered to have been sent by God to the Indians as Christ was sent to the White man, and it is even identified with Christ.

In Mexican tribes the ceremony is usually held outside and is characterized by movement and dancing. The Huichol Indians, for example, dance in a circle to the sound of peyote chants, the clacking of deer bones and the beating of the water drum. The men carry deer tails and the women bamboo sticks.

The North American Indians usually hold their ceremonies in specially erected

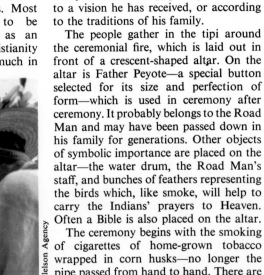

Kal Muller/John Hillelson Agency

tipis. Beginning on Saturday evening, they continue until the next morning, though in the more Christianized sects the ceremony starts on Sunday. Meetings are called for various purposes, usually by a sponsor as a special act of piety or thanksgiving for the birth of a child, or to pray for recovery from an illness. It is often the sponsor who provides the peyote, though at some ceremonies everybody brings their own. The ceremony has to be presided over by a Road Man (one who shows the Road), who may be the sponsor himself, or someone he invites to take this role. The Road Man is not a priest in any formal sense; anyone could lead the worshippers. He conducts the ceremony in his own way, perhaps according to a vision he has received, or according to the traditions of his family.

The people gather in the tipi around the ceremonial fire, which is laid out in front of a crescent-shaped altar. On the altar is Father Peyote—a special button selected for its size and perfection of form—which is used in ceremony after ceremony. It probably belongs to the Road Man and may have been passed down in his family for generations. Other objects of symbolic importance are placed on the altar—the water drum, the Road Man's staff, and bunches of feathers representing the birds which, like smoke, will help to carry the Indians' prayers to Heaven. Often a Bible is also placed on the altar.

The ceremony begins with the smoking of cigarettes of home-grown tobacco wrapped in corn husks—no longer the pipe passed from hand to hand. There are then prayers and a ritual blessing, and the peyote is eaten. Accompanied by the drum, each person takes his turn to sing four songs—songs which are the living history of peyotism. Men often sing of their visions and peyote experiences—many of which relate to their tribal traditions. A common feature is the invocation of the great Indian past—life on the prairies, the buffalo, victories over other tribes, and skill in hunting and war.

Not all peyote songs are old; modern songs have been composed to honour the Indians who fought in the Korean and Vietnam wars. Some of the songs are of almost unrecognizable Mexican origin, others are close to Christian hymns. The songs are passed from tribe to tribe, and some, as they pass to tribes who speak different languages, acquire nonsensical words, unintelligible to the worshippers. The Road Man may himself sing ritual songs, lead the prayers and read passages from the Bible. The music, with its strong rhythmic beat, is a major factor in drawing the members of the cult together.

The effects of the peyote, the chanting, the cedar incense and the incessant drumming leads to an intense experience for the participants. The principal object of meetings is contemplation, and the experience of communicating with the spirits, from whom the worshipper hopes to receive help and guidance. Peyote is invariably regarded as a teacher.

Individuals may see visions of various kinds. They may see supernatural figures twirling in the smoke from the fire: God, Christ or the Virgin Mary might appear; the actual bearers of supernatural power may enter the tipi in human or animal form. The visions are not always pleasant. Among the Apaches particularly they are often horrific. Monster owls and bears—both regarded with dread by these tribes—may appear, and so may cannibal spirits and demons who sometimes cause panic.

When the stars show midnight, the Road Man steps outside the tipi and blows four short blasts on a whistle made from an eagle's wing bone. A woman, often a relative of the Road Man, or someone he wishes to honour, brings water for the worshippers. It is ceremonially passed round and everyone drinks. Water is considered sacred since it is essential to all life and an incarnation of 'power' second only to peyote itself. This ritual water is blessed and prayed over so that it acquires additional power. The water ceremony seems to be an example of the ritualization of a physical need since the drug causes dehydration and the worshippers become thirsty. The woman who brings the water may symbolize womanhood as the source of life; although in some tribes she symbolizes the Peyote Woman, the woman to whom peyote was revealed in a dream.

The role of water-bearer is, in some of

The 'Road Man' lights a taper for a child in a Huichol peyote ceremony. Unlike more Christianized North American Indians, the Mexican Huichol still relate the visions induced by eating the peyote to their traditional beliefs.

the tribes where peyotism was first introduced, the only one which women are allowed. But in many of the more Christianized sects, women now participate in the ceremony.

The woman comes again in the morning to bring more water, and is followed by other women bearing dried, sweetened meat, dried corn and fruit. When the worshippers have broken their fast, the praying and chanting are resumed, at least until daylight, and often until well into the morning. After the ceremony a feast is customary, usually provided by the sponsor of the meeting.

There is a strong ethical implication to the eating of peyote. It is frequently said that a man cannot use peyote unless he is 'straight', that he must have a clean heart and lead a devoted life. The peyote 'Road' can be a hard one. The ethics of peyotism are similar to those of Christianity. They teach brotherly love, friendliness, honesty, helpfulness, care of one's family, unselfishness, hard work and self-reliance. John Wilson, the half-white leader who helped to spread peyotism in the 1890s, exhorted his followers to abstain from alcohol, fighting, gambling, sexual excess, witchcraft and love magic. One of the strengths of peyotism was the ethical code and new social values it offered to a demoralized people.

Besides its use in religious ceremonies, peyote can also be used by the *shaman* of the tribe, a spiritual leader believed to have special powers. Under the influence of peyote the *shaman* can prophesy, tell fortunes, control natural events, find lost property and hear confessions.

Peyote also continues to be used as a medicine. As a sedative and pain-killer its efficacy is proven although in many Indian tribes it tends to be used as a panacea for all ailments from toothache to blindness.

In addition to the peyote eating cere-

monies, the Mexican Indians have elaborate pilgrimages and picking ceremonies which involve the worship of the peyote plant. One tribe, the Hikori, live some 640km (400 miles) from where the cactus grows. In early October about 12 men from the tribe set out on a pilgrimage to collect the tribe's yearly supply. They prepare themselves for the journey by religious rites and by abstaining from sex. To retain a spiritual contact with the rest of the tribe, one man who has taken part in the ceremony in the past stays behind. As they know the journey takes 43 days, he has a string tied with 43 knots, and he unties one each day. The leader of the pilgrimage has a simililar string and unties one knot each day.

Both the pilgrims and the man they leave behind take peyote throughout the journey to heighten the feeling of spiritual contact that exists between them.

When the party arrive at the peyote fields they first pray to be saved from madness. This is a real danger as for the next few days they will eat nothing but peyote. In gathering the cactus they go through the ritual of a hunt. Arrows are fired both in front and behind the sacred plant to prevent the spirit escaping. And before the plant is dug up, they pray for forgiveness.

After four or five days of gathering the peyote cactus the pilgrims return. On the journey home they fast and smear their faces with the yellow juice of the peyote. They arrive at the village completely exhausted and almost unrecognizable. The year's supply of peyote is threaded on a string and kept in the temple.

The Indian tribes further north have to buy their peyote from dealers. And this has not always been easy. Since the use of peyote has become widespread among the North American Indians there has been harassment and legal restriction on its use and sale. Although many American states retain their anti-peyote statutes the law tends to turn a blind eye to its use for religious purposes by the Indian community.

Partly because of persecution in the past, few Indians admit to being peyotists, and the Native American Church itself has no organized structure or heirarchy of officials. But it has been defended by many anthropologists and others concerned with the rights of the Indian people of North America. Peyotism, with its strict moral code, has brought a dignity to a defeated and demoralized people. With its stress on contemplation it has encouraged a resignation and acceptance of life as it is, while allowing a temporary escape from its harsher realities. But above all it has provided a means of uniting Indians nationally, giving them a sense of identity and enabling them to preserve many facets of their ancient cultures. □

Kal Muller/John Hillelson Agency

Witchcraft in Africa

Death at a distance, death which occurs without any physical contact between the killer and the victim, death caused by envy and malice or even by an unconscious feeling of hostility, these are the ideas which lie at the heart of witchcraft beliefs. Such beliefs about death and misfortune are still found in many pre-industrial societies throughout the world, and although few people in the West now believe in the efficacy of such ideas, it was only two or three centuries ago that people were being tortured and executed all over Europe because they were believed to be witches.

Anthropologists have always been fascinated by witchcraft and sorcery, although they have often had great difficulty in producing any satisfactory and comprehensive definition of the subject as there is a great deal of variation from culture to culture. Among the Azande people of Central Africa, for example, a witch achieves power by having a witchcraft substance, *mangu*, in his or her belly, and this is inherited from the parent of the same sex. Although this power may lie dormant for a whole lifetime, it can be activated by feelings of envy, greed or spite and may cause harm even without its possessor doing anything or being aware of it.

In other cultures the 'witch' may have to perform certain rites or manipulate physical substances to achieve power. Among the North American Navajo Indians certain forms of 'witchcraft' need the hair or nail parings of the victim before they can become effective, and both the Gusii and Mandari of Africa believe witches are taught their skills by their parents and, in the case of the Mandari, by learning how to dance in the dead of night.

Difficult though it is to produce a definition of witchcraft which suits all cases, it usually involves the idea that some human beings can harm others without recourse to direct physical assault. The harm caused in this way is almost always unusual, undesirable and utterly without justification.

Among the Azande, whose belief in witchcraft was first explored in detail by the great anthropologist Sir Edward Evans-Pritchard in the 1920s and 1930s, it is believed that the activities of perverted, anti-social witches create almost all

those misfortunes of life which do not have any other obvious causes. If a man is careful to take all normal precautions and still wounds himself with his cutlass when clearing a farm; if his beer fails to ferment even though he has carefully prepared it in the correct way; or if his hut catches fire and burns down for no apparent reason, then these events may be taken as *prima facie* evidence of the activity of witches.

Similarly, among the Asanti of central Ghana it is anything unusual and evil which serves to arouse suspicion that male or female witches, *abayifo,* may be practising their evil among their local kinsmen. Road accidents, infertility in women or impotence in men, the deaths of children or the sudden descent into drunkenness and poverty of a previously sober and successful man, are also attributed to the work of witches by the Asanti.

It is this linking of misfortune to the malignant personal feelings of other individuals in the society which forms one of the key elements in witchcraft beliefs. It is for this reason that these beliefs have often been interpreted as methods of explanation; tribal philosophies tend to explain not only *how* but *why* certain events occur.

In support of this view, it is clear that most of the societies in which these beliefs are found have only a relatively limited power to control the world in which they exist. They are usually at the mercy of drought and famine, and life expectancy is low; many of those born into these societies sicken and die in their first few years and few reach old age. Treatment for physical illness is often ineffective, and the universe in which such tribes see themselves as existing is far less mechanistic and predictable than the one Western people have constructed for themselves.

Such a world view requires explanations of why things go wrong, and any explanation which allows some positive human response is more useful than a feeling of complete impotence. However, this cannot offer a complete explanation of the existence of witchcraft beliefs, for there are many similar societies with limited technological control over their environment and which do not believe in the power of individuals to cause the misfortunes which assail them. In these societies the cause of such events is attri-

buted to God, to the ancestors or to the breaking of some behavioural or deitary prohibition. The Nuer of the southern Sudan, for example, care little about the existence of witches; they see God, and the relationship of people to God, as the cause of events in their lives.

Nevertheless, it is clear that witchcraft beliefs flourish in those societies where face to face human relationships form the essential basis of social life, where there are few or no impersonal institutions and where formal bureaucracies and a highly developed division of labour have yet to appear. Such 'universes' are highly personal; where the cosmos and the events which occur within it are directly linked to the behaviour of individuals; where each person is both actually and theoretically their brother's keeper. Events such as famine and disease commonly considered to be beyond human control and responsibility are seen as the responsibility of erring and perverted individuals.

The image of the witch to whom these evils are ascribed varies from society to society. But in all cases the things he or she is supposed to do can be seen as involving a perversion or inversion of some of the most basic values of that society. In many cases, the witch is thought to be physically, as well as morally, perverted—a creature who not only twists and distorts the ordinary rules of social life but one who is himself upside down.

Thus among the Ewe, Ga, Fanti and Asanti of Ghana those men who have 'medicines' which enable them to see witches, tell how men and women, who to normal eyes appear to be walking in the ordinary way, are really striding about upside down. By kicking dust or sand at their 'ankles' such witch-seers really kick it into their eyes so that next day these should be red and sore—a clear sign that a person is a witch.

Witches are supposed to be perverted in other ways. They go out naked at night, and consort with wild animals such as hyenas and lions. They travel at great speed, flying through the dark at the time when all normal people are asleep; or they meet in trees, or in the bush, and turn the village into a latrine.

But the values that witches attack are more central than this: they do what is most likely to destroy what their societies

Weidenfeld & Nicolson Ltd/Denise Paulme

(Above) This carved 'rubbing board' is used as an oracle by the Lele of West Africa. Special roots are ground on it and men may ask if witchcraft threatens their lives. A reply is given when the knob sticks.

(Below) This Kongo carving represents a powerful supernatural being. Those people who seek aid from the spirit drive a nail into the statue, thereby releasing the spirit's power.

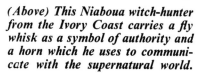

(Above) This Niaboua witch-hunter from the Ivory Coast carries a fly whisk as a symbol of authority and a horn which he uses to communicate with the supernatural world.

see as the good and moral life. Asanti witches are supposed to devour the blood of those closest to them, those with whom they should co-operate and live in amity. They devour the very blood which links them to their relatives. They also kill chidren and make mothers die in childbirth or cause them to become infertile, thus preventing their group from having children.

The Nyakusa of Southern Africa, who live in age-set villages, place great emphasis on the fair sharing of food among neighbours as one of the basic bonds of social life. Their witches, roused by the smell of roasting meat, are driven by greed and selfishness to attack their closest allies.

Among the nearby Pondo, witches are supposed to be sexually perverse and driven by their lusts to couple with familiars. Monica Wilson, who studied their beliefs, suggested that this could be attributed to the fact that a large number of Pondo social encounters in everyday life are between people among whom sexual

relations would be incestuous. The witch in this case is a figure who articulates the suppressed and forbidden urges of people living under such restrictions.

Very often it is people who are physically unusual or socially graceless who are suspected of being witches—the blind, the malformed and the sterile, or the greedy, the noisy and the gossipy. It has even been suggested that in some cultures such beliefs serve to make people conform to a strict code of behaviour, for showing too much self-interest, greed or envy may lead to a person being accused of witchcraft.

All these factors make it clear that the relationship between the victim and the supposed witch is of crucial importance, and most recent anthropological field-studies of witchcraft have concentrated on this fact. In many societies witchcraft is thought to be restricted to one of the sexes, or to particular sections of the community, and it is believed that it can only operate within certain limited sets of relationships.

Among the East African Kaguru it is said that witches are more likely to attack people who are not members of their own clan (although an actual examination of incidents shows this is not true). The Zande believed that witchcraft only

Axel Poignant/British Museum

occurred between people of about the same status and that men never bewitched women; while among the Asanti, witches are said to attack only co-members of their local matrilineal group, and they are adamant in their belief that witchcraft cannot operate outside that group.

Among the polygamous Pondo and Nyakusa, the rivalries and jealousies of a man's co-wives, bidding for his favour and affection, lead to the recognition that witchcraft is most likely to fly back and forth between squabbling women. And accusations of bewitching between wives are frequent.

Among the Lugbara of Uganda and the Cewa of Central Africa, witchcraft accusations have been linked to the build-up of strains among local groups such as those created by land shortages or over-population. Outbreaks of accusations and counter-accusations of witchcraft lead to divisions, each of which goes off to set up on its own as a more viable unit.

Witches are generally considered to be either more or less than ordinary human beings, and as super- or sub-human creatures they can only be identified by extra-ordinary means. Many societies have therefore made use of various tests and oracles to show whether a suspect was a witch or not. These varied greatly, but over much of Africa the usual method was to test the accused person with a poisonous bark or with a drink made from it. Those who took this poison ordeal were judged on whether they vomited up the preparation or whether they managed to keep it down. On the principle that only the poisonous would not reject the poison, those who did not vomit at once were seized and executed.

Witchcraft beliefs do not necessarily disappear with the introduction of Western theories of causation and sickness into smaller-scale societies. In many African societies the old witchcraft and sorcery beliefs continue to exist, although often in somewhat modified form, alongside the new 'scientific' knowledge. Thus local people often begin to draw a distinction between illnesses which can be dealt with by Western medicines and those, caused by witches, which can only be treated in a traditional way.

It has also been noted that witchcraft beliefs, rather than disappearing with European contact, take on a new lease of life and even expand their field of operations. This observation is based on the fact that over the last 50 or 60 years, cults dedicated to eliminating witchcraft by capturing, curing or killing all the witches

(Left) Physical pecularities of any kind are often interpreted as indications that a person is a witch. This Lugbara man was suspected because of his squinting eyes and his constant benign smile.

(Above) These masked witch-doctors from Sierra Leone act as policemen among the Mende people. They lead those suspected of thieving through the village then check their pulse to ascertain guilt.

(Below) This shrine house is used by members of the Blekete cult among the Ewe people of West Africa. People who believe themselves the victims of witchcraft consult a diviner in the cult house.

in a particular area have rapidly spread in many parts of Africa. The activities of such anti-witchcraft cults have been reported from the Congo, Nigeria, Ghana, Uganda and Zambia and many other regions. A few men move from village to village offering anti-witchcraft 'medicines' to 'protect' the hundreds of people who flock to join the movement. These witch-finders 'sniff out' witches in various ways. Many of those apprehended confess to past misdeeds and ask to be cleansed of their evil. Not all these confessions are forced, and many people may freely and willingly come forward and claim to be witches.

The reasons for the spread of these cults are complex. To a certain degree they can be linked with social disruptions and breakdowns caused by Western colonial contact. In many cases old methods of finding witches such as using chiefs' oracles or the poison ordeal were banned by the European rulers, and the original penalties, such as exile, death and mutilation for supposed witches were made illegal. In addition, the powers of those who were traditionally responsible for finding and controlling or eliminating witches were severely curtailed under the new régimes.

In such circumstances new methods of controlling witches, whom local people viewed as menaces, had an obvious appeal. Moreover, it seems clear that with the traditional political structure changed and blocked by the colonial régimes many young and ambitious men saw that active participation in an anti-witchcraft cult could offer prestige, power and profit.

But attempts have also been made to link such cults to a more general disruption of society caused by the introduction of cash-crops, a money economy, schooling and a general break-up of the old tribal order.

From this point of view, the fears, suspicions and accusations aroused by the practice of witchcraft may be a means for people to try to deal with the decay and disappearance of the old moral order. If the witch is personified as the opposite of correct behaviour in the old moral order, any change in this order (and such changes were the essential aim of a 'successful' colonial system) can be attributed to the witches becoming more active.

Change can well produce insecurity in those people who are unable to adapt. In these circumstances their own failure and misfortune and the obvious—but to them inexplicable—success of others, may well inspire them to put the blame for all that happens on witchcraft. But the causes of the strain can only be alleviated and not cured by these attitudes and before long a new cult may arise and the cycle begin again. □

Brian Bond/Colorific!

Jak Kilby

Witchcraft in Europe

It is difficult to arrive at a satisfactory definition of witchcraft. The word itself means the craft of the wise—'witch' deriving from the Anglo-Saxon 'witan', to know. The Egyptologist Margaret Murray made a distinction between what she called Operative Witchcraft and Ritual Witchcraft. In the former she classified all the charms and spells for good or evil, curing or healing, which are common to societies throughout the world: in effect the cultural heritage of the human race, practised by priest and layman alike. Ritual Witchcraft, on the other hand, was the term she applied to the supposed beliefs and practices of those people who, in the late medieval period in Europe, were called 'witches'.

Whether or not the whole of Margaret Murray's theory regarding witchcraft is satisfactory, the distinction she draws between Ritual and Operative Witchcraft is useful. The idea that certain people possess, or may obtain, the power to affect others without physical contact is fundamental to witchcraft beliefs throughout the world. But it is dangerous to assume that European witchcraft and that studied by anthropologists in pre-industrial societies are analogous. Undoubtedly there are similarities, but whereas the witchcraft beliefs of the Zande of the Sudan may still be studied directly as part of a living society, historical records are the only source of information about the witch cult in Europe. For this reason European witchcraft must be treated separately.

In England the legal definition of a witch was 'a person who hath conference with the Devil to consult with him or to do some act'. It is interesting that only during the period of persecution in the Middle Ages which the German scholar Hansen called *Zauberwahn*—witch madness—did the god worshipped by the witches become identified with the Christian Devil. The word 'devil' simply means 'little god', but the different interpretations which may be put upon the word suggest the two main theories regarding the origin of the witch cult in Europe.

Margaret Murray believed that the Devil of the witches was literally a 'little god': the deity of an old religion who had become the Devil of the new. There were parallels with other religions which made the theory that medieval witchcraft was the last remnant of an old pagan cult both plausible and attractive. Other, more pragmatic, scholars argued that witchcraft, where it existed, was anti-religion: a reflection and a parody of Christianity engendered and nourished by pressures within contemporary society.

There were three great periods of witch persecution in Europe, and ironically it is from the inquisitors that most of the documentary evidence comes. The vast majority of those tortured and put to death were undoubtedly innocent; 9 million—this number could be an exaggeration but there may have been many more. The entries in ecclesiastical records of the

This figure, painted on a cave wall in Ariege, France, is known as the 'Sorcerer'. More than 30,000 years old, it is said to depict a man wearing a red deer mask performing a fertility dance. Some historians suggest there are connections between such ancient rites and witchcraft.

trials were concise: 'convicta et combusta'.

The dates of the periods when the persecution was at its most ferocious give a good deal of weight to the argument that the witch trials were a kind of release, a skin eruption on the body of a sick society. When economic and social pressures become unbearable, and society places an intolerable burden on the individual, blame must be allocated—a scapegoat must be found.

The Church was the principal organ for prosecuting suspected witches through the ecclesiastical courts. And it is interesting that the three peaks of persecution correspond to times when the Church, as the upholder of traditional values, felt itself threatened by the tides of change. The first great persecution followed the end of the Crusades in the 13th century. Although the forces of Islam had been successfully prevented from sweeping into Europe by Norman expansion in the Near East, a more insidious enemy had won victories in the minds of the crusading knights—dualism. This uncomfortable doctrine reinforced other heresies already existing in Europe. The Church reacted by creating the Inquisition.

The second outbreak of persecution came in the 15th century, and by this time the Inquisition was a subtle and remorseless machine for detecting and exterminating heresy, particularly anything which suggested a return to paganism. This was also the period of the Black Death, which brought incalculable misery and an overturning of the old social order. It was the time of the Hundred Years War, with England and France locked in mutually exhausting conflict. King Phillip the Fair of France found a scapegoat in the Knights Templar, but this did not prevent an increase in witch persecution: witches died in their thousands all over Europe.

The development of nationalism brought further disillusion, and the number of witch trials increased steadily until the final orgy of persecution in the 16th and 17th centuries. Paradoxically, coming at the end of the Renaissance and the dawn of the Age of Reason, the final wave of persecution was the most severe. The Inquisition killed 400 people in one execution at Toulouse, and 600 supposed witches were burned by a bishop in Bamburg.

If the light of reason was casting dark

shadows, the causes were not difficult to see. It was a time of unprecedented social change. The questions 'does it work' and 'will it pay' which were applied to all things, were being asked by a new middle class. Prices had soared, and in the countryside enclosure was destroying the old system of demesne agriculture. Uncertainty and alarm at the rapidity of change was felt throughout society.

In the 16th and 17th centuries the Church dominated the minds and the lives of the people just as the towers and spires of its churches dominated the towns and villages. But a New World was being colonized, and new ideas spread rapidly after the invention of printing, finding avid readers among the merchant classes. It is not surprising that the Catholic Church felt itself threatened, but the Inquisition rose to the challenge: greater strictness, not greater tolerance was seen as the answer.

In 1484 Giovanni Battista Cibo became Pope, and as Innocent VIII he issued his famous Bull. In it he denounced all heresies: Protestantism, dualism and, of course, witchcraft. Six years later two Dominicans, the Chief Inquisitors of Germany, produced a detailed and exhaustive handbook of the campaign for the detection, examination and extermination of witches. This was the notorious *Malleus Maleficarum*—'the Hammer of the Witches'.

Malleus Maleficarum was an appalling document, a legal textbook totally opposed to what we would understand as natural justice. Guilt was automatically assumed, torture was recommended as a means of securing confessions, and any trick or deception which might trap a witness was encouraged. Allowing no defence, the book sent countless thousands of innocent people to their deaths (which, it advocated, should be as protracted and horrible as possible).

But it must be remembered that in 1490 the problems of contemporary society were not linked with economics or even political structures. The Church saw all evil, including social evil, as emanating from the Devil. Suffering, confusion and disillusion were attributed to an attack launched against the Church, and therefore against society, by Satan and his followers—the witches. Given this total conviction, any means by which the Devil might be thwarted and his minions eliminated was considered justifiable.

The same was still true more than 100 years later. The voices of the men of reason, like Erasmus, were as yet unheard and the imagination of a genius like Durer could still be haunted by the nightmare images which lie in wait, ever ready to trap the traveller, in his engraving 'The Knight, Death and the Devil'. But changes had occurred since the Papal Bull of Innocent VIII. The intellectual speculation and questioning of the Renaissance had given birth to the Reformation.

The reformers, however, had not yet learned tolerance. If anything the Protestants sought out witches more ruthlessly than the Catholics; of all that he rejected in Catholicism, Luther accepted the principles of the *Malleus*. 'I would have no compassion on the witches', he said, 'I would burn them all.' And in Geneva, Calvin had not relaxed the cruel witchcraft laws, but increased their severity. Protestantism brought no relief from the insanity and hysteria of the mass persecutions. Instead, as the Catholic Church armed itself against this heretical religion which threatened its very existence, and the Counter Reformation clashed with the Reformation, the numbers of those accused of witchcraft increased.

Economic and social pressures at the lower levels of society created new grievances and made old ones unbearable; and the way of expressing a grievance was very often an accusation of witchcraft. The Inquisition seized every new opportunity to fix the blame on someone, and not to be outdone in piousness the Protestants equalled every outrage. No-one was safe. The Italian philosopher Giordano Bruno was burned at the stake as a heretic for saying that those witches who actually existed were no more than mentally disturbed old women.

James I's *Daemonologie* replaced the *Malleus* in Protestant Britain. The witch persecution there had never been so severe as on the Continent, partly because the most extreme forms of torture were not permitted for securing confessions. The years between 1598 and 1607 were particularly bad, although only an estimated 40 per cent of those accused were subsequently convicted. The worst period of persecution in England came during the Civil War between 1642 and 1649. This was the time of the famous witchfinder of Essex, Matthew Hopkins.

Hopkins and his assistant John Stearne, supposedly dismayed at the number of people who practised witchcraft in their native Essex, appointed themselves to root out the heretics and present them to the courts. Hopkins may have been sincere. His methods of ascertaining guilt by 'pricking' and the 'swimming ordeal', although barbarous, were enlightened compared with the brutal tortures employed as a matter of course elsewhere in Europe.

The most interesting aspect of Hopkins' period as witchfinder, however, was the introduction of the idea that a pact with the Devil was a necessary factor in determining the guilt of a witch. At this time numerous pamphlets from Europe dealing imaginatively with the Faust legend were circulating in Britain. There can be little doubt that the idea that a mortal can make a pact with the Evil One, bartering his soul for earthly power, captured the popular imagination. Soon, by a kind of osmosis, the pact with Satan became an essential fact in the catalogue of a witch's guilt.

The process was more wide-ranging. Because witchcraft was a statutory offence and the ruling classes who made up the courts were highly literate, folklore and popular fantasy from literature all tended to adhere to the witch image. Gradually, like the 'pact' idea, the witches' sabbath, flying on broomsticks, hideous concoctions, and every kind of sexual excess became essential features of all witch trials. In a time of strict ecclesiastical censorship the book illustrators, with Sunday newspaper piety, depicted in explicit detail every sexual enormity they could devise—so long as they could be attributed to witches, the enemies of God, they were acceptable.

But who were the witches? Although the history of all the persecutions proves that any individual, however faultless, was susceptible to envy and malice and could therefore be accused of witchcraft, there are certain categories who appear again and again. The greatest number of witches were female, a fact which can be linked with the medieval attitude to women. The *Malleus* was quite clear on the subject: the primary cause of witchcraft was 'carnal lust', which in some women was 'insatiable'. Drawing their power from sexual intercourse with male demons, incubi, they caused impotence, sterility, disease, famine and murder.

Anyone, who was in any way 'different' was liable to be classed as a witch. Physical peculiarities or deformities of any kind—lameness, unusual skin or eye pigmentation, speech impediments—were considered indications of possible witchcraft. In a society holding these beliefs and possessing no concept of disease caused by micro-organisms or scientific cause and effect, it only needed crop failure or a series of coincidental miscarriages in a village, for someone who was in some way different to be accused of witchcraft. Once the accusation had been made the Church authorities were always ready to investigate.

There are some parallels between the witch persecutions and the persecution of the Jews in Nazi Germany: the same sickening reasoning is at work, the same principle of finding a scapegoat on whom to blame the nation's ills. In fact, Jews often appeared with witches in Papal Bulls: confederate heretics in league with the Devil. Witch meetings were sometimes referred to as 'synagogues' in court proceedings, and the word 'sabbath' may be either derived from the French *s'ebattre*, to be gay, or it may have more obvious Jewish connections.

The typical witches' sabbath which appears with certain alterations through-

This 15th century Flemish painting shows a young witch preparing a love potion. Elements from art, popular myth and ancient folklore attached themselves to the witch image until fantasy was almost indistinguishable from reality.

11th century the laws of King Canute still emphasize the pagan rather than the Anti-Christian aspects of witchcraft practices: 'We earnestly forbid every heathenism: heathenism is, that men worship idols; that is that they worship heathen gods, or stones, or forest trees of any kind.' The standing stone or another phallic symbol appears regularly in descriptions of the witches' sabbath even of the latest period.

A quite different view of witchcraft is displayed in an Epistle of Pope Adrian VI in 1521. He described the witches as: 'a Sect deviating from the Catholic Faith, denying their Baptism, and showing Contempt of the Ecclesiastical Sacraments, treading Crosses under their Feet and, taking the Devil for their Lord, destroying the Fruits of the Earth by their Enchantments, Sorceries and Superstitions.' The witches had become identified with Anti-Christ. All the paraphernalia of trampling crosses, perverting the Mass and ridiculing God—no doubt suggested by the inquisitors during torture—became commonplace in confessions. Accusations of the 'obscene kiss' which had been levelled at earlier sects were made also, and became something of a favourite with contemporary illustrators.

The unresolved question in all this is of course whether witchcraft actually existed. And if it did exist, whether it was a parody of Christianity, the last remnant of a pagan religion, or a mixture of both. As we have seen, the argument in favour of viewing the persecutions as a kind of safety valve in society, and looking on witches as scapegoats, makes a good deal of sense—particularly in the light of what we know of the history of the three periods when the persecutions were at their worst. But because the witch persecutions may have been caused by the social conditions of the time, does not necessarily mean that witchcraft did not have a separate existence of its own. The Church may not have created a cult; it may have deliberately maligned an existing one for its own purposes.

Assuming that the vast majority of those tried and convicted during the witch persecutions were innocent—which few would now dispute—there still remain cases which demand a different explanation. The notorious trial of Joan of Arc, for example, seems quite clearly to have been politically motivated. The trial and subsequent execution of her mentor Gilles de Retz (the original Bluebeard) is, however, quite different: for one thing it

out the medieval period is a curious mixture of fantasy and possible reality. These sabbaths were supposed to take place four times a year: on February 2 (Candlemas), May Eve (Roodmas), August 1 (Lammas) and November Eve (All Hallow E'en). A joyous occasion rather like a great fair, the sabbath was attended by hundreds of men and women, young and old. The dancing, singing, feasting and copulating began in the evening and lasted until dawn. The god they had come to worship was represented by a man dressed in an animal skin: a stag with antlers, a goat with horns, or in England very often a bull. During the course of the festivities as many of the women as possible would couple with the god. This was the very centre of the ritual: to become one with the god incarnate.

In each district the witches were supposed to be controlled by a priesthood or coven, which consisted of 13 people (including the god) who would be consulted on matters of witchcraft for good or evil. The earliest mention of the coven is in the tract *Handlyng Synne*, in which 12 'fools' and a woman danced at night as a 'coueyne'. In addition to its organizing function, the coven was credited with the handling of the most important rite of all: the sacrifice of the god. This was said to take place every seven or nine years, either by fire or ritual bleeding to death.

This description is really a composite picture of how the witch cult was described in the early documents; it is both simplified and idealized, and some of it is inference. One important omission is the Anti-Christian element, which from the early Middle Ages occurs with increasing frequency. As early as the 9th century the Council of Ancyra had identified Satan with the god of the witches, but in the

Snark International

2484

seems to have been completely justified.

Enormously rich, and one of the most powerful men in France, even de Retz's wealth could not finally conceal his crimes. Under threat of torture he admitted a list of hideous acts, committed he said, to obtain supernatural power. The skeletons of hundreds of boys he had procured and sacrificed were found in the moat of his castle. But the crimes of de Retz had little to do with witchcraft, either imagined or actual. He was probably a paranoiac, who happened to possess the means to indulge his sexual perversions.

Throughout the witch trials, explicit details of sexual behaviour occur again and again. To a certain extent this was undoubtedly a reflection of the interests of the inquisitors. But it also suggests another category of 'witch'. In the light of modern psychology it seems clear that the outbreaks of 'demonic possession' which affected numerous nunneries during the 16th and 17th centuries—notably at Loudun—were the result of sexual hysteria. It was in fact the witch as a scapegoat again: women with no religious vocation were placed by their families in

An illustration from the Compendium Maleficarum published in Milan in 1608, showing witches trampling the Cross. Accusations that members of the witch cult were Anti-Christian became increasingly common in the late Middle Ages.

closed orders, and when their frustrated sexual energy found an outlet in neuroses and hysterical delusions, blame had to be allocated. Ironically the man on whom their sexual fantasies were centred, was very often denounced as the 'witch'.

Sexual fantasy is clearly the basis for many of the 'spontaneous' confessions of witchcraft where no inquisitor was involved and torture was not employed. One young woman when asked to renounce witchcraft replied: 'No, I will not be other than I am; I find too much content in my Condition; I am always Caressed.' An adolescent girl confessed that her devil 'Caressed her Night and Day'—the implications are obvious.

But something far more important comes to light in studying the accounts of witches' relations with the Devil which occur in every trial from the early Middle Ages right up to the 17th century: the similarity of the descriptions. Almost without exception witches—young and old, married and unmarried, from every country in Western Europe, over a period of hundreds of years—describe the Devil in the same way. He is cold, heavy and hard; his sexual organ is universally said to be cold and hard, and to inflict pain on the witch. Margaret Murray had no doubt as to the explanation for this: she believed witchcraft to be the remains of a pagan fertility religion in which intercourse with the god incarnate was the aim of every worshipper. Naturally, since the god was a man disguised, an artificial phallus had to be used if he was to

serve many women.

The disguise, possibly of leather, accounted for the weight and hardness of the rest of the 'Devil's' body. The idea was far from absurd. As an Egyptologist, Margaret Murray backed up her argument by citing as evidence the statues found in ancient Egypt which have a detachable phallus of different material, and the Roman custom of a bride sacrificing her virginity to the god Priapus. It was not difficult to imagine that in a more ancient cult the god was personified by a man rather than an image.

Of course it would be absurd to base the entire argument that witchcraft was a pagan fertility religion on this evidence alone. But working from the hypothesis that in spite of an overlaying of Anti-Christianity, popular myth and private psychosis, witchcraft was a Neolithic cult, a great deal of evidence does slot neatly into place. Firstly, the dates of the two great festivals on May Eve and November Eve indicate the use of a calendar which is pre-agricultural and earlier than the division of the year into solstices. This would fit, because the cult was evidently for increasing the fertility of animals rather than crops.

Another argument in favour of the theory is the extraordinary consistency in reports of the witches' activities. These reports span many centuries, among people of different countries, and the pattern which emerges is only reasonably explained in terms of some kind of fertility cult. The 'horned god' appears from the earliest times: as an image on a cave wall in France dating from 30,000 BC, as the Isis cow of the Egyptians, and as the Golden Calf the Israelites worshipped when they turned away from Yahweh. The identification of the 'Devil' of the witches with this totem animal is therefore quite reasonable.

It is unfortunate that the simplicity and pleasing logic of Margaret Murray's argument was obscured by disconcerting leaps in her anthropological technique. The theory was done further disservice in later books in which she suggested that almost every English monarch up to the Hanoverians was the leader of the witch cult. Nevertheless, the basic concept remains reasonable.

The social pressures of the time may have led some people to parody Christianity; the same pressures may have caused a frightened Church to accuse quite innocent people of doing so. Witchcraft may have degenerated through the Christian era, from a Neolithic fertility cult, to an excuse for a Baccanalian orgy and finally ending as an obscene parody of the New Religion. Or possibly the forms and organization of the Old Religion did survive in isolated areas, and some witches died in the flames as sure of the truth of their god as any Christian martyr. ☐

Voodoo

To the Western mind voodoo is the embodiment of dark superstition and macabre rites. The image of the voodoo temple, with mystical designs drawn in chalk on the floor and strange objects on the altar, echoes the practice of magic long-since discredited in Europe. The drumming, dancing, chanting and finally the moment of 'possession', when the spirits are thought to take hold of the worshippers to 'ride' them, may all seem exaggerated, and even bizarre.

In practice, however, voodoo is a system of belief which provides its followers with the same kind of benefits that all religions do. It has survived within the Haitian social context because it works. It answers to some very basic and perhaps universal human needs which are by no means peculiar to the practitioners of the cult in Haiti.

Most of the slaves who were carried to the New World in the course of the infamous slave-trade came from West Africa. The appalling conditions they suffered on board the ships, and the harsh realities of life as a slave, intensified the need for some system of belief which would help them to cope with the many difficulties they faced.

Most of the problems faced by voodoo followers in Haiti are faced by everyone: success and failure, love and hate, strength and weakness, acceptance or rejection by relatives, friends and other members of society, health and sickness, joy and sorrow, and ultimately life against death. As with other religions, it is the need to maximize the good and to mitigate the bad in life which animates voodoo.

The means to this end related, naturally, to the ancestor cults the slaves had known in West Africa. There, the land, the ancestors who are buried in it, and the living who occupy it, are all closely related.

The first source of help in any difficulty is the spirit of an ancestor. If a person falls sick, for example, the people believe it is an ancestor causing the sickness, perhaps because his spirit has been neglected, or because he is calling attention to himself for another reason. If the crops fail, or if no rain falls, the ancestors must be consulted at the Earth Shrine to find out what is wrong and how to put it right. If people are attacked, whether in war or by malicious witchcraft (or indeed if they wish to attack someone who has

A voodoo initiate rhythmically beats a drum which helps to induce possession. Drums are important in voodoo ritual and are believed to possess the power of revitalizing those who touch them.

offended them) they will ask the spirits for help. The idea of omnipresent spirits, constantly concerned with human affairs, is fundamental in West Africa and to voodoo.

But pure ancestor worship has limitations, particularly if the political units in which people live and co-operate grow large. By definition, an ancestor cult relates only to a particular group of

people who belong to one family, lineage or clan. As larger states developed in West Africa, most of them solved the problem by adding systems of high gods 'above' the ancestors. These gods could be worshipped by everyone, often at the same time as they worshipped the particular ancestor spirits of their own smaller group. And just as people from different groups might be formed into nations, so also might the individual ancestors be grouped into 'nations' under a higher god.

The Fon of Dahomey were one of the West African peoples who adopted this principle and built a most successful centralized kingdom upon it and many slaves came from this area. Fon gods were grouped in pantheons, and their name for god or spirit—the distinction is naturally imprecise—is *vodu*, from which the word 'voodoo' derives. Each Fon *vodu* has a cult-house or temple, and priests or priestesses to care for it. Worship of the *vodu* often takes the form of becoming 'possessed'—an initiate is 'captured' by the spirit he chooses, or who chooses him, towards the end of his period of initiation. For the rest of his life he will seek its help, and will support the temple and its priests or priestess.

It is a particular feature of Fon belief that each clan is said to descend from a part human and part non-human ancestor: an ideal person to be the intermediary between the world of the living and the world of the dead. Yet the most striking feature of this system is the great variety of choice it offers the individual. A person may belong to any one of a wide variety of cults; in effect there are many spirits to choose from when asking for help.

Such a system was ideally suited to the conditions in which the slaves found themselves in Haiti. They came from many different tribes, and could find in voodoo a means of coming together in a community of belief. But choice was still possible, and there was room for ancestors as well as the universal spirit-gods. Even the structure of temples, priests and initiates was taken over in very similar detail.

In Africa such beliefs and practices had developed as a response to changing circumstances, and they were easily adapted to further change in the New

Henry Grossman/Transworld Feature Syndicate

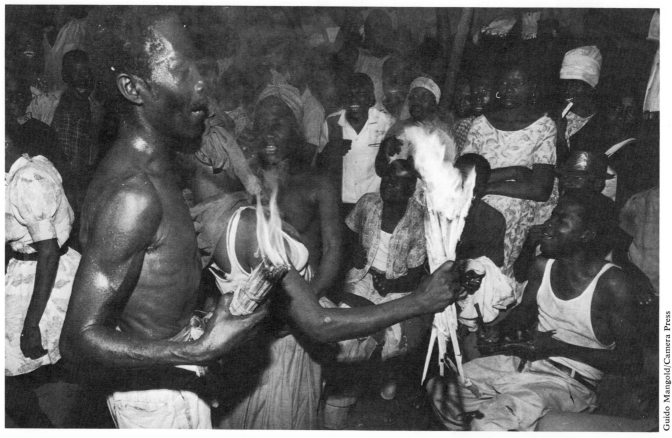

Guido Mangold/Camera Press

(Above) This man and woman are undergoing 'brule zin' or trial by fire. When possessed by their gods, initiates are able to handle the burning tapers without pain.

(Below) A voodoo altar dedicated to Baron Samedi—'Lord of Cemeteries'. His title, and the formal clothes and high hat which are his symbols, recall the slave-owning French plantation masters of the 18th century.

Popperfoto

World Voodoo could, for example, incorporate elements of Christian belief without difficulty, and the 'altar' of a voodoo temple carries a wide range of symbols. Within voodoo, many ideas derived from Amerindian beliefs and the traditions of magic and folklore brought by the Spanish and the French have combined with the basically African structure.

The largest 'nation' of spirits is that of the *Petro-loa* and is mainly of local origin. The thunder-spirit Ogoun, on the other hand, is named after St John the Baptist, and his characteristics, while clearly deriving from West African beliefs, have parallels in past mythological gods such as Zeus. Voodoo believers accept that Christianity, especially the Roman Catholic Church, has spiritual and even magical powers. Since part of this 'power' is thought to reside in church properties like holy water and candles, Christian priests have to guard such movable things carefully against theft for use by voodoo priests. The connection is also perceptible in the celebration of certain Christian festivals by voodoo followers.

Many Christian beliefs and practices have been assimilated into voodoo ritual and in the town of Saut d'Eau, for example, the Feast of the Virgin of the Palms in early July is an occasion for prayers to the *loa*, (the gods of the spirit world) as much as to the Virgin Mary. And, as befits a god of the dead, the chief of the *Petro-loa*, the dreaded Baron Samedi,

Graham Finlayson

(Below) Voodoo priests work them-selves into an ecstatic state around a post dedicated to Legba, the 'messenger of the gods'. The 'loa' or spirits are believed to descend the posts to possess initiates.

(Above) This voodoo priest has been possessed by Damballah, the 'sacred serpent', and all his move-ments are snake-like. When the goat has been sacrificed, the blood will be drunk.

Guido Mangold/Camera Press

Lord of Cemeteries, has his great day on All Souls' Day. Even the notion of the individuals soul, called the *gros bon ange,* the 'great good angel', is a composite notion derived from both African and Christian beliefs.

Because voodoo is a 'total' belief system concerned with all aspects of life, its practices have both a positive and a negative side. White magic pre-supposes the possibility of black magic, and it is part of the job of a voodoo 'priest' to counteract the work of a voodoo 'sor-cerer', To do this both techniques must be understood, and in fact there is no way of distinguishing the roles as both may be performed by the same people.

Medicine which is used to protect can also be used malevolently. It has both pharmacological and magical properties, and all voodoo practitioners (the magi-cians, sorcerers and priests), as Francis Huxley expresses it, 'use two stones to kill one bird'.

Magic works mainly on the soul, the *gros bon ange* which is visible in the shadow and associated with the breath. The *'ti bon ange,* or 'little god angel', is more like the spirit or the conscience, and is sometimes call the *zombie* meaning the kind of bodiless spirit that sorcerers can manipulate. Both of these 'angels' inhabit the *corps-cadavre,* the corpse-body. Bodies, it is also believed, can be raised from the grave by magicians to act as *zombie*-slaves. If a magician should succeed in removing the *gros bon ange* he can even turn a living person into a *zombie,* because without it the spirit and the body lose contact. Many mental defectives, and even the deaf or dumb or blind, are called *zombies* and greatly feared.

The *gros bon ange* is always at risk because it is easily affected by strong emotion. The social relevance of voodoo is clearly seen in the emotions which are thought to have the greatest effect upon it —emotions such as suspicion, envy or resentment. Anger, lust or shock from a family death, business failure or love problems, all put the soul at risk. It can be worked on by spells or 'medicine', and is strongly influenced by music and drumming. It is strongly susceptible to the expectations aroused by a belief in voodoo. When the psychological pressures generated either by such external in-fluences or by self-suggestion have reached a certain degree of intensity, the individual experiences a crisis. This usually takes the form of a seizure, or a *saisissement,* when the victim is thought to be possessed or 'ridden' by a spirit.

A seizure appears somewhat like an epileptic fit. The victims lose control of their muscles, and often collapse and become rigid. Their eyes turn up so that they may appear to be white with none of the iris showing, and the heart-beat

Graham Finlayson

The surreal images in this painting derive from the mythology and ceremony of the voodoo cult. The school of painting inspired by voodoo is becoming increasingly important.

fluctuates wildly. They may roll about and foam at the mouth, and in this state of dissociation may cause themselves serious injury—for example, by falling into a fire. This is the most severe form of *saisissement,* of course, and matters do not always go this far. There may indeed be no actual seizure at all: perhaps just a severe depression or *mauvais sang*, a fit of 'bad blood', will be all that appears.

If the seizure has been induced by bad magic, a voodoo priest will have to be called in for help in diagnosis and treatment. A common preliminary form of treatment is to cool the head with special water which will bring the *gros bon ange*

back, for it is the departure of the soul that brings on the crisis.

A victim who is fortunate may eventually experience a vision in which the spirit appears. This spirit may be the embodiment of a malady which the individual has generated himself, or it may have been 'sent'. But with a priest's help, the spirit itself will probably prescribe a cure, and may subsequently remain at hand as a beneficial spirit so that a formerly 'sick' person will be in a position to cure others. Where the crisis takes the form of vomiting, objects like a lizard or a needle may be 'found' by the doctor-priest and held responsible for the original sickness. They may then be preserved and used to treat similar infections in other people.

The process of initiation into voodoo similarly involves 'possession', but the *saisissement* takes place under the control and guidance of a priest. Individuals may feel that a *loa,* or the spirits of their dead parents, require them to become initiates. Both are called the 'invisibles' and personify grandeur, pride and power. These characteristics respond to the positive feelings, emotions and aspirations of believers in voodoo just as the malicious spirits embody negative equivalents: the fears, weaknesses and emotions of oppression and failure. The initiation than follows a pattern of death and re-birth, with parallel associations of disease and cure.

The individual will have to choose a particular 'nation' of *loa* to follow. The *Rada* are based on spirits known in Dahomey, the *Wangol* from Angola, the *Siniga* from Senegal and so on. Or an initiate may choose the local *Petro-loa.* Since families tend to serve the same 'nation', the initiate may already know which spirit will be his; but if he does not, the priest will be able to help. The initiate's behaviour will reveal which spirit is involved, since each spirit expresses itself differently.

On the acceptance for initiation, the individual will buy the necessary magical and ritual apparatus, and undergo a week's preparation and a further week's seclusion. During this period he or she will learn the correct passwords, songs, prayers and gestures, and will eat only 'dead' (that is white) food. When the time comes, the novices emerge dressed in white, to resemble the dead. During the period of dissociation which precedes 'possession' by the *loa*, the priest preserves each novice's soul in a special pot, protecting it carefully while it is away from the body.

The *loa* enter the novices by travelling down the central post of the temple against which each individual stands. This post is the tree sacred to Legba, the messenger of the gods, *Legba Grand Bois Chemin*, Legba the Path of the Great

Tree. The tree also represents the backbone, and it is partly to let the *loa* enter the novice, that the *gros bon ange* (located for this purpose at the nape of the neck) has to be taken away. Once the soul has gone, subverted by music, dancing and drumming, dissociation sets in and the *loa* can take control. The initiate is now a *hounsi*—a spouse of the god, a servant of the spirit and a member of the congregation.

The sexual connotations of this relationship are considerable. Possession often takes an actual sexual form. Many of the initiates are *jeunesses* (women whose regular lovers are a source of income) or even *bousins* (prostitutes), and part of the voodoo magic is used to gain and keep lovers. The priests, too, sometimes take advantage of their positon to exploit followers sexually.

Baron Samedi may appear at any voodoo ceremony to devour the offerings destined for other *loa*. On All Souls' Day women flock to the rural cemeteries, dressed in the Baron's black and purple colours, and perform an erotic dance, waving sticks as mock phalluses. These echoes of the Dahomean cult of Legba—in which is regarded as irresponsible Legba and violent, and a phallus symbolizes his constant demands and the difficulty of constraining him—may be particularly appropriate in a social situation which owes much to the past history of slavery. Social patterns still owe much to this past history: marriage, for example, is still rare in Haiti and a woman's life may be even harder than a man's. Legba is an appropriate comment on the situation because it highlights male irresponsibility and offers the women an opportunity to express their defiance symbolically.

The voodoo priests maintain control of the whole ceremonial complex by a special position. They balance on the borders of the various spheres of death, magic and sexuality, and of the interdependent worlds of the spirits and their followers. They possess a special power, the *prise des yeux*, which enables them to remain conscious while listening to the *loas* whispering in their ears. They do not reach a state of either full dissociation or full possession. Like the Dahomean ancestors they perform the role of a kind of intermediate midwife.

It is through the priests that the 'invisibles' can be turned from enemies into friends, from hostile and uncontrollable forces into useful associates. It is a dangerous game because the forces involved are very powerful. Both black and white magic must be employed. The mystery is fearful but the price has to be paid if power is to be acquired. Acceptance of god means accepting the devil, for the individual is composed of evil as well as good. To be neither one nor the other is, in truth, to be a *zombie*. □

Curing and primitive medicine

The healing of the sick is one of the permanent preoccupations of the human race. But our approaches to this task differ sharply. Observing the conduct of Western doctors or surgeons going about their business, and the the incantations of a tribal *shaman* or witchdoctor, we might find it hard to believe that these had anything whatever in common.

And yet they do share a common purpose, a common structure of diagnosis followed by treatment, and even a certain degree of effectiveness. It is in the method, and the underlying assumptions about disease, that the great differences between them lie.

The fact that many diseases appear to have no visible cause is a problem shared by all medical systems. And although Westerners may all be familiar with bacteria and viruses—which are certainly invisible to the naked eye—it is easy to forget the extreme novelty of the idea that disease is caused by pathogenic organisms. The idea itself is the result of a long tradition of scientific observation and experiment, and of course, the development of instruments like the microscope.

Over most of human history, no such tradition has prevailed and no such technology has been available. And so, for the most part, doctors were obliged to fumble in the dark. They guessed that many diseases were caused by (real but invisible) living entities or agents; but on the other hand they supposed them to be far more personal, human and even spiritual than they really were.

Any form of medical treatment has to begin with diagnosis. The observation of symptoms is then followed by some conclusion about their cause. In modern Western medicine, this involves what we call the science of pathology, and by methods not available to many societies, modern doctors can study the processes at work in the body. They can then classify disease by their causes and their charac-

For many tribal peoples, like these from Chimbu in New Guinea, an invisible ailment may still be regarded as the result of sorcery—and so best treated by the tribal doctor. Here, pig-fat is used to remove the evil influence which causes the child to suffer a bronchial infection.

Axel Poignant

teristics instead of by symptoms alone.

Western doctors will not, for example, distinguish a disease which causes bleeding from one which cases vomiting. In terms of cause and effect, they will know that the same disease may cause bleeding in one patient and vomiting in another. Above all, they will not consider any question of either motivation, purpose or intention. If patients ask *why* they are suffering, the doctor will answer in terms of infection or something of that sort. All deeper questions are left to the philosopher or the theologian.

This specialized and technical approach to diagnosis is only made possible by the science of pathology. Where that science is absent, as in all primitive medicine, disease can only be explained and diagnosed along moral and motivational lines. In that situation, there is no basis for cause-and-effect thinking: if a man falls ill, the first question to be asked is: Who *wanted* him to fall ill? Who had a grudge against him?

To questions of this kind, there are many possible answers. The illness may have been intended by a human enemy, a dead relative who feels neglected; or perhaps because the victim cut down a tree or fouled the river in which a spirit lived. The possibilities are numerous, and depend on the beliefs of the people.

In this situation accurate diagnosis— the identification of whatever enemy has caused the disease—will also lie beyond the competence of ordinary people. It will be the business of a specialist. And since the enemy to be identified will often be a spirit, or can only be tracked down with the aid of spirits, the specialist will often need to be a priest quite as much as a doctor.

In order to effect a diagnosis, he may go into a trance and converse with good and evil spirits. He may allow them to 'possess' him, or may even experience an *ekstasis*—a separation from the body— and journey into their world, in the sky or under the earth. A priest-medium of this kind, acting from motives which are ultimately medical, is usually described as a *shaman*.

Once the cause of illness has been established along these lines, the treatment follows quite logically. If a spirit or a dead relative is responsible, the doctor will prescribe a suitable placatory sacrifice. If the offence is particularly serious, however, he may pronounce the disease incurable, and everybody will then expect the patient to die. But if another human being is deemed responsible, it may be possible to fight back— and where there are fierce enmities or vendettas between different groups, this will often be the most obvious diagnosis.

In this case, the enemy may possess a power of his own which can harm others, using what is usually called 'witchcraft'.

In many parts of the world, illness is believed to result from an evil spirit entering the body. This Malay man withdraws a demon from his wife by smearing lime on her forehead and chest.

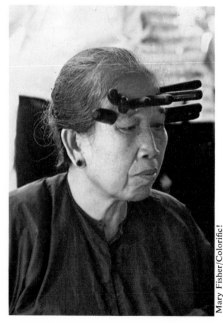

Mary Fisher/Colorific!

A Vietnamese woman has 'bad blood' removed. Hollow tubes with pieces of smouldering cotton inside are placed over cuts in the skin. This creates a vacuum which draws out the poisoned blood.

Alternatively he may have engaged in 'sorcery', the manipulation of magical substances. This can take many forms. He may have stuck pins into an effigy of his victim, or fired invisible darts into his body. He may have surreptitiously acquired hair or nail-clippings, or even excrement from his victim and mixed them with poisons or cooked them over a fire. He may have sent spirits or demons to steal one of his victim's souls in order to sap his strength. And the victim's symptoms—his feelings of being pierced, poisoned, burned or just weakened—will provide the 'doctor' with an accurate guide to the method chosen by his enemy.

The enemy, witch or sorcerer, wielding some kind of magic force, leaves the victim's doctor with only two options: he can either wield some stronger kind of magic and so neutralise the attack, or he can strengthen his patient's power to resist. In the former case he attempts to

Ivan Polunin/Susan Griggs Agency

strengthen a sick person today may be used to strengthen an arrow tomorrow, or a canoe, or a field of food-plants.

For many tribal peoples, medicine tends to be only one specialized application of a general concern with magic. Their doctors therefore need a range of skills which include not only the ability to converse with spirits and invoke their power, but also understanding the whole of a patient's life, the moral and social circumstances, and even the guilts and resentments of which even the patient may be unconscious. This is an ancient wisdom which is now being re-discovered. A virus can be identified in a laboratory by somebody who knows nothing of the patient's life, but for the overall task of healing a doctor will often need to know the whole background.

Primitive medicine often involves a great deal of psychotherapy. Among the Ndembu of Central Africa, for example, and in many other parts of the world, a doctor will call the patient's friends and relatives together and make them take part in a public confession of their grudges towards him. The easing of tensions that results is of definite therapeutical value.

There are many such accounts which make it clear that these doctors can be extremely skilled in the arts of manipulating people to good effect. One Ndembu

Elaborate dress and dancing establishes this Tiv tribesman as a person 'outside' society—and so in a better position to ask the help of the spirits and effect cures on his patients.

A. Baring

retrieve, the sorcerer's materials and destroy them, suck the magic darts out of the patient's body, or deploy other spirits to fight those doing the damage. In the latter case, he can draw on a wide range of tonics and medicines for internal and external application. But in both cases the treatment will usually be accompanied by dances and songs. In this way the doctor solicits the goodwill of the spirits, asks for the medicines to be effective and gives the patient encouragement. Even on its own account the act of singing is widely believed to have magical results.

Where cause-and-effect is not considered, specific medicines are not always prescribed for specific diseases. But prescription usually follows a kind of logic, often based upon similarities between the disease and the remedy. If some limb or organ is swollen, for example, a kind of homoeopathy will suggest large round fruit as a remedy. If jaundice leads to a yellowing of the skin, it will suggest the flesh of a yellow animal. Thought and practice alike are governed by the association of ideas, and the effects of a single magical power can be very diverse: the substance which can belief is that anybody with a grudge can cause a human tooth to become magically lodged inside an enemy's body, only to be removed by the enemy's confession. The doctor must then call the people together and during intervals between singing and dancing the patient's body is cupped. Each time the tooth fails to appear in the cup, the doctor will deliver a homily to his audience. In so doing, it is clear that the doctor is familiar with all the relevant personal relationships.

Of one such session, an anthropologist who worked among the Ndembu wrote: 'Ihembi's' greatest skill was in managing this stop-start routine so that, after several hours of it, the congregation felt nothing but a unanimous craving for the removal of the *ihamba* (the tooth) from the patient's body. The intensive excitement whipped up by the drums; the patient's trembling; mass-participation in the sad-sweet or rousing hunters' cult songs, which are sung to "please *ihamba*", followed by a spate of confessions and the airing of grievances; the reverent or hortatory prayers addressed not only by the doctor but also by village elders to the shade (spirit) to "make our kinsman strong"; the sight and smell of blood . . .'

Inevitably, we ask what was the likelihood of the patient being healed? But this question needs careful answering. These forms of curing have always covered a far wider area of life than our modern notion of medicine, which is rather narrowly directed towards the physical health of the individual. They have served the well-being of the community, especially by releasing and easing its tensions. In an isolated community, for example, people depend upon one another, and find it very hard to avoid those whom they dislike: the primitive doctor—in the role as social psychotherapist—then becomes an important and successful figure.

Where the individual is concerned, the doctor's success will obviously be greater with illnesses of psychological origin. But even Western medicine has come to recognise the presence—and sometimes the decisive influence—of psychological factors within even the most physical of diseases. People's mental or emotional condition has a most powerful effect—for good or for ill—on their resistance to infection and their powers of recovery. A patient given correct treatment in a modern hospital, but who feels a sense of loneliness and despair, may well be less likely to recover than the patient of tribal *shaman*.

It has also transpired that a surprising number of herbal and other folk-remedies in fact do have considerable therapeutic effect. Gypsies, for example, were applying mouldy food to their septic wounds, with good results, long before Fleming discovered penicillin. But even if the remedies are useless, a *shaman's* or witch-

This Dayak charm is believed to have magical properties and is worn at all times. If the wearer becomes ill, a witchdoctor will prepare a remedy with small chips of wood from it.

Werner Forman Archives

doctor's patients become the centre of the community's care and attention. They are made to feel that a disturbed relationship with their fellows or with the supernatural is being set in order. And such feelings, combined with nature's own healing power, often leads to recovery.

Yet it should also be pointed out that the converse can also be true. The power of mind over body is such that if a healthy person believes they are incurably poisoned by a sorcerer or cursed by a spirit, they may be beyond the help of any doctor, primitive or modern, a poisoned imagination can kill just as surely as a poisoned bloodstream, especially if friends and relatives avoid the doomed person in fear, and even speak of them as though they were already dead. Before long they will, in fact, be dead—through terror and loneliness and, in a real sense through 'faith'.

What of the tribal doctors' belief in their own powers? Like Western doctors they

expect some failures. If they try to explain them, it will be in terms of the continuing anger of the spirits or the stronger magic of his adversary. As for the belief in the effectiveness of their treatments, it is hard to be sure: those who know something of science, and whose minds run along the lines of cause-and-effect, cannot easily enter into the minds of those brought up to think differently. But we should be cautious, at the very least, about assuming that the witch-doctors are merely fakes.

There may be a great temptation to see them in that light. In the *ihamba* ritual when the doctors decide that all latent grievances have been expressed and released, they will triumphantly produce a human tooth as though from inside the patient's body and then pronounce the patient cured. A more colourful 'performance' of the same kind takes place among the Iban of Western Borneo whenever a monkey-demon is believed to have been stealing women's souls. The doctor will go into a closed hut and wrestle there with the demon. The bystanders outside hear the noise of a fierce scuffle and the shrieks of a wounded monkey. Eventually they rush in to find the furniture overturned and a blood-spattered trail leading out of the back door. The doctor stands there breathless, with a spear covered with warm blood and authentic monkey-hairs. The demon has fled, mortally wounded.

The instinct of Westerners may be to call this trickery—a human tooth, monkey-hairs and blood were carefully hidden beforehand and brought out at the right moment. Yet the doctor could not be persuaded to admit it, and it would be wrong to call the performance simply wilful deceit. The profession—like its counterpart in our culture—is a demanding and most exhausting one, and its practitioners are mostly conscientious people who would not go in for trickery. More to the point is that the visible phenomenon symbolises something which is genuinely believed to be happening—albeit at an invisible, deep level. When the doctors contrive a visible phenomenon, perhaps by sleight-of-hand, they probably feel that they are enacting the reality of the matter rather than departing from it. By 'pretending' to pull a tooth out of the patient's body, they are actually pulling out an invisible but hostile power.

Like doctors everywhere, their concern is to diagnose and then to restore health by appropriate treatment. They differ from modern Western doctors in their notion of what *causes* illness and of the treatment that will cure it. Their failure-rate, although higher than that of our own doctors, is certainly not total; and if they can sometimes be suspected of show-manship and pretence and self-importance, such failings are not unheard-of even in Western medicine. □

Great World Religions

Hinduism

The term Hinduism refers to the whole complex of social custom and religious belief of the majority of people in India. Itself strongly syncretic (see following article), this gave rise in turn to other religious systems such as Buddhism, Jainism and Sikhism.

Hinduism remained strong in India, where in 1948 it formed the basis for division of the sub-continent between India and Pakistan which has a predominantly Moslem population.

The influence of Hinduism also spread eastwards to Indonesia, where it has mingled with other religions in a complex amalgam of various beliefs. There are about 516,000,000 Hindus.

Buddhism

In the 6th century BC, when·Brahmanism was still growing into Hinduism, the same religious tradition gave birth in India to Buddhism. It takes its name from the Buddha, or 'Enlightened One', who formulated a doctrine to counteract the evils of violence, 'self' and death.

Buddhism was popular in India for 1,500 years; from there it spread to Tibet, China and eventually all of South-East Asia. In India its doctrines were reabsorbed by Hinduism and Buddhism thus disappeared in its original homeland.

The religion developed in different ways. Mahayana, the 'Greater Vehicle', elaborated the Buddha's godly role; Hinayana, the 'Lesser Vehicle', was a more orthodox doctrine with less popular appeal. Today there are about 230,000,000 Buddhists in the world.

Shinto

The folk-religion of Japan, Shinto is a compound of nature and ancestor worship, which places little emphasis on death or an afterlife. For over 1,000 years 'the way of the gods' was united with Buddhism, which arrived in Japan during the 6th century.

In the 18th century, a group of literary patriots purified the religion, removing all alien elements. 'State Shinto' later became closely associated with Japanese militarism, and was used to justify imperial expansion.

After Japan's defeat in the Second World War, 'State Shinto' was dismantled, and the religion has reverted to its origins with about 84,000,000 adherents.

Judaism

Judaism is the religion of the Jews, a Semitic tribe which settled in Palestine. Divisions between the sub-tribes long made them vulnerable, but Judaism, with its insistence on a single, omnipotent God, became a powerful force for unifying the tribes, and prophets often gained considerable political influence. The Torah (Bible) relates this turbulent history.

After the destruction of the Jewish state by the Romans, refugees spread throughout the world. Religion was the main support of Jewish identity until, nearly 2,000 years later, Israel was established as a Jewish state in 1948. There are an estimated 14,000,000 Jews in the world.

Christianity

The Christian religion was formed by the followers of Jesus, whom they regarded as the Son of God. From its beginnings in the Middle East, the religion spread rapidly through the Roman Empire.

Although missionaries travelled widely from the earliest times, it was the expansion of European peoples to all parts of the world which gave Christianity its present wide distribution.

The split between the Orthodox and Catholic Churches was a by-product of the division of the Roman Empire. The later split between Catholicism and Protestantism in Europe reflects political changes at the end of the Middle Ages and the emergence of capitalism. There are now about 91,600,000 Orthodox Christians, 552,000,000 Roman Catholics and 325,000,000 Protestants.

Islam

The latest of the great world religions, Islam derives from the preaching of the Prophet Mohammed in the early years of the 7th century. It is based on the same Semitic foundations as Judaism and Christianity and incorporates many similar beliefs.

Arab conquest rapidly carried Islam throughout the Middle East and North Africa, but Persian resistance to the Arabs led to the development of a separate branch of Islam, Shi'ism. The majority of Moslems remain orthodox, or Sunni.

Mysticism has also found its place within Islam: its followers are Sufis or Dervishes. There are about 530,000,000 adherents of Islam.

Chinese Religions

In the earliest religions of China the divine ruler of the universe was seen as a remote god, perhaps the sky, T'ien. There was a prolonged stage in which nature gods and various house and nature spirits were worshipped. Ancestor worship remained important, even after the coming of Taoism and Buddhism.

Taoism derives from the teachings of Lao Tsu, who believed ritual was useless and recommended conformity to the 'Tao' or 'Way' of right conduct. Later, a whole religious paraphernalia of temples was adopted, along with ceremonial, vestments, liturgies and the sanction of Hell.

Buddhism became important in China in the mid-1st century AD, and for the next 250 years many missionaries came to China from India. By the 11th century Buddhism was found all over China.

Confucius was born in 550 BC, when many small states existed largely independently of central control. There was widespread suffering and Confucius's teaching was designed to bring order to a chaotic world: Confucianism is thus a political philosophy more than a religion.

Tribal Religions

Central and Northern Asia, Africa and the Americas have been less affected by the major religions than the rest of the world. In these areas, many smaller-scale religions are widely followed.

They differ widely: some have high gods and elaborate prayer; some have more nature spirits than others; still others have *shamans* or witch-doctors as priests.

Missionaries from all the world religions have tried to gain converts from tribal societies, often with great success. Yet despite these alien influences, the indigenous faiths are still followed by many millions of people.

Communism

In the course of the 20th century Communism has become a complete social, economic and political philosophy for many millions of people. Consciously atheistic, it has attempted to suppress traditional religious beliefs in many countries, while co-existing with them in others. It is impossible to give accurate statistics of religious adherence in the Communist world today.

Great World Religions

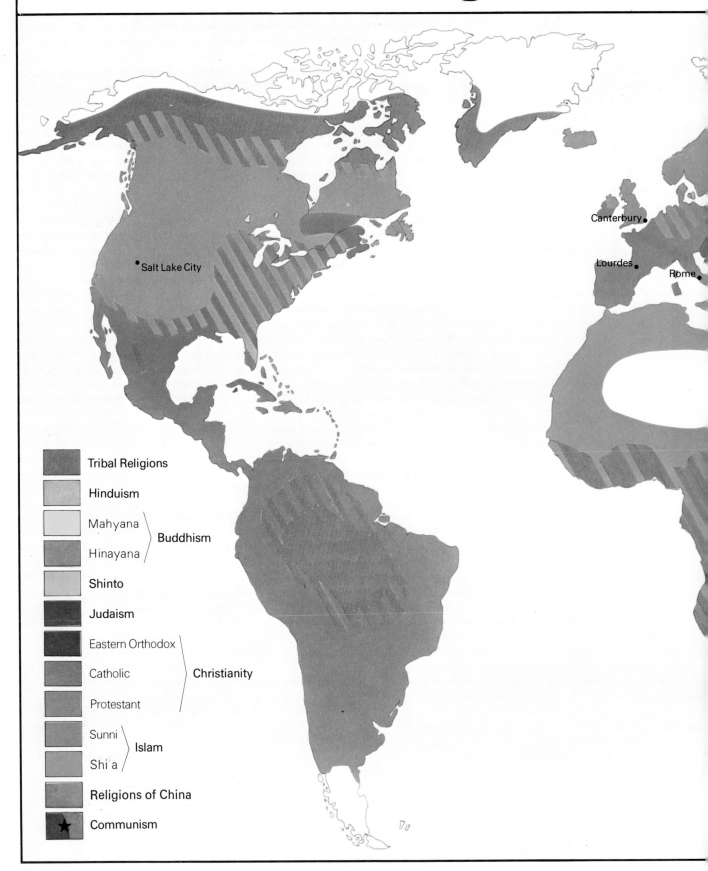

Canterbury

Lourdes

Rome

Salt Lake City

Tribal Religions

Hinduism

Mahyana ⟩ Buddhism

Hinayana

Shinto

Judaism

Eastern Orthodox

Catholic ⟩ Christianity

Protestant

Sunni ⟩ Islam

Shi′a

Religions of China

★ Communism

Istanbul

Meshed

Jerusalem

Karbala

Mecca

Lhasa

Benares
Budd Gaya

Kandy

Mt. Fuji

Hinduism

'Hinduism is more like a tree that has grown gradually than like a building that has been erected by some great architect at some definite point in time'. The origins of the oldest living religion in the world are not to be found in one single authoritative text nor in any single founder, for Hinduism was born out of the culture of the Aryan invaders of India in the second millenium BC as it fused with the beliefs and cults of the indigenous peoples they conquered.

The Aryans were aggressive, martial peoples; their religion was masculine, ritualized and organized. But as waves of Aryans invaded India, the process by which the many indigenous peoples were incorporated into the Aryan political system involved a parallel assimilation of many beliefs and cults.

This was a gradual process, taking place between 600 BC and 650 AD, but it transformed the Aryan culture and resulted in the formulation of the basic tenets of Hinduism. In social terms the non-Aryans were related to the Aryan social structure by the division of society into four classes.

When the Aryans entered India a simple class division already existed in their tribal structure. Some of the earliest hymns of the Vedas—a collection of four books of hymns, prayers and ritual formulae—distinguish between the nobility and the ordinary tribesmen. The four *varnas*, or classes, developed out of this stratification as the conquerors settled among the conquered. For *varna* is a Sanscrit word meaning colour, which suggests its origin lay in the attempt of the fairer-skinned Aryan minority to maintain its supremacy over the darker native majority.

The first mention of *varnas* comes in the Rigveda, the most important of the Vedas. One of its hymns describes the creation of the world through primeval sacrifice. The gods offer a primeval being, identified as Prajapati (lord of all creatures), as a sacrifice to himself. From his body are born the four great classes of society: from his head the Brahma, from his arms the Kshatriya, from his thighs the Vaishya and from his feet the Shudra.

Originally the fourfold division was based on occupation. The prime duty of the Brahman was to study and to teach,

I am He who causes:
No other beside me.
Upon me, these worlds
        are held
Like pearls strung
        on a thread.

I am the essence
        of the waters,
The shining of the sun
        and the moon:
OM in all the Vedas,
The word that is God.
It is I who resound
        in the ether
And I am potent in man.
I am the sacred smell
        of the earth,
The light of the fire,
Life of all lives,
Austerity of ascetics.

Know me, eternal seed
Of everything that grows:
The intelligence of those
        who understand,
The vigour of the active.
In the strong, I am strength
Unhindered by lust
And the objects of craving:
I am all that a man
        may desire
Without transgressing
The law of his nature.

while the Kshatriya was a warrior and a ruler. Strictly, the duty of the Vaishya was to keep cattle, but members of this class were soon extending their activities, and they became recognized primarily as a class of traders.

A sharp distinction was made between these three higher classes and the Shudra. The former were 'twice born': once at their natural birth; then at their initiation, when they received the sacred thread and were received into Aryan society. The Shudra had no initiation, and no place within Aryan society. They had no rights; they were servants, to be disposed of at their masters' whim. The Shudra class was itself divided into the 'pure', or 'not excluded', and the 'excluded'. Those who belonged to this last group were virtually indistinguishable from the great mass of people who were later termed 'untouchables'. They had to live outside the boundaries of Aryan settlements, and in theory their prime duty was the transporting and cremation of corpses.

The organization of class sanctioned by *samsara* and *karma* aided the Aryan conquest of India; it provided a legitimate political and social framework for a huge sub-continent characterized by diverse languages and practices. And while the division of society was static, it did allow for the social mobility of certain groups.

The Kshatriya class was the most open. It could accommodate various groups, both indigenous and alien, since the basic qualification for belonging to this class was the possession of political power. But to legitimize his power a king or a chief had to become a Kshatriya. This was achieved by linking his genealogy to a Kshatriya lineage and, most important of all, by following the classical life-style of the Kshatriya.

Within each of the great classes are a myriad of castes, or *jati*. Each caste possesses its own method of conduct, or *dharma*, which is set out in the texts on law and human conduct, known as the Dharma Sutras and the Dharma Shastras. The methods of conduct are aimed at preserving the traditions and way of life of the castes intact. Certain basic rules, such as endogamy (marrying only within the group), commensuality (eating food only in the company of members of the group), and following only those trades or crafts practised by the caste, have to be observed. The penalty for breaking the rules was severe—loss of caste. This meant complete social ostracism, for the man without caste had no place in society.

To the Aryan doctrine of *varna* were added the non-Aryan, indigenous doctrines of *samsara* and *karma*, which made the inequalities of Aryan society less intolerable to the lower classes. *Samsara* is the doctrine of continual reincarnation—the belief in the repeated rebirth of the soul. *Karma*, which literally translated means 'work' or 'deeds', is the belief that the individual's actions in one life determine his status in the next. It is through *karma* that the physical form of the next life is determined, and it is a man's *karma* in one life which shapes his character, fortune and social position in the next. *Samsara* is seen as a constant process, and is often represented as an ever-spinning wheel.

The twin doctrines of *samsara* and *karma* led to a desire to escape from the endless chain of birth, death and rebirth, and this was formulated in the great mystical writings of the Upanishads, written in about 800 BC. While the Vedas describe the dead as passing either to the 'World of the Fathers' or to the 'House of Clay' where they remain indefinitely, the Upanishads maintain that the souls

of those who have practised sacrifice, austerity and alms-giving go beyond the World of the Fathers. From there they pass 'into the moon, where they become food . . . When their karma is exhausted, they return to air, from air to wind, from wind to rain, from rain to the earth where they become food, where they are offered as sacrifice to the fire of man; offered as sacrifice to the fire of woman; then they are born again. Once more they rise, once more they circle round.' The unrighteous are also reincarnated, but as 'poisonous worms and insects'.

From the doctrine of *samsara* the Upanishads develop the most fundamental of Hindu tenets. Starting with the concepts of Brahman (the All-Pervading) and Atman (Breath: the individual essence) they stated that a Supreme Being manifests himself in every soul. In the words of the Upanishads: 'Whatever lives is full of the Lord . . . The Self is everywhere, without a body, without a shape, whole, pure, wise, all knowing, far shining, self-depending, all transcending . . .' From this flows the doctrine that the ultimate aim of human life is to achieve unity with the Supreme—that is, with the self.

When a man achieves unity with the Supreme he realizes *saccidandanada*: Bliss (*sat*), Consciousness (*cit*) and Delight (*ananda*). 'Of a certainty a man who can

see all creatures in himself, himself in all creatures, knows no sorrow . . . How can a wise man, knowing the unity of life, seeing all creatures in himself, be deluded or sorrowful?' All a man's sufferings, and the limitations imposed by self which prevent him from realizing this blessed state, are due to ignorance; thus a man must seek true knowledge.

Out of the synthesis of the Aryan concept of the *varnas* with the non-Aryan doctrines of *samsara* and *karma*, therefore, grew the fundamental Hindu tenet that the ultimate aim of human life is to achieve union with the Supreme. This in turn led to the formulation of an ideal way of life designed to facilitate this goal. According to Hindu doctrines there are four stages of life for members of the three higher classes.

After initiation, which takes place at puberty, a Hindu should embark on the first stage—*brahmacarya*. This is a period of discipline and education in which *jnana* (knowledge) and *yoga* (a physical and mental discipline) play an

The mystic tradition of North India was influenced during the Middle Ages by Islamic Sufis. Millions of pilgrims still bathe yearly in the sacred lake at Pushkar, where the first Sufi teacher settled at the end of the 12th century.

important part. The second stage, *garhasthya*, is one in which an active married life and the ideals of social life are legitimate goals. However, material success is not held to be sufficient, because of the ultimate aim of obtaining release from *samsara*. Thus in the third stage of life, *vanaprasthya*, a man should prepare for the loosening of earthly bonds so that he might enter the fourth stage, *sannyasa*, and follow the life of the hermit.

The four stages, in particular the ascetic, represented an ideal. While seldom followed exactly in practice, they provided a pattern for the Hindu way of life. The Hindu explanation for the discrepancy between the ideal and its practice is that in the earlier stages of the world's development, when people were closer to perfection, Hindu ideals were followed automatically, but as the cosmic cycle progresses, the rules are increasingly broken.

The process of syncretism was strikingly illustrated by the emergence of the divine trinity of Brahma (the Creator), Vishnu (the Preserver) and Shiva (the Destroyer). The Aryan Vedas (collected together in their present form in the first millenium BC) describe a polytheistic

An ice-cave 3,140m (10,300ft) up in the Himalayas is the source of the Bhagirathi, a headstream of the Ganges. Hindu pilgrims travel to nearby Gangiroti to wash away their sins in the sacred waters and gain eternal happiness.

A 7th century painting shows the god Vishnu reclining on the thousand-headed serpent Sesha in the primeval ocean. Devotees of Vishnu believe that he appears in many different incarnations: some theologians have included Buddha amongst these, in an attempt to absorb his religion into Hinduism.

Raghubir Singh/John Hillelson Agency

Werner Foreman Archive

religion, whose central theme is the appeasement of its gods through elaborate sacrificial rituals. These gods, who are associated with nature and usually male, did not disappear, but gave way in importance to the trinity or *trimurti*. Vishnu, originally a minor deity, and Shiva, a fertility god, gradually took on some of the aspects of the ancient Vedic gods and in this way became 'High Gods'. The process was facilitated by the doctrine of divine reincarnation, which allowed gods worshipped in animal form and as divine heroes to be revered as incarnations of the great gods.

The development of the *trimurti* coincided with the discarding of the elaborate Vedic rite of sacrifice in favour of the rite of worship (*puja*) and the religious attitude known as *bhakti*, the path of devotion. Inspiration and religious devotion are the outstanding characteristics of *bhakti*, and the most important early *bhakti* literature is the Bhagavad Gita. Inserted into the great epic of the Mahabharata War, it takes the form of a poetic dialogue between the great warrior Arjuna and his charioteer, the god Krishna, an incarnation of Vishnu.

The new gods were worshipped with offerings of food, flowers and incense as well as prayers. The practice of image-worship appears to have played no part in the Aryan culture, but gradually the worship of images in stone temples became an integral part of Hinduism. The worship of female deities also became firmly established: the principal cult being that of the Mother Goddess in a variety of guises or aspects.

Vishnu, Shiva and the Mother Goddess became the most popular gods of Hinduism. Although a bewildering variety of other and lesser gods are still worshipped today, most Hindus look ultimately to one of these three. Thus, generally speaking, the majority can be divided into the followers of either Vishnu, Shiva or Shakti (the female power). The Vedas, the Upanishads and the Bhagavad Gita are respected by all, but each following also has its own scriptures.

These scriptures offer different versions of the world's origin and time-span. Shivaites believe that Shiva created the world through dancing and will destroy it at the end of time by the same process, and this legend produced one of the most glorious images of Hindu art: dancing Shiva.

Shaktas maintain that the Mother

Known as Lord of the Dance, Shiva is one of the great gods of Hinduism and represents death and time. Shivaite Hindus believe he created the world through dancing and that his wild rhythms will destroy it at the end of the cosmic cycle.

Michael Holford/Musee Guimet

Goddess gave birth to the universe. But the most widely accepted version among Hindus, the Vishnuite version, is that the universe is of immense size and duration. The cosmic cycle, or 'day of Brahma' spans four thousand million years and is called *kalpa*.

At the beginning of the 'day of Brahma' Vishnu is asleep on the cobra Sesha, who is the symbol of eternity. From Vishnu's navel springs a lotus, and from its bud the god Brahma. Brahma creates the universe on Vishnu's behalf and then Vishnu awakes and controls the cosmos for the duration of the day. At its close, the world is destroyed, and once again absorbed into Vishnu's body. After another *kalpa*, 'the night of Brahma', the process begins again.

Within the *kalpa* are 1,000 smaller cycles, which are each divided into four aeons. Aeons become progressively shorter and more degenerate. The world is now in the fourth aeon, which dates from 3102 BC and will continue for over 400,000 years when Vishnu, incarnated as Kalkin, will destroy the world and initiate a new golden age.

Vishnu is usually worshipped in his *avataras*, or incarnated forms. Their number and variety again reflect the process of syncretization. Of the many *avataras* there are ten which the god is believed to assume in order to save the world from the threat of total destruction. These include the Fish, the Boar, the Man-Lion and the Dwarf, but the most important are Krishna and Rama. Krishna is the more popular, his history is long and complex and he appears in many forms—the child prodigy, the divine warrior, the charismatic lover, the wise teacher and the dying god. Rama is the perfect husband, the brave leader and the ideal ruler. He is often depicted together with his wife Sita, who represents the ideal, loving and faithful wife. The last of the ten most important *avataras*, Kalkin, is a future incarnation. At the end of this age, Vishnu will appear as a man on a white horse, holding a flaming sword, to pass sentence on the wicked, reward the good, and restore the golden age.

Shiva is an older deity, more austere than Krishna. He sits in perpetual meditation on a high peak in the Himalayas, sustaining the world through his immense spiritual power. In this aspect he is depicted as wearing his long hair in a topknot, secured with the crescent moon. From his hair streams the sacred River Ganges, and in the middle of his forehead is a third eye, the symbol of superior vision and wisdom. Befitting his origin as a fertility god, Shiva is often worshipped in the form of a lingam, a phallic symbol, although this aspect of his character is seen less, now.

The Mother Goddess appears in many

different forms. In her benevolent aspect she is variously 'Daughter of the Mountain'; 'the Virtuous', 'the White One'; 'the Bestower of Much Food' or 'the Mother'. In her dreadful form she is known as Kali, 'the Black One'; Durga, 'Inaccessible' and Candi 'the Fierce'. In one of her most famous aspects, Kali, she is depicted as garlanded with human skulls, waving different weapons in her many hands.

Despite its apparent polytheism, there is no contradiction in Hindu thought between the omnipresent, all-pervading God and the worship of different gods and goddesses. They represent some of the infinite aspects of the Supreme Being who is manifest in all. In the Bhagavad Gita Krishna says: 'The Lord dwells in the heart of every creature . . . through His divine power moving all beings, as though guided by mechanism'.

The identification of a lesser god with the aspect of one of the greater gods brought together the many different cultural traditions of India, while the pantheistic idea that everything is animated by god provided a rationale for the reverence of objects such as trees, stones, animals and rivers, within the Hindu creed.

The structure of Hinduism was essentially complete by the middle of the 7th century. The period has also witnessed the birth of a number of heterodox, notably Buddhist and Jainist sects which became religions in their own right. Indeed, Buddhism became the state religion of India during the third century BC, particularly under the patronage of the emperor Asoka.

When Hinduism re-emerged, Buddhism did not disappear from India; rather, some of its concepts were absorbed into the body of Hinduism, which again displayed its remarkable power of assimilation. For example, the Buddhist practice of using parables as a method of teaching was adopted, the Buddhist emphasis on the importance of organized education recognized, and Buddha himself was seen as one of Vishnu's *avataras*.

One reason why Buddhism was successful was that it offered another means of lessening some of the harsher effects of the caste system for those at its lower end, while it also attracted the more intellectual members of the upper classes. Similarly, when Islam spread to India, it also gained some adherents who wished to 'opt out' of the caste system.

In both cases Hinduism responded by assimilating some of the new ideas. During the medieval period, for example, Moslem influence stimulated the North Indian mysticism associated particularly with the poet Ramananda (1370–1440) and his famous disciple Kabir, who lived in the 15th century. Both emphasized *bhakti*, simple faith and devotion,

Bury Peerless

brotherly love and fellowship, and strongly rejected elaborate ritualism and caste pretensions.

However, by the end of the 17th century Hindu mysticism had declined: Hinduism stagnated and the social order became increasingly rigid. But increasing contact with the West tended to revitalize rather than erode Hinduism. A renaissance took shape in the teachings of Raja Rammohan Roy (1774–1833). He founded a reformed Hindu church, the Brahmo Samaj, which was based on the central teaching of the Upanishads that there is one all-pervading, omnipresent Being who dwells in all. He also stressed the need to learn from Western science.

The renaissance was also expressed in a very different form, in the teachings of the Bengali mystic Ramakrishna Paramahamsa (1834–1886). Centred firmly in the *bhakti* tradition, his preachings emphasized simplicity, devotion and unity with god. His disciple, *swami* Vivekananda, founded the Ramakrishna Mission which has at present over 100 teaching centres in the West and is concerned not only with spiritual matters, but with social, educational and medical needs. A further outstanding figure in the modern renaissance was Mahatma Ghandi. Influenced by Christian ideals, his teachings focussed on those of the Bhagavad Gita, but stressed the need to adapt traditional beliefs and practices to the modern day.

It has been said that Hinduism is as much a way of life as a religion. In practical terms there are an infinite variety of religious ceremonies attached to every aspect of daily life. Some consist of meditations, prayers and rites to be performed daily in the home, usually by high-caste Hindus. The many ceremonies connected with personal life begin with a child's conception and continue through every stage of his life.

Hindu funerals usually involve cremation, after which the ashes are thrown into water. Hindus believe in reincarnation, and the family of the deceased will pass several days in ritual observance to ensure a propitious rebirth.

A stone lingam, the phallic symbol of Shiva, stands outside a temple in Bangkok. Like many non-Aryan deities, Shiva was assimilated gradually into Hinduism and much of his original significance as a fertility god has since disappeared.

William Macquitty

The most important ceremonies include that of initiation, which is performed at puberty when a child is invested with the sacred thread and learns the *Savitri* verse of the Rigveda which is repeated at all ceremonies. (This practice is today generally confined to Brahmans, and the initiation means a Hindu is eligible to study the sacred Vedas, and embark on

the first stage of life, *brahmachari*.)

The long and complicated marriage ceremony marks the advent of the *garhasthya* stage. (Marriage is indissoluble, even before consummation, and widows are not allowed to remarry). Funerals usually involve cremation, after which the bones are thrown into a river, preferably the Ganges or other sacred waters. For at least ten days the family of the deceased is ritually impure. They are supposed to confine themselves to the home, where they perform ceremonies which will enable the dead to achieve eventual rebirth.

Although in practice old customs lapsed and new ones were adopted, the traditional Hindu social system was, and is, fundamentally conservative. The existence of castes, independent of governments, was a powerful factor in ensuring the survival of Hinduism. For in India, particularly in the North, successive waves of foreign invasions contributed to long periods of anarchy. But the Indian, living under an alien political order whether it was Aryan, Moghul, Portuguese or British, as a Hindu could retain his cultural identity through his caste, which was the focus for much of his loyalty.

The caste system has remained so strong that, until very recently, all attempts at breaking it down have foundered. The present century has seen some erosion of the system mainly through the spread of Western education, the development of national feeling and the campaigns of Indian leaders such as Ghandi and Nehru.

Religious practice in modern India varies from region to region and within communities living in the same region; it differs according to caste, age, sex, cultural background and social status. Since Hinduism recognizes that there are infinite number of paths to the Supreme and that each while valid is not exclusive, no particular practice is compulsory for everyone. Hinduism is a religion flexible enough to accommodate monism, dualism and pantheism. To survive in and to give some coherence to the hetrogeneous nature of Indian society it has remained syncretic.

Its recognition of 'many paths' sharply distinguishes Hinduism from Western religions. While they tend to reject all other religions and their gods as false, Hinduism can concede some validity to them all. Centuries ago in the Bhagavad Gita Krishna said: 'In whatever way men approach me, in that way I love them, in all ways the sons of man follow my way'. The contemporary philosopher Savepalli Radhakrishnan has expressed the same concept in a modern idiom: 'Hinduism is not a sect but a fellowship for all who accept the law of right and earnestly seek for the truth.' □

Buddhism

Buddhists believe that a person called 'Buddha', or 'the Enlightened One', rediscovered an ancient, indeed an ageless, wisdom, and that he did so in Bihar in India, round about 600 or 400 BC. The exact date of Buddha's life is unknown, but his reformulation of the wisdom of the ages, designed to counteract three evils of Man's life, spread in due course through the whole of East Asia.

Buddha abhorred violence first of all, and enjoined his followers to avoid it in every form, from the killing of humans and animals to the intellectual coercion of people who think differently. In the second place he accused the 'self', or the fact that one holds on to one's individual personality, of being responsible for all pain and suffering. Suffering could be destroyed systematically until in the end a state of self-extinction was attained, technically known as Nirvana. Thirdly, Buddha did not fear death, and promised to overcome it by opening to his followers 'the Doors to the Deathless', 'the Gates of the Undying'.

Apart from the antidotes he provided for these three ills, Buddha formulated no definite doctrines or creeds. He put his entire trust into training his disciples through a threefold process—of moral restraint, secluded meditation and philosophical reflection. The results have been of immense significance for the Far East, profoundly influencing social attitudes.

Buddhism was one of many movements reacting against the tyrannies which arose in Asia about 3000 BC and whose technical projects and military operations led to widespread and often senseless violence and destruction of life. About 600 BC onwards, a wave of disillusion with power and material wealth went through the whole of Asia, from China to the Greek islands off the coast of Asia Minor, mobilizing the resources of the spirit against the existing system.

In India the reaction grew up in a region devoted to rice culture, as distinct from areas further west which relied on animal husbandry and wheat cultivation. For the last 2,000 years Buddhism has flourished mainly in rice-growing countries, with little success elsewhere. It arose in a part of India—around Benares and Patna—where the Iron Age had thrown up ambitious warrior kings, who established large kingdoms with big cities,

What then is the Holy Truth of Ill? Birth is ill, decay is ill, sickness is ill, death is ill. To be conjoined with what one dislikes means suffering. To be disjoined from what one likes means suffering. Not to get what one wants, also that means suffering. In short, all grasping at any one of the five components involves suffering.

What then is the Holy Truth of the steps which lead to the stopping of Ill? It is the holy eightfold Path, which consists of right views, right intentions, right speech, right conduct, right livelihood, right effort, right mindfulness, right concentration.

widespread trade, a money economy and a rationally organized state.

Most of Buddha's public activity took place in cities, which helps to account for the intellectual character of his teachings, the 'urbanity' of his utterances and the rational quality of his ideas. The Buddha always stressed that he was a guide, not an authority, and that all propositions must be tested, including his own. With such a liberal education, Buddhists reacted to the unproven with a benevolent scepticism, and they have been able to accommodate themselves to every kind of popular belief, not only in India, but in all countries they moved into.

In regard to death, the Buddha shared the conviction, widely held in the past, that death is not a necessary ingredient of our human constitution, but a sign

that there is something wrong with us. It is our own fault, for essentially we are immortal and can conquer death to win eternal life by religious means. Buddha attributed death to an evil force called Mara, 'the Killer', who tempts us away from our true immortal selves.

On the principle that 'it is the lesser part which dies', we are tied to Mara's realm through our cravings and through the individual personality which is their invisible embodiment. In shedding our attachment to that personality, we move, 'beyond the death-king's sight' and win relief from an endless series of repeated deaths.

Buddhist society normally requires three components: a body of monks, who are held to be in direct contact with dharma, the Truth; a king, who has been consecrated by these monks in return for his promise to obey the dharma, and who provides society with a centre; and laymen, who are devoted to the monks and have some commitment to act as Buddhists. Rituals centre around the countless stupas (buildings containing relics of the Buddha) which are scattered over all Buddhist countries, uniting the entire society in common celebrations, performed at intervals throughout the year.

Buddhism has traditionally been approached in six different ways. It may be viewed as a matter of morality, whose adherents try to keep at least the five basic precepts—not to take life, not 'to take what is not given', to reduce and regulate one's sex and food drives, not to tell lies, and to shun intoxicants 'liable to confuse the mind'. Secondly, one may take care of the monks—give them food and clothes, repair their dwellings, look after their financial affairs. Or, prompted by faith, one may 'take refuge' with the Buddha, the dharma and the community of monks. This involves the worship and adoration of many Buddhas and Bodhisattvas — Buddhas-to-be — with murmured mantras (such as the famous Om mani padme hum!), and with incense, garlands and the other requisites of traditional Hindu puja (worship).

A fourth category of Buddhists withdraw from society, if possible into jungles or remote mountain caves, in order to practise a huge variety of meditations, which all stem from Buddhist yoga. Others are at heart philosophers, who

(Right) This giant statue of the Buddha is carved into the cliff of the Bamyan Valley in Afghanistan. Buddhism flourished in India itself for 1,500 years, until the invasion of the Moslems who forcibly suppressed the religion.

(Below) A novice from Chiang Mai in Thailand. Buddhist monasteries are found throughout South-East Asia: some monks spend their entire lives in the religious community, others remain only a short time before returning to their families.

(Below right) Buddhists consider it meritorious to multiply images of the Buddha. Many temples, like this one in Burma, contain statues of 'the Enlightened One'.

Alan Hutchison

Brian Culley

glory in metaphysics and thoughts both subtle and profound. The sixth group comprises the magicians and *shamans*, who cultivate and display their supernormal powers, such as thought-reading and flying through the air. Their function is to establish a harmony between society and the cosmic and spiritual forces on which its prosperity depends.

For a long time most monks, and certainly the more influential among them, came from the upper strata of society, having been Brahmans, warriors or rich merchants. And although class divisions were muted and almost entirely abolished within the monastic order itself, the general tone of the teaching was upper-class. The doctrine of deliverance was essentially aristocratic and made high demands on both intellect and moral demeanour. With this went an emphasis

on gentlemanly behaviour: there was little fanaticism or emotional exuberance, and good manners were observed in controversy and debate.

The Buddhists addressed one another as sons and daughters 'of good family' and looked with some distain upon the general populace. They referred to the mass of their fellow men as 'the foolish common people' who were addicted to pleasure and at the mercy of their senses; they derided their sexual activities as bovine habits; and they had nothing but pity for the perpetual worries of householders, imprisoned in their dusty homes and consumed with ambition for their paltry families.

Far from believing in progress, Buddhists assume that their religion has declined constantly. At first it was like 'freshly made cream', but then deterior-

ation set in, step by step every 500 years, until now, after five times 500 years, the spirit has departed almost in its entirety and the holy doctrine is good only for contentions and squabbling.

After the first 500 years, at the beginning of the Christian era, there was a renewal of the religion, known as *Mahayana* (the Great Vehicle). In many ways, it was a reaction against the conceit of self-centred monks and was accompanied by the rehabilitation of those who had formerly been disparaged—ignorant laymen, women and the rich.

After 500 AD the lower orders took over, both in the Indian *tantras* (a combination of Buddhism and primeval magic) and in Ch'an (from *dhyana*, 'meditation') in China. The founders of the tantric systems were often artisans, and took their cues from the most primi-

mercial acquisitiveness. On the assumption that 'property is theft', and that one can only become rich by cheating others, well-to-do Buddhists feel uneasy about their wealth, because they fear that the evil deeds by which they gained it will be punished in the next life.

Before they die they often get rid of their ill-gotten gains by giving them to the poor, to the monasteries, or best of all to the Buddha himself, by building monuments to his memory. Families with vast inherited wealth therefore rarely oceur in Buddhist societies; in addition, greed is constantly disparaged as an evil thing, and frugality and simple living are valued highly. Not to hoard is dufy when generosity is a great virtue; and material, as distinct from spiritual, happiness is considered merely contemptible.

In general, however, Buddhism has greatly enhanced the authority of govern-

(Left) Mara, 'the Killer', is the equivalent of Satan in Buddhist mythology. This Central Asian painting depicts Mara's temptation of Buddha.

(Right) Buddhist monks do not generally cut themselves off from the rest of the community. These monks in Laos are receiving food from peasants in return for the guidance they give them in their daily life.

(Below) Images from the Sanjusangendo temple in Kyoto, Japan, built by the Shinshu sect. Shinshu emerged in the 12th century, and gained popularity by preaching simple doctrines intelligible to the masses.

Michael Holford/Musée Guimet

tive strata of Indian society. Ch'an was founded by peasants who were proud of their illiteracy and bad manners, and constantly asserted their superiority over everyone else. About 800 AD the Ch'an monks took the unprecedented step of maintaining themselves by manual or agricultural work, for 'a day without work is a day without eating'.

In Japan, the apparent collapse of the *dharma* provided the main justification for all later developments, on the principle that 'if we offer you only these pitiful remnants of the *dharma*, this is because that is all this corrupt age can bear'. During the 13th century, a clamorous demagogue named Nichiren emerged as spiritual leader, despite being the son of a fisherman—a tabooed and sinful occupation. He was chauvinistic, rude, intolerant and aggressive.

Nichiren flattered the innate tribalism of the people by making the salvation of all living beings dependent on first achieving the salvation of Japan. And he

claimed for himself an enormously exalted status as the re-incarnation of a Bodhisattva mentioned in the *Lotus Sutra* (c. AD 100). thus compensating for his lowly birth.

Yet Buddhism continues to have a profound influence on Asian societies. It has greatly reduced the level of violence—in India the death penalty went out of use, all classes except the outcasts adopted a vegetarian diet, and animal sacrifices were abolished. Even violence against the physical environment was censured, and the people were urged to take care of trees and to avoid unnecessary burning of forests. The Tibetans and Mongols, who were the fiercest militarists in Asia, were pacified by Buddhism. In the social hierarchy, soldiers became regarded as the lowest of the low.

Buddhist influence has also impeded the accumulation of wealth in private hands. This is in accordance with the injunction 'not to take what is not given' —a precept distinctly inimical to com-

William Macquity

Alex Langley/Aspect

(Right) Stupas surround a stone Buddha at a large shrine in Indonesia. The Buddha is often shown seated, and the positions of his hands indicate such activities as meditation or teaching.

Alex Langley/Aspect

ments. It provided the ideal social cement for those who had to rule over vast heterogeneous areas and so it was taken up by the great conquerors of Asia: first the Emperor Asoka, about 250 BC, and last the Emperor Ch'ien Lung in China about 1750 AD. Few political leaders are always successful, or even regularly so. They therefore seek a quality which will ensure the allegiance and obedience of the ruled even when things go wrong—the seal of 'legitimacy'.

The Buddhist monks could bestow legitimacy upon a ruler by representing him as in some way the anointed of the Lord, as a manifestation of the benevolent spiritual forces which were known as Buddhas or Bodhisattvas. In Tibet, for example, to act against the Dalai Lama would be to act against the great compassionate Bodhisattva Chen-re-zi, and this is a real deterrent. Furthermore, such peaceful, frugal and other-worldly populations, conditioned by Buddhism to be non-violent and indifferent to material wealth, were easy to rule.

But Buddhism also promoted the material welfare of the people. Asoka built hospitals for people and animals; along the roads he set up rest-houses, dug wells and planted mango groves and banyan trees; and did everything 'in order that my people might conform to the *dharma*'. Buddhist governments regularly provide famine relief, medical help, homes for the aged, the infirm and the orphaned, and care for the poor—Japanese empresses even purified themselves of their sins by bathing lepers.

Buddhist co-operative and charitable societies used to be widespread in China, sometimes with unexpected results. They lent a Buddhist colouring to some of the subversive secret societies which sprang up after 1200 AD—the White Lotus Society for instance, weakened the alien Manchu dynasty by a long-planned rebellion from 1796-1804. At other times the monasteries organized their economic activities with such efficiency that they made vast commercial profits.

Beauty has been another by-product of Buddhist culture—over many centuries Asian countries have been adorned with millions of splendid buildings, fine statues and paintings; and enhanced by lovely and solemn sounds from bells, gongs, musical instruments and trained human voices. Ordinary daily life was beautified and harmonized by the tea ceremony and the art of flower arrangement, while poetry, dancing and gardening were totally remoulded.

But local conditions were inevitably varied, and Buddhism has borne the imprint of the national character in each of the dozen or so countries to which it migrated in the course of time. It remained a fairly alien body for three or four centuries, then produced local adaptations, often of great originality, during the next centuries before the vigour waned and it became just one added flavour in the life of society.

Buddhism entered China in AD 60, to encounter a well-established civilization which had already, in its own well-developed language, formulated a number of solutions to the problems of life and death. Many Buddhist technical terms had aready been pre-empted by the native Taoist mysticism, while for others, no appropriate word could be found. The style of thinking was also quite different. Indians loved a profusion of scholastic categories, with countless divisions and sub-divisions, and with the most elaborate logical apparatus to sustain them. In China all this counted for nothing. Simple, natural and poetical forms of expression were valued, and intuition counted for more than reasoning.

Over the years, the Buddhists also had to accommodate themselves to the ethical principles of Confucius—in particular, the virtue of filial piety—and after a long struggle the monastic communities were finally subordinated to the imperial bureaucracy. The Chinese attitude to nature, which added the aesthetic appreciation of natural beauty to the discovery of the Buddha's work within it, gave Buddhism a further new dimension.

In Japan Buddhism underwent vast changes after it was introduced during the 6th century, often becoming the opposite of what it had been in India. When the *samurai*, the professional warrior class, adopted 'Zen' Buddhism, they used it to become more efficient fighters, to improve their skills in archery and sword fighting. The monks themselves banded

(Below) A monk from Ulan Bator in Outer Mongolia prostrates himself in penance for his sins. Buddhism spread to Mongolia from China, where it had taken root as early as the 1st century AD.

(Right) Buddhism appeals to people of all classes and occupations, throughout Asia. It plays a vital part in the lives of these Tibetans, who are lighting candles as part of the New Year festival.

John Massey Stewart

together in huge feudal castles and indulged in large-scale internecine warfare. Monastic celibacy was soon abolished, and the temples were handed down in families from father to son. In the 1950s and 1960s 'Zen' became popular in the West with its emphasis on achieving enlightenment through meditation.

Doctrinally, an extreme simplification took place and demands on the faithful were reduced to a minimum. Shinran Shonin (1173-1262) proclaimed that men are salvaged by merely invoking the name of the Buddha *Amitabha* ('Infinite Light') just once in their lives, even without belief of commitment to any of the Buddhist precepts. Unrepentant sinners were particularly welcome in *Amitabha's* paradise, since they exercised his saving grace.

Japanese intellectual life, compared with Indian, was characterized by a lack of logical coherence and precision, a reliance on intuition and emotional moods, and a tendency to avoid complex ideas and simplify everything out of concern for the practical needs of the common people. Japanese, as distinct from Indian, Buddhists accepted the phenomenal world as if it were absolute, and looked for nothing outside, above or beyond it.

In keeping with their native Shinto, Japanese were inclined to accept people's natural desires as they are and do little to repress or fight against them. The scholar Hajime Nakamura commented that 'religion, in the true sense of the word, never deeply took root in Japanese soil'—and the Buddha's religion seems indeed to have fulfilled itself there through more or less total negation. From the standpoint of Buddhist logic, which loves paradoxes, this is not necessarily a criticism.

Like most other traditional religions, Buddhism has fared none too well over the last two centuries and on the whole it has suffered even more than its rivals. The forces of the modern world, whether capitalist or communist, have removed, by military force or economic pressure, the majority of the monks, as well as taking their lands, their temples, and most of their influence over the people. The Buddhist religion has initiated nothing of its own over the last five centuries, but has remained on the defensive throughout, constantly retreating before the hostile forces which threaten to engulf it altogether quite soon.

If Buddhist society needs a king, a community of monks and faithful laymen, then at present Thailand, small and imperilled as it is, alone fulfils all three requirements. The Buddhist kings and emperors have all been toppled, the latest victim being the Cho(s-r)gyal ('*dharma*-king') of Sikkim in 1975. Monastic institutions provide the lifeblood of

Buddhism, but over the last 400 or 500 years the monks have faded away, initially because they became indolent and found celibacy nearly everywhere too onerous. The married 'priests' of Nepal, Tibet, China, Japan and elsewhere, failed to inspire much awe.

As for the attempts to spread Buddhism to the West, the results have been derisory from an organizational point of view. Western religious thinking is being enriched by a few additional ideas or points of view, but none of these are

Buddhism is characterized by detachment from the illusory sensations of the world. The extraordinary serenity some Buddhists have achieved is exemplified by this Vietnamese monk, who burned himself to death in protest against Government persecution.

particularly new, merely part of the heritage of perennial philosophy.

Buddhism remains a social force where it has allied with the two most potent forces of contemporary Asian society—nationalism and the desire for social justice. In Burma and Sri Lanka the monks were in the forefront of the fight against the foreign imperialists; in Vietnam the serene countenance of the monks who burned themselves alive foreshadowed early on the ultimate futility of American military might when faced with a fearless moral force.

In Sri Lanka and Burma all kinds of combinations between Buddhism and Marxism are being tried out in an attempt to build a non-acquisitive, non-exploitative and co-operative socialist society. It should never be forgotten that the *sangha* has always been communistic in its property relationships, that the monks were forbidden to handle gold, silver or money of any kind, and that Buddhist values are unlikely to thrive in a capitalist economy. In China those Buddhists who have survived the Maoist revolution welcome the ejection of foreign intruders and admit that much of the social programme of the new rulers carries out Buddhist social ideals envisaged centuries ago.

In Japan, likewise, Buddhism is nourished by nationalism. Zen Buddhists marvel at the sublimity of Nipponian spirituality, 'incomparably incomparable'. The laymen of the Nichiren lineage have created organizations which grew from 350,000 members in 1955 to 15,700,000 in 1968—run by and for merchants, craftsmen and the people in general, they combine an intense national pride with efforts to improve the quality of their daily lives.

In India, his original homeland, the Buddha has become an object of national pride: the Congress Party has resuscitated him as 'India's greatest son', and his 'Wheel of Dharma' adorns the national flag. In 1956, Dr Ambedkar, author of the Constitution of the Republic of India, tried to integrate millions of outcastes into Hindu society by reviving the Buddhism which had disappeared from its country of origin more than eight centuries ago, although he greatly curtailed the Buddha's teachings and reduced them to a belief in the equality of men and a repudiation of the caste system.

The prospects for the future are bad everywhere. None of the forces of modern society favours Buddhism as a religion, and increasing decay may prove to be its fate. But a religion which has Impermanence for its main theme will not be too downhearted if it finds itself doomed temporarily to disappear. For in due course, so we are promised, another Buddha, Maitreya by name, will appear in the world and reveal again the eternal Truth to a mankind by then so much more willing and capable to receive it. ☐

Associated Press

Shinto

Shinto is the national religion of Japan, with neither moral teaching nor scriptures. A cult which celebrates the life of the spirit after death, it recognizes neither Heaven nor Hell and offers neither reward nor punishment. The spirit of Shinto stirs deep in the Japanese imagination: embodied in the racial mythology, the religion has survived as a constant expression of national identity.

Born from ancient knowledge of the natural elements, Shinto has infused the experience of nature with religious veneration. At the same time, its mythology and its emphasis on ancestor worship have linked the legends of prehistoric Japan to historical fact. Shinto provides the framework for social organization and a channel to release powerful and volatile national emotions—the Emperor is believed to be a direct descendant of the sun goddess Amaterasu, the principal deity of the Shinto pantheon.

The word 'Shinto' literally means 'the way of the spirits', who themselves are known as *kami*. The term first appears in the 8th century chronicles, the Nihonshoki. It is believed that the term was widely used from the 13th century onwards to distinguish the native *kami* faith from Buddhism and Confucianism, which entered Japan from China.

The worship of *kami* emerges from the earliest myths, and it is through the imagery of myth that Shinto retains its power and significance today. The Japanese have traditionally preferred intuition to intellect. Similarly, they have focussed their attention on the present, avoiding speculation on the past and future; in consequence much of the early history of Japan is vague, for the Japanese found myth more appealing than historical fact.

In Shinto myth, the islands of Japan were created by the gods Izanagi and Izanami, who descended to the ocean on a rainbow from their celestial land. The divine pair gave birth to the sun goddess, Amaterasu-o-mikami, and to her two brothers, Tsuki-yomi-nomiko, the moon god, and Susanowo-no-mikoto, the storm god. Susanowo was violent and unruly. On one occasion he visited Amaterasu to apologise for previous misdeeds, but set loose a group of wild, piebald colts, which ran amok and destroyed the walls dividing the rice fields. Amaterasu re-

We of the Japanese race who have been brought into existence through the creative spirits of the ancestral Kami are, each and every one, in spontaneous possession of the Way of the Gods.

A man of Michi (the Way) is a man of character, of justice, of principle, of conviction, obedient to the nature of his humanity. To be accused of having wandered from the Michi is to suffer an insult, for it implies perversity to that which is most essentially manly. Michi is a heaven-given constituent, the ideal of heaven to be realized in humanity.

The course of nature is the will of the Gods. The will of the Gods performed in all that acts naturally. Here is extreme simplicity, utter faith in the rightness of the natural. Such is the core of the Japanese Michi.

treated to a cave in disgust and the world was plunged into darkness.

The other deities, or *kami*, gathered outside the cave and planted a sacred *sakaki* tree. In the centre of the tree they placed a mirror and on its upper branches a jewel; these are now two of the sacred treasures of Japan. A goddess then performed a bawdy dance, to the great enjoyment of the assembled *kami*.

Hearing their laughter, Amaterasu peered out of the cave. She caught her reflection in the mirror and once again ventured out into the open. Thus was light returned to the world.

This legend is full of the imagery of a primitive agricultural society, whose survival was dependent on the natural cycle of the seasons. The force of the storm encounters the power of the sun; the storm disrupts the land and the sun retreats. Only by ritual entreaty does the light of spring return to renew the cycle. The animistic beliefs of prehistoric Japanese society are preserved in the myth: the legend of Amaterasu has retained its significance and her shrine at Ise is the holiest shrine in Japan.

The *kami* are the object of Shinto worship; there are said to be eight million of these spirits. The concept of *kami* endows the natural elements and phenomena with holy properties, and implies a divine order where the *kami* function in harmonious co-operation. The Shinto pantheon includes the creator, sun, moon and stars, the spirits of fertility and production, the wind, thunder, mountains, rivers, sea and fire, plants, animals and ancestral spirits.

The typical dwelling places of the *kami* are the summit of the holy mountain, forests (especially the sacred tree *sakaki*), caves and rocks. Shrines are placed close to these abodes, on top of mountains, on solitary crags of rock or in the forests; within the precincts of the shrine particular trees or rocks are adorned with prayers, in the form of slips of white paper, and ropes of worship, known as *shimenawa*.

Shinto shrines are examples of devotion to the *kami* rather than evangelical symbols. Through the worship of the *kami*, forms which we would consider inanimate are instilled with vitality. Delight in natural form is characteristic of Japanese aesthetics; it is a sensibility born from the Shinto tradition.

It was not until the 12th century that Shinto was transformed from an animistic folk belief into a philosophical system. The development of an intellectual school of Shinto was the result of Buddhist and Confucian influence, which had appeared in Japan six centuries earlier. There was some conflict between the foreign religions and the native faith, but by the 8th century a curious

2510

D. Turner Givens/Rex Features

Ian Berry/Magnum

fusion between Buddhism and Shinto had already taken place.

The *kami* were thought to be pleased to receive Buddhist temples. Amaterasu was absorbed into the Buddhist pantheon and was identified with the Tantric god, Vairocana; according to the doctrine of Horiji-Suijaku, Shinto *kami* were regarded as manifestations of Buddhas and Bodhisattvas.

But throughout Japanese history, the pendulum of national reaction has swung from one extreme to another.

(Left) The shrine at Ise to Amaterasu, the Shinto sun-goddess, is the home of the sacred mirror, brought from the celestial land by her grandson Ninigi. The shrine, a perfect example of pure Japanese architecture, is pulled down and faithfully reconstructed every 20 years.

(Right) An old woman breathes in incense smoke, supposed to ensure good health and fortune, at a Tokyo shrine. Shinto is very much a folk religion, and many Japanese perform daily rites to the deities.

(Left) A festival in the Kanda district of Tokyo. Before 1945, most Japanese national holidays were based on Shinto festivals, but many have since lost their religious significance.

(Below) Shinto priests walk through Kyoto, Japan's holy city. Anyone with the proper training can become a priest; only they and their attendants may enter the inner sanctuary of a shrine.

Ian Berry/Magnum

Ian Berry/Magnum

between myth and history.

The early emperors, who held power over the tribal chiefs of ancient Japan, acted not only as military leaders or civil administrators, but also as the chief participants in the rituals of *kami* worship. Religious rites and secular administration were linked by a common word, *matsurigoto*, meaning 'worship affairs'. The performance of these rites was not merely associated with administration but was the actual means of government —*saisei itchi*, 'the unity of worship and government'. The key to power was held by those who controlled the ritual; *saisei itchi* was the spiritual foundation of Japanese society.

The strength of that foundation was demonstrated most clearly in 1868, with the return to direct rule by the emperor, who had been politically impotent for centuries. The so-called Meiji Restoration was made possible by the revival of Shinto *kami* worship as a basis for government and social order. A Government Department of Shinto was established, modelled on the 7th century Office of Divine Affairs. In 1869, the Emperor Meiji conducted Shinto rituals in the Imperial Palace before an assembly of dignitaries, assuming the role of a priest engaged in worship before the entire Shinto pantheon. This ceremony marked the adoption of Shinto as a State cult.

In more recent history, Shinto has provided a channel for patriotic fervour. The Japanese suicide pilots of the Second World War, though trained in Zen Buddhist monasteries, were *kamikaze*, 'the divine wind' or 'wind of the *kami*'. But after Japan's defeat, the American military occupation ended the official status of Shinto; a strict separation of religion and government was enforced. Today the shrines exist as institutions independent of the state.

Kami worship is practised by observing four rites: purification (*harai*), the offering (*shinsen*), prayer (*norito*) and the sacred feast (*naorai*). Purification is performed to remove evil spirits which may hinder communion with the *kami*. Shinto recognizes no concept of original sin— the world of Man and the *kami* is inherently good. Evil therefore originates outside the world, in darkness; it is propagated by spirits known as *magatsuhi*, who upset the balance and stability of the *kami*. The purification itself is achieved by abstention and by cleansing, which the priest performs by sprinkling salt and water, and the worshipper by rinsing the mouth and washing the hands.

Purity was also a Buddhist concept, which was a significant principle of the Japanese tea ceremony, *cha-no-yu*. Simple offerings of rice, salt, water and sprigs of the *sakaki* tree can be seen in wayside shrines all over Japan. More elaborate

After a period of contact with the Buddhist doctrine, the Japanese have reacted strongly with a wave of nationalism. The 'Fukko-Shinto' sect advocated the exclusion of all intellectual concepts from Shinto practice and a return to the purity of the mythological ideals. And the sect soon became a weapon for extreme political factions.

Shinto has always assisted political unity in Japan, for it reinforced the status of the Emperor at the summit of the social hierarchy and linked him directly to the legendary Amaterasu. Ninigi-no-mikoto, the grandson of Amaterasu, received instructions to descend from the celestial world and govern Japan. With the sacred treasures, including the jewel and the mirror, as symbols of his authority, and accompanied by the *kami*, Ninigi established his court at Izumo on the west coast of Honshu. Jimmu, the first Emperor of Japan, who died in 585 BC, is said by legend to be the great-grandson of Ninigi and their relationship forms the bridge

Marilyn Silverstone/Magnum

Prayer slips hang from the trees around a shrine in Kyoto. Shinto was Japan's state religion from 1869–1945, with 110,000 shrines controlled by the Home Ministry. The religion was disestablished after Japan's defeat in the Second World War.

offerings of fish, seaweed, vegetables, rice cakes and fruit are made at the large shrines—silk, cotton, money, jewels and even animals may sometimes be offered.

At Ise, where the sacred mirror is housed at Amaterasu's shrine, two white horses are stabled as offerings from the Imperial Household. Three times a month these horses are decked in robes and led before the main sanctuary. At the other end of the spectrum, Japanese families make offerings of rice wine (*sake*) and rice cakes to their ancestral spirits at a family altar in the home.

Prayers were often chanted in the most solemn, archaic Japanese, free from any sounds of the Chinese vocabulary which entered the language over the centuries. Many of these prayers have been preserved in an important oral tradition, but Shinto priests are free to compose their own words of praise and respect to the *kami*. The prayers also express thanksgiving, announce the offerings and make reference to the particular festival or occasion that is being celebrated. Shinto ceremonies are completed by the sacred feast, when the worshippers eat sym-

bolically with the *kami*. This involves the sipping of *sake*, and often an informal meal.

In addition to formal worship, the shrines are places of entertainment where sacred dance, *bugaku*, classical drama, *noh*, archery contests and even *sumo* wrestling is performed for the divine amusement (*kan-nigiwai*) of the *kami*. In rural areas, Shinto ceremonies may also accompany important stages of the agricultural cycle such as the sowing, the transplanting and the harvesting of the rice. Fishermen may also praise the *kami* of the sea.

It is understandable that people whose livelihood is dependent on the elements should still observe the Shinto tradition. However, Shinto has a place even in the industrial centres of post-war Japan and among the great urban populations. Over the New Year a million people are said to pay their respects at the shrine of the Emperor Meiji in the centre of Tokyo. And Shinto shrines are to be found in most modern Japanese factories. Amidst the concrete, glass and steel of the new Japan, the *kami* are still recognized.

The strength of the Shinto tradition can be observed most clearly at the shrine dedicated to Amaterasu at Ise. This shrine, which houses the sacred mirror brought from the celestial land by Ninigi, is the earliest and finest example of a pure Japanese architectural style. But every 20 years since the reign of the Emperor Temmu in the 7th century, the shrine has been pulled down and faithfully reconstructed on an immediately adjacent

site according to prescribed ritual.

The last reconstruction ceremony, *Shikinen-sengu* was completed in 1973. Starting with *Yamaguchi-sai*, a ceremony to honour the god of the mountain and to pay respect for the thousands of trees that will be cut for the new shrine, the ritual reaches its climax eight years later when the sacred mirror is installed in the new building.

During the final ceremony in 1973 a procession of 130 people accompanied the mirror to its new shrine, while the Emperor in his palace in Tokyo, 200 miles to the north, ceremoniously turned and faced the direction of Ise. More than 10,000 worshippers watched the torchlit procession of dignitaries, wearing Shinto costumes from the 10th century, make their way to the new shrine. The sacred mirror was carried in a box within another box, which was wrapped in white silk. Nobody may see the mirror except the Emperor, who has never made use of the privilege. By renewing the materials of the shrine and replacing the edifice, the underlying belief is preserved intact.

The pendulum of history has taken Japan from the ashes of defeat to vast economic power. The transformation has been sudden and extreme, but the significance of Shinto is undiminished. Its characteristics are both elusive and diverse, popular and esoteric, yet it remains the touchstone of the Japanese identity, the current with which the spirit of this island people is charged—the pulse of their vitality.

Judaism

A well-known Jewish prayer runs: 'Blessed art Thou O Lord our God who has given His Torah to His people Israel'. For the basic idea of Judaism is that the God of all the universe communicated His will, contained in the Torah, to the Jews, who thus become God's people. But it must be realized that this is the language of prayer: emotional and spontaneous, sacrificing any deep reflection on what such an extraordinary statement involves.

The whole of Jewish history can be seen as a sustained meditation on the three themes of God, Torah and Israel. These were interpreted and re-interpreted, applied to the realities of Jewish existence and studied at different levels to avoid crudity and narrowness of thought. For example, Jews often asked 'How does God 'communicate' His will? In what sense can He be said to have a 'will' at all? How can any one people be said to be His people since He is the Creator of all men?'

There has never been any gathering of representative Jewish teachers to try to answer these questions. There is nothing in Judaism to correspond to the great Councils of the Christian Church with the purpose of defining doctrine. Yet a kind of consensus has emerged among the faithful that the three basic ideas are true, but with considerable elasticity and room for individual interpretation.

Some Jews have tended to place the greatest stress on the notion of God, understanding Judaism in universal and individualist terms, though never to the total exclusion of the other two ideas. Other Jews have tended to put the emphasis on Jewish peoplehood while others again have preferred to devote most of their intellectual energy to the Torah.

The consensus works by declaring that any religious position which rejects any of these three ideas completely is incompatible with Judaism. Thus no one can be an adherent of Judaism if he embraces Christianity or Islam at the same time, to say nothing of religions with a plurality of gods, or atheistic philosophies.

There has been considerable development in Judaism. The concept of Torah itself was gradually extended from the Five Books of Moses—the Torah of Moses—to the prophetic writings and the

The Lord is my shepherd; I shall not want. He maketh me to lie down in green pastures: he leadeth me beside the still waters.

He restoreth my soul: he leadeth me in the paths of righteousness for his name's sake.

Yea, though I walk through the valley of the shadow of death, I will fear no evil: for thou art with me; thy rod and thy staff they comfort me.

Thou preparest a table before me in the presence of mine enemies: thou annointest my head with oil; my cup runneth over.

Surely goodness and mercy shall follow me all the days of my life; and I will dwell in the house of the Lord for ever.

rest of the Hebrew Bible—the books of Psalms, Proverbs, Job and so forth—then to the later interpretations of these books by the scholars and teachers and eventually to the sum-total of Jewish teaching throughout the ages.

As Solomon Schechter (1847–1915) said, when a devout Jew asks a scholar to 'tell him some Torah' he does not expect the scholar to open the Bible and read him a verse, but to give him some original idea, some fine exposition of a Biblical verse or some new understanding of a Jewish idea.

It follows from this that God is understood as giving the Torah not only *to* the Jewish people but also *through* them.

The different cultural environments in which Jews lived had an influence on the way Jews thought and consequently on the way they applied and interpreted the Torah. It is possible to see these influences at work throughout Jewish history down to the present day.

The major classical work of Judaism, after the Bible, is the Talmud. There are two Talmuds in fact: the Palestinian, compiled around the year 400 AD, and the Babylonian, compiled around 500 AD. Both are in the form of elaborate commentaries on the Mishnah, a work compiled in Palestine around 200 AD, which is a digest of the whole of post-Biblical Jewish law and doctrine.

The two thousand and more teachers whose names occur in the Talmud are known as the Rabbis. The word Rabbi means 'teacher' and was subsequently applied to all the teachers of Judaism. The Rabbi is not, therefore, a priest; he is not singled out from the rest of the Jewish community except as an expert in the 'teaching', as one who knows the Torah and can make his contribution towards the further development of the Torah.

The Talmud should be seen as a gigantic attempt at translating into action the ideals of the Bible. For instance, the prophets speak of justice as mandatory and see people's aim in life as the pursuit of justice and righteousness. But how is justice to be realized in daily life? What is a fair wage? How are the relationships between employer and employee to be regulated? And what duties do parents owe to children and children to parents, the individual to the community, the Jew to the nion-Jew, husband and wife to one another?

All these and other numerous questions are discussed in the Talmud, with the result that Judaism acquired a strong legal character, criticized at times as legalism but defended passionately as an excellent example of what has been called 'prophetism in action', the mighty quest for the will of God in every human situation.

The Talmud, however, contains much more than legal material. Nothing human is foreign to it. In the Talmud all human civilization is surveyed. There is geography, history and folk-lore; science, medicine and magic; profound specu-

(Above) Jews gather with their prayer shawls at the Wailing Wall in Jerusalem, to celebrate the Feast of the Tabernacles. The site of the ancient Temple, destroyed by the Romans, has become a focus for Judaic sentiment.

(Left) A Hasidic teacher guides his pupils through a Hebrew text. The Hasidic movement, founded in Poland during the 18th century, emphasized the mystic need to be attached in the mind to God, and stressed traditional Judaic practice.

Cornell Capa/Magnum

lations on philosophical questions and simple but charming tales; ethical standards and the way in which a gentleman should behave; the needs of women as women and men as men; the achievements of Rome, Persia, China and India; the activities of pearl-fishers, merchants, sailors, camel-drivers, soothsayers and necromancers; the temptations of the rich and the sorrows of the poor; the heights of human saintliness and the depths of their brutality; all surveyed in the light of the Torah as life's guiding principle. And all this is a matter of learning and study.

The chief contribution of the Talmud to Jewish life was the tremendous importance it attached to learning. The study of the Torah became the Jewish ideal not only for the scholars but for all Jews, who according to the Talmud are

obliged to set aside some time each day, no matter how busy and preoccupied they may be, for the study of the Torah. A revealing though extreme Talmudic passage states that if a man can only afford to ransom either his father or his teacher from bandits he must ransom his teacher, since his father only brings him into this world while his teacher brings him to eternal life.

The philosophical element in Judaism came to the fore in post-Talmudic times, especially among Spanish Jewry in the Middle Ages. In this period Greek philosophy in its Arabic garb came to exercise a powerful fascination for the Jewish mind. The towering figure of Maimonides (1135–1204) represents this trend at its best, though it is worth noting that Maimonides was a distinguished exponent of Jewish law as well as the most out-

standing theologian Jewry has produced.

The problem of reconciling faith with reason was prominent in the works of the medieval Jewish philosophers. Uncompromising in their acceptance of the authority of the Torah, they insisted nonetheless that if its teachings appeared to be in flat contradiction to human logic these teachings had to be understood differently, so as to be in full accord with reason.

In particular, these thinkers declared that the Biblical and Talmudic passages describing God in all too human terms should be interpreted in a non-literal fashion. God does not really have an eye or a hand, nor can He really be angry or jealous. In their determination to develop a purely spiritual understanding of the Deity the scholars went so far as to deny that anything positive can be said about God—even to say that God is One is merely to affirm that He is not a multiplicity of beings.

For Maimonides and many of the other thinkers of this period, the true aim of the religious life is profound contemplation of metaphysical ideas so

said to mirror some divine reality, and, in turn, the Jewish way of life influences the upper worlds. Thus, every human action has cosmic significance. If people are virtuous, they send on high those impulses which promote the flow of divine grace to the world below; however, if they are wicked, they send forth baneful influences which impede the flow of divine grace.

Although the majority of Jews accepted the Kabbalah as part of revealed religion and the Zohar as a sacred text, throughout subsequent centuries there were some who saw the Kabbalah as a foreign importation into Judaism and, in its doctrine of the ten different potencies in the Godhead, as a breach of pure monotheism.

After the expulsion of the Jews from Spain at the end of the 15th century, new centres of Jewish life were established, one of them in the town of Safed in Palestine, where Jewish mystics worked and taught during the 16th century. The two most prominent were Moses Cor-

dovero and Isaac Luria, the latter the founder of the Lurianic Kabbalah, in which the older Kabbalistic ideas are elaborated in a rich but bewildering symbolism.

At the heart of the Kabbalistic system, as at the heart of Judaism in general in this period, is the idea of cosmic redemption. The Messiah who had been promised by God will come to redeem the Jewish people from exile, to restore the Jewish State in Palestine and usher in the Kingdom of God for all mankind.

In Safed, too, there lived towards the end of his life the great lawyer and mystic Rabbi Joseph Karo, author of one of the

This famous painting by Marc Chagall shows a Jew with his Torah—the book of 'teaching' or 'doctrine', which contains God's will. The Torah also includes interpretations by scholars and rabbis— a compilation of Jewish teaching through the ages.

that the human soul can come closer to God, who is pure Spirit. Other aspects of general culture also found their full expression among Jews during this period. In the Golden Age in Spain there were poets, grammarians, statesmen, musicians and physicians active as equals in the society of their non-Jewish neighbours.

It is precarious to generalize too much, but on the whole it seems that in times of persecution, of which there were many, the Jews tended to retreat within themselves, with a consequent narrowing of Jewish vision. In times of acceptance by the non-Jewish world, the Jew's spiritual horizons were widened and the spirit of Judaism became more embracing.

Partly in reaction to the cold austerity of the philosophers, partly as a result of the religious ferment produced by Christian movements, the Jewish mystical system known as the Kabbalah ('Tradition') developed in 12th century Provence. Its major work, the Zohar ('Illumination') appeared mysteriously in Spain at the end of the 13th century—to this day the question of the Zohar's authorship is much discussed.

The Kabbalah is an esoteric doctrine, theosophical in nature, concerned with the Godhead in all Its manifestations and the relation between God and humans. The Bible is interpreted in the Zohar as a mystical text. The narratives of Genesis are said to be not primarily about Abraham, Isaac and Jacob and the other heroes and heroines, but about the dynamic life of the Godhead. Abraham, for example, is the representation on earth of the divine Mercy, Isaac of the divine Judgement and Sternness and Jacob of the harmonizing principle on high.

Every detail of Jewish observance is

most influential Jewish works of all time, the Shulhan Arukh ('Arranged Table'). This is a summary of Jewish law, divided into four gigantic books dealing with the daily life of the Jew, the special religious requirements of Judaism, the laws of marriage and divorce, and with law proper—the whole range of jurisprudence. The Shulhan Arukh, governing every possible situation, became the standard of Jewish piety. Faithful Jews adhered strictly to its laws until the rise of Reform Judaism in the early 19th century.

New currents of thought began to penetrate Jewish communities during the 18th century. In Germany the Jewish philosopher Moses Mendelssohn (1729–1786) and the circle which gathered around him founded the Haskalah ('Enlightenment') movement, which sought to incorporate the advantages of Western culture. Increasingly, the Jews were forced to come to grips with the new system of ideas and culture from which they had been excluded.

Some Jews sought to resolve the tension by embracing Christianity and giving up their Judaism. The Haskalah encouraged its followers to take a sterner stand, to appreciate that, as they saw it, a full and rich Jewish life was compatible with complete involvement in Western society. The followers of the Haskalah translated the Hebrew Bible into German, encouraged the study of the German language, stressed the universal idea in Judaism and generally tried to see Judaism as a perfectly rational way of life rather than a set of dogmatic assertions.

Revivalism was also in the air during the 18th century. In Podolia and Volhynia in Poland, there arose the Hasidic movement, founded by Rabbi Israel Baal Shem Tov ('Master of the Good Name of God') who died in 1760, leaving behind disciples and disciples of disciples. His intensely mystical movement, emphasizing the need for people to be constantly attached in their mind to God and the joy and rapture of such attachment, spread to such an astonishing degree that it had been embraced by about half of the great mass of Jews in Eastern Europe by the end of the 18th century.

In this movement a new type of Jewish leader emerged, the Guru-like, charismatic personality, the holy man whose function it is not so much to teach the Torah as to be himself an example of the Torah. One of the leaders of the movement said that when he was a disciple he journeyed to his master not to study the Torah but to see how he tied his shoelaces.

At the beginning of the 19th century in Germany, and slightly later in England, France and the new world of America, there arose the Reform movement, aiming to adapt Judaism to make it easier for

The head of an orthodox Jewish family presides over a meal during the Passover Feast, held annually in remembrance of the Exodus from Egypt. Some of the Torah's ritual requirements are a source of controversy today, but the Passover is celebrated by all practising Jews.

Jews to be socially and culturally at home with their neighbours, while adhering to their own religion.

At first this meant changes in synagogal worship. Sermons were given in the vernacular; prayers for the restoration of the Temple in Jerusalem and for the coming of the Messiah were abolished—this doctrine was re-interpreted to mean the advent of a Messianic age, in which all people will acknowledge the One God and peace will reign supreme on earth. A choir was introduced, along with Western standards of decorum.

But a more radical concept of Reform soon emerged, in which practically all the distinctive features of the Jewish religion, such as the dietary laws (the prohibition for Jews to eat pork and shell-fish, for example), were ignored in favour of a way of life that would bear the strongest resemblances to the Christian way, without, of course, adopting any of the distinctive dogmas of that religion. Against such radical Reform a reaction set in, and a Neo-Orthodoxy emerged in which the values of Western society were frankly and whole-heartedly accepted, but without any surrender of the traditional Jewish forms and observances.

At the end of the 18th century the anti-

Semitic tendencies in many parts of Europe dashed the hopes of Haskalah and Reform and encouraged a more nationalistic interpretation of Judaism, resulting in the birth of political Zionism. The importance of the holy land was stressed again, although the return to Palestine was thought of more in secular than in religious terms. The exceptions were the many religious Zionists who tried to combine the demand for a national home in Palestine with a religious longing for the advent of the Messiah.

The general philosophy of this latter group, particularly after the establishment of the State of Israel, was to see Zionism as the necessary first step to be taken by humans to pave the way for divine intervention in the person of the Messiah. Other religious Jews refused to accept Zionism as a legitimate option, holding the dream of a return to the holy land to be impious without direct divine intervention. However, after the terrible events of the Nazi period and the establishment of the State of Israel, most religious Jews came round to the view that the hand of God was to be seen in the emergence of the new state and they prayed for its continuing success.

In the US there developed the movement known as Conservative Judaism, adopting a middle-of-the-road position, rejecting the inflexibility of Orthodoxy and the radicalism of Reform. In practice, this movement accepts the tradition but allows considerable freedom of thought to its followers, especially in scholarship. It would see no harm, for instance, in Biblical criticism and would not normally see the Bible as an infallible work.

In contemporary Judaism the idea of God is universally understood in a traditional form, with the exception of a few naturalistic thinkers who understand God as a process or as the power in the universe that makes for righteousness. The notion that the Jewish people are central to God's plan for mankind is similarly adhered to, though a few Jews have been prepared to give up the notion of a 'chosen people', arguing that while the idea is traditionally interpreted in terms of service not of privilege, it is liable to be misunderstood.

The differences among contemporary Jews with regard to Torah are chiefly in connection with the ritual rules. No Jewish group has abandoned these entirely but, as stated above, Reform does not consider many of them binding; Orthodoxy insists that the rituals are part of the immutable Torah of God; and Conservative Judaism holds them to be binding as a general rule but wishes to preserve what it sees as the dynamic character of Judaism in which the ritual laws must inevitably change, if gradually, in response to the changing conditions of human life. □

Christianity

Blaise Pascal, the 17th century French philosopher, once complained of Jesus that 'out of 33 years, he lived 30 without making an appearance'. It is an interesting observation, and one which raises a problem of fundamental importance to any study of Christianity. More than any other faith, Christianity is the religion of one man, one teacher; it is not an exaggeration to say that Jesus is the only common denominator among some of the many branches of the Church which claim him as their founder. Yet cross-reference between the Gospels—the only record we possess of his life and words—reveals the fact that only 50 days in his life have been recorded.

Nevertheless, so important is the man and his teaching, that Christianity can only be understood in terms of his life. The process of development—of action and reaction—which has continued for nearly 2,000 years is extremely complex: the Christian Church has modified political structures, and they in turn have effected changes within the Church; individuals have at times united the Church and at other times caused schisms. More importantly, Christian ethics have become part of the fabric of Western civilization.

To try to understand Christianity, the way it has developed, and the impact it has had on society, there is no better starting point than a simplified and selective account of the life of its founder, as told by the Gospels. In this way, highly complex processes and ideas are reduced to their essentials: rather like the parables of which Jesus was so fond. However, it is essential to be aware of the different versions of the life of Jesus presented by the four Gospels (and to a lesser extent, the various apocryphal writings which never became part of the Canon or Holy Scripture), because the changes in emphasis between them are the only clues we have of the ideas and aspirations of the early Judaeo-Christian community.

Mark, probably writing in Rome for the benefit of non-Jewish Christians, is concerned with Jesus the teacher and healer, the bringer of good news. Matthew aims his Gospel at Christians who, like himself, are still Jews: for him Jesus is the Messiah and Christianity is the fulfilment of Judaism. Matthew delights in parallels with the Old Testament and

Blessed are the poor in spirit: for theirs is the kingdom of heaven. Blessed are they that mourn: for they shall be comforted. Blessed are the meek: for they shall inherit the earth. Blessed are they which do hunger and thirst after righteousness: for they shall be filled. Blessed are the merciful: for they shall obtain mercy. Blessed are the pure in heart: for they shall see God. Blessed are the peacemakers: for they shall be called the children of God. Blessed are they which are persecuted for righteousness' sake: for theirs is the kingdom of heaven. Blessed are ye, when men shall revile you, and persecute you, and shall say all manner of evil against you falsely, for my sake. Rejoice, and be exceeding glad: for great is your reward in heaven: for so persecuted they the prophets which were before you.

comparisons between the old law and the new. Luke is a Gentile writing for Gentiles; his concern is the personal grace and compassion of Jesus, the universality of his teaching and its application to human pain and suffering.

The Gospel of John is radically different from the other three. In Matthew, Mark and Luke, Jesus is shown as a human being—a man inspired with the Spirit of God, and in that sense the 'Son of God', but nevertheless a man. But

John portrays Jesus uncompromisingly as a divine being: he is the 'Word made flesh' and the 'Light of the world'. The key figure behind this fundamental change in the representation of Jesus is Paul of Tarsus.

St Paul was, without doubt, the most significant single influence on the development of Christianity in the whole course of its history, and the extent of his doctrinal changes will be considered later. But important as he was, Paul was only one influence among many which helped to shape the vast and diverse Christian Church of today. Through the centuries the fathers and doctors of the Church laboured to interpret and adapt the original message of Jesus, often perverting it and even introducing opposing ideas in order to make the teachings conform with new needs and pressures in society and within the organization of the Church.

The story of Jesus begins in Nazareth. En Nasira, as it is now called, is a typical Near Eastern village which lies in a narrow, rocky valley in Galilee. The houses, with their low, flat roofs and brilliant white-plastered walls are perfectly adapted to the Palestinian climate and the design can have changed little in 2,000 years. Nor has the way of life altered radically since the childhood of Jesus: the women still dry figs and dates in the closed courtyards, and walk through the narrow alleys to fetch water from Nazareth's one fountain. Today the fountain is dedicated to Mary, the mother of Jesus; it was here that Mary—a young woman betrothed to Joseph, a carpenter—learned that she had been chosen to bear the Son of God. The form of words which the angel used at the Annunciation have become a prayer: 'Hail Mary, full of grace, the Lord is with thee; blessed art thou among women, and blessed is the fruit of thy womb, Jesus.'

Surprisingly, only one of the Gospels describes the Annunciation or gives any prominence to the Madonna. The New Testament is centred on Jesus, and except for two chapters in Luke (and a few lines in Matthew) Mary is scarcely mentioned: her position is subordinate, even unimportant. This would not be remarkable if the worship of the Madonna had not—at certain times among some branches of the Christian religion—almost rivalled

make the Mother of God as comely as possible. Intending no disrespect, Filippo Lippi used his serenely beautiful mistress as a model for several Madonnas and thereby incurred the thundering invective of Savonarola; Sandro Botticelli gave Mary the same features as Venus. The connection with paganism is significant, although it would have been more appropriate if it had been Cybele, the mother-goddess, and not Venus who had resembled the Madonna.

When Christianity became the official religion of the Roman Empire under Constantine the Great in 313 AD, the majority of people were still pagan. It was therefore both natural and expedient that Christianity should absorb many aspects of paganism—among them the concept of a mother-goddess. In different parts of the Empire different goddesses were worshipped, but all the cults were essentially the same. From the 2nd century the cult of Isis spread from Egypt and gained considerable popularity, and later many statues of Isis were used to represent Mary. Christian churches were built on the sites of pagan temples and in some cases the original building was adapted and consecrated to the new religion. Some of the practices associated with the worship of the mother-goddess were also continued, including self-mutilation. The Christian theologian Origen castrated himself, and this practice became so common that Constantine and later emperors were forced to prohibit mutilation altogether.

But the veneration of the Madonna was not simply a development of the cult of the mother-goddess: it is most useful to see it as fulfilling the same basic human need. For the Church, Mary became the archetypal mother. As a woman and a human being, Mary was more accessible, more readily understandable than Jesus.

In 325 AD the Council of Nicaea had identified Jesus with God for the first time (previously he had been known rather ambiguously as The Son of God). This further exalted Jesus, and had the effect of increasing both the importance of Mary and the need for an intercessor—a being closer to the majority of Christians. (It also, incidentally, led to the doctrines of the Virgin Birth and the Immaculate Conception). It is not known when the two chapters in Luke venerating the Madonna were interpolated, but it was from the 4th century onwards that Mary became a significant figure in the Christian Church. For 1,600 years her importance grew, until 1964 when Pope Paul VI proclaimed Mary 'Mother of the Church'.

The cult of the Virgin exemplifies several important aspects of the Christian faith. The relatively minor position of Mary in the Gospels and her subsequent importance show that many of the most fundamental beliefs and practices of the

Salvador Dali's disturbing interpretation of the Crucifixion was suggested by a vision of St John of the Cross. The Crucifixion symbolizes the central Christian themes of self-sacrifice and redemption: even on the cross, Jesus could say 'Father, forgive them; for they know not what they do'.

that of Christ himself. Some Protestant theologians have suggested sarcastically that Roman Catholicism is not so much Christianity as 'Marianity'. Images of Mary, depicting her traditional beauty, were an obsession with Renaissance artists, reflecting the power and appeal of the image as much as the tastes of the patrons. Naturally it was important to

Marion Morrison

fication of Mary, the elaboration of the Nativity story arises out of the need to make all aspects of the life of Jesus remarkable as befits a divine being. Birth and death are recurrent themes in Christianity and, like the Crucifixion, the Nativity is a ritual dramatization full of symbolism and fulfilled prophecies.

In the West, the traditional date for Christmas is December 25. It is interesting that in the 3rd century, when the worship of the sun was the national cult of the Roman Empire, December 25 was known as Dies Natalis Sol Invictus: 'The birthday of the invincible sun'. There is no doubt that the political dexterity of Constantine I was largely responsible for the identification of Jesus with the sun god; and, like the fusing of Mary and Isis, this formed a solid pagan foundation for the new religion. As important as the

(Above) The Pope is the ultimate authority within the Roman Catholic Church, Christ's Vicar on Earth. Massive crowds stand in the rain outside Bogotá Cathedral to welcome Pope Paul VI during his visit to South America in 1968.

(Right) The Virgin Mary has been the subject of veneration since Roman times. By the Renaissance, when Filippo Lippi painted this altarpiece, the popular appeal of the Madonna almost rivalled that of Jesus. Mary's importance continued to grow, and in 1964 Pope Paul proclaimed her 'Mother of the Church'.

religion are later developments and have little to do with the teachings of its founder. It also shows that Christianity is a synthesis of many cultural elements apart from those which fused in the mind of Jesus and gave birth to his original teachings. But none of this detracts from Christianity: it is its strength rather than its weakness. The process shows the adaptability of the religion, its responsiveness to the needs of humanity. The same may not be true of other developments which will be dealt with later, but there is nothing in the veneration of the Madonna which is at variance with the teachings of Jesus. Christianity needed a mediator, someone to intercede on behalf of mankind; and this is the role which the Madonna fulfills: 'Holy Mary, Mother of God; pray for us sinners, now, and at the hour of our death'.

Jesus was born in Bethlehem, a small village which lies about 12km (8 miles) from Jerusalem. The beautiful story of the Nativity appears only in Luke and in a much abbreviated form in Matthew—it is significant that the Gospels of Mark and John both begin with the mission of John the Baptist. Like the later glori-

Scala/Galleria Uffizi

2520

Many pagan elements were incorp-orated into early Christianity, and in some parts of the world a process of fusion continues. While the Mass is recited in Spanish, a Bolivian witchdoctor makes offerings to the earth-mother, Pachamama.

conversion of Constantine was for the ultimate triumph of Christianity, it was based on a naive belief that a monogram of 'Christ' on his standard made him invincible in battle, rather than any deep-felt conviction. Nevertheless, from the beginning of the 4th century the new religion and the State became inextricably intertwined.

John the Baptist is, after Jesus, the most remarkable figure in the Gospels. When the priests came from Jerusalem to question what they saw as a potentially dangerous heretic with a sizeable follow-ing they asked him to describe himself. John's reply, with its thundering poetry and tragic insight, is typical of the man and his life: 'I am the voice of one crying in the wilderness'.

As we have seen, both Mark and John begin their Gospels with the Baptist rather than with Jesus. Except for a few references in the other Gospels and a good deal of apocryphal writing, the childhood and early manhood of Jesus are given little coverage. Although the intention of the Gospels is clearly to portray John as subordinate to Jesus (which in every important sense he is) it seems probable that Jesus was at first a disciple of the

man who later recognized that the teacher could learn from his pupil.

Palestine under the Roman occupation was a hotbed of revolutionary splinter groups: some political, some religious and some combinations of both. These ranged from the nationalistic Zealots who believed in armed resistance, to the ascetic Nazarites who believed in morti-fication of the flesh and who renounced society and its evils.

John the Baptist was an important figure in the turmoil of 1st century Palestine, and is even mentioned by the Jewish historian Josephus. He lived in the Judean desert close to the Dead Sea, preaching on the banks of the Jordan. The site is significant: together with other evidence it indicates that John may have belonged to one specific religious splinter group, the Essenes.

In 1947, a Bedouin shepherd boy searching—like a character in a parable—for one of his flock which had strayed, stumbled into a cave which had once been an Essene refectory. Jars which were found in the cave contained the oldest Biblical manuscripts in existence: these were part of the library of the Essenes, the famous Dead Sea Scrolls. The implications of the scrolls are wide-ranging, but so far as Christianity is concerned they show a continuity, a progression of which the religion is a culmination.

One of the scrolls, the Manual of Discipline, sets out the rules of the com-munity. The organization of the Essenes

was almost indistinguishable from that of the early Judaeo-Christian community. They believed above all in charity, in love of one's fellows and a duty to heal the sick. Baptism, the ritual used by John and re-interpreted by St Paul, which is an important rite in every branch of the Christian Church today, was practised by the Essenes. The confession of sins and a eucharistic meal of bread and wine also formed part of their beliefs. Equally fascinating in view of the early history of the Church is the fact that they turned towards the sun for their daily prayers.

Jesus and John the Baptist may well have belonged to the Essene community at some time. In any case, the discovery of the scrolls at Qumran shows that the teachings of Jesus were not solitary or erratic, but were rooted in contemporary belief. More important—since the Essenes, contrary to popular belief, were in many ways strongly 'orthodox' Jews, almost Pharisaic in their strictness—is the essentially Jewish context in which this places the creed of Jesus.

Christianity is more Jewish than many Christians (and indeed many Jews) would like to think: in its forms and beliefs, and in the special intimacy which both Jews and Christians have with their God. For this reason the anti-semitism with which some parts of the Christian Church have been associated at certain times is all the more disgusting and tragic. During the Middle Ages the Church wielded enormous power. This power was often used to suppress Jewish communities, either for financial gain, or through perverted Christian ethics which found expression in the idea that the Jews were the 'nation that murdered God'—a stupid misunderstanding of the circumstances on every possible level. The 'Holy' Inquisition was responsible for thousands of deaths and untold misery, lumping together Jews, witches and heretics in the ecclesiastical courts, and prosecuting them all under a legal system which was a travesty of natural justice.

But the taint of anti-Semitism was not restricted to the medieval Church. In 1936 Cardinal August Hlond of Poland declared: 'It is an actual fact that Jews fight against the Catholic Church . . . it is also true that Jews are committing frauds, practising usury, and dealing in White slavery'. During the 1930s members of the Catholic Church hierarchy also incited anti-semitic feeling in French Canada, Argentina, Romania, Slovakia and the United States. Protestant anti-semitic movements were also active during the same period, although principally among laymen.

These outbreaks of anti-semitism did not, however, represent the feeling of the Churches themselves. During the Nazi occupation of mainland Europe many leading churchmen, both Protestant and Catholic, publicly condemned the treatment of the Jews at great personal risk. It was right that they should do so: anti-semitism is the antithesis of the charity and tolerance which are at the heart of Jesus's teaching. And of course Jesus was himself a Jew, he worshipped in the temple like his disciples: the Catholic writer Jacques Maritain saw the real implication of anti-semitism, describing it as 'a psychopathically disguised Christophobia'. Pope Pius XI explained it more simply: 'Through Christ and in Christ we are all the descendants of Abraham . . . spiritually we are Semites'.

In contrast to the Dead Sea, the Sea of Galilee is surrounded by human settlements and is rich in fish; in the days of Jesus it was known as the Lake of Gennesaret, which means 'valley of flowers'. It was here in Galilee—recruiting disciples from among fishermen and tradesmen—that Jesus began his mission. The climate of the country is in many areas unhealthy: even today the dust, the glaring sun and the rapid changes in temperature are the cause of a great deal of illness. Perhaps because of his Essene background, or simply through compassion, Jesus became known to his contemporaries as a healer as well as a teacher. But the two parts of his ministry were not really separate, not divided between the physical and the spiritual—to the Jews illness was intimately connected with the idea of ritual 'uncleanness', and

it was believed that disease was in some way the consequence of sin.

The most feared of all diseases, and that most strongly associated with uncleanness, was leprosy. The disease was incurable, although sometimes its development arrested naturally, and there were complex rituals for the purification of sufferers by priests. The 'curing' of the leper is one of the most moving stories of the healing ministry and appears in all three synoptic Gospels. A leper kneels before Jesus and asks to be made clean. Risking priestly anger, and overcoming the horror which a man in his society must have felt, Jesus was 'moved with compassion, put forth his hand, and touched him and saith . . . be thou clean'.

Compassion is the fundamental Christian principle and the belief that it is a Christian duty to care for the sick and needy has made a greater impact on society than almost any other aspect of Christianity. The story of the Good Samaritan is one of the most popular in

the New Testament, and from the earliest times Christian communities have run hostels for travellers and almshouses for the poor. It was St Jerome who described the task of the Christians as 'clothing Christ in the poor, visiting him in the sick, feeding him in the hungry, and welcoming him in those who have no roof over their heads'.

Since the 19th century the idea of 'loving God by loving the needy' has gained even more ground. Today there is no area of social welfare in which the Christian Churches are not active, often providing more effective grass-root help

St Jerome described the task of the Christian as 'clothing Christ in the poor, visiting him in the sick, feeding him in the hungry, and welcoming him in those who have no roof over their heads'. Mother Teresa and her Missionaries of Charity have dedicated their lives to caring for the destitute.

In the 20th century the Christian Churches have placed increasing emphasis on social welfare. These nuns belong to the Order of St Vincent de Paul which runs schools and hospitals for the mentally and physically handicapped.

Burt Glinn/Magnum

than government bodies. Millions of pounds flow through international organizations such as Christian Aid; Catholic nuns run hospitals and homes for the destitute and the aged throughout the world; the Salvation Army helps alcoholics, the homeless, drug addicts and the mentally ill; the Anglican Church runs orphanages and other institutions; while thousands of human beings (both ordained and lay) devote their lives quietly and anonymously to helping others in the name of Christ.

The opening-up of world-wide com-

munications in the 18th and 19th centuries, and the beginning of the colonial era, saw the development of the missionary societies. Together with Buddhism and Islam, Christianity had from the earliest times been a 'missionary' religion: St Paul, the most tireless and energetic of all missionaries, had begun the spread of the new faith beyond the country of its origin by evangelizing most of Asia Minor and the principal cities of Greece. The 19th century missionaries believed that no part of the newly discovered (and newly subjugated) world should be allowed to continue in ignorance of their own particular version of Christianity.

It has become fashionable to condemn the activities of the missionary societies in their entirety: an attitude which requires the same bigotry which too many of the missionaries possessed. It has been said that missionaries in every

part of the world inflicted moral codes appropriate to the Victorian middle class on peoples whose cultures they would not, or could not, understand. They allowed themselves to be an organ of suppression under colonial governments; they insensitively overturned the old gods and prohibited the old customs out of ignorance, taking away the self-respect, even the will to live, of the peoples they professed to love. They were guilty of every kind of narrowness, spitefulness and ignorance. And all of this is true.

But missionaries were also responsible for introducing Western medicine, building hospitals and leper colonies, eradicating disease and reducing infant mortality rates. They raised the status of women and stimulated social reform. Countless missionaries devoted their entire lives to serving the needs of others, ignoring personal hardship, and doing only good; worshipping their God by helping mankind. In many cases the missionaries ameliorated the worst abuses of colonial government. And it should not be forgotten that the leaders of many of the emergent nations of the Third World were educated at mission schools.

Mount Tabor is the traditional site for the Sermon on the Mount. The similarity of this impressive background to Mount Sinai where Moses composed the Ten Commandments invites comparison between the old law and the new, between the prohibitive rules of the old patriarch and the promissory 'beatitudes' of Jesus.

It is a simple fact—at once both obvious and extraordinary—that the ethical codes of all the great religious teachers and philosophers of the world are remarkably similar. The differences, and the difficulties, come in the methods of persuading others to follow the code. Pagan philosophy had taught the necessity of being unselfish and loving one's fellows long before the mission of Jesus. Socrates believed that justice was inherent in Man: he did not make it the object of a divine commandment like Jesus. But like Jesus he died for his beliefs. Indeed so close are the analogies between Socrates and Jesus that Erasmus felt constrained to pray to 'Saint Socrates' and Voltaire described Jesus as the 'Socrates of Galilee'.

The Beatitudes which form the backbone of the Sermon on the Mount were not the original creation of Jesus, who brought together ideas from many Biblical sources to serve his purpose, particularly the Psalms and Proverbs. Of course the collection and re-interpretation of the ideas was all-important, but some Christian writers have tended to over-emphasize the separateness and uniqueness of Jesus's teaching, refusing to see him in the context of the Jewish prophetic tradition. The old law and the new were very different, but one had grown out of the other and both were part of the same faith: 'Think not that I am come to destroy the law, or the prophets: I am not come to destroy but to fulfil'.

The Temple of Jerusalem at the time of Jesus was a new and massive structure built by Herod in 18 BC to replace the temporary building which had served the Jews since Nebuchadnezzar destroyed the temple of Solomon five centuries earlier. Just as today the great Christian cathedrals are plagued by parasitic shops and stands, the Temple was a popular pitch for vendors and traders of all kinds who set-up their stalls in the outer courts. The story of Jesus's angry outburst in the Temple, when he overturned the tables of the money-changers and merchants, lashing them with a 'scourge of small cords', appears in all four Gospels. The incident presents a different facet of Jesus's character; the very incongruity of the episode lends it authenticity.

In the Sermon on the Mount and on

Martin Luther was the dominant figure in the Reformation which divided Christian Europe between the Protestant North and the Catholic South—although initially the emergence of Protestantism was as much political as theological. This woodcut was made by Luther's friend Lucas Cranach.

other occasions, Jesus had already railed against the rich and wordly, and to find commercial transactions taking place in the Temple itself was more than he could stand. Jesus was uncompromising on the subject of wealth, consistently aligning himself with the poor and underprivileged: 'How hard it is for them that trust in riches to enter into the kingdom of God'. As in so many other areas, the Church has generally chosen to ignore this most basic of Jesus's teachings. The accumulated riches of the Churches contrast appallingly with the extreme poverty of many of their flock.

The identification of the Church with the rich and powerful was an inevitable consequence of the connection between Church and State. The connection has been important: if Constantine had not adopted Christianity as the official religion of the Roman Empire in the 4th century, the world and Christianity (if it existed at all) would be very different. But the Church-State liaison has brought Christianity a long way from the simple teachings of Jesus.

The identification of the Church with the State meant that the Church was carried along by the tide of change. The various major divisions which have taken place in the Church have been political and economic, rather than theological. The schism between the Churches of the East and West was not caused by such minor doctrinal differences as whether leavened or unleavened bread was used for the Eucharist—the reason was entirely political. On Christmas Day 800 AD, Charlemagne was crowned by the Pope as Roman Emperor of the West. From that moment the break with the Eastern Empire, with its own Patriarch and Emperor in Constantinople, was inevitable. The differences between the Eastern Orthodox Church and the Catholic Church today are largely the result of the diverging paths these two branches of Christianity have taken since that time, they were not important in initiating the split.

An archbishop in the Greek Orthodox Church officiates at an Easter service in Jerusalem. Orthodox priests, unlike their Catholic counterparts, do not take vows of celibacy; they play a role in the community similar to that of a Protestant minister.

Flip Schulke/Transworld Feature Syndicate

Economic and political considerations also underlay the Protestant Reformation. In the 16th century, nascent capitalism and the growth of the nation state gradually undermined the old concept of a united Christendom. These developments coincided with (and to some extent stimulated) a reforming trend in Christian theology in the newly powerful states of northern Europe. Luther in Germany, Cranmer in England, Calvin in Geneva and Knox in Scotland sought to simplify Christian doctrines and forms of worship. A split suited many rulers who resented papal authority, and a second great schism in Christianity was inevitable. The reaction of the Catholic Church was to become doctrinally more rigid, and the Reformation was opposed by the Counter-Reformation. Bloody wars between the opposing camps, in which religion was again less significant than territorial and economic considerations, were followed by relative peace.

Jesus was adamant in attacking the wealthy—('Woe unto you that are rich'). But the dedication to accumulating wealth through hard work came to be considered a virtue in Protestant Europe. There was soon a return to the Eastern Orthodox concept of a minister who

The Baptist minister Martin Luther King was awarded the Nobel Peace Prize for his non-violent struggle against racial inequality in the United States. King combined direct action against discrimination with a doctrine of love and understanding towards those who upheld it. He was assassinated in 1968.

marries and is part of the community (like a Jewish rabbi), rather than a celibate priest. The Protestants also abolished the monasteries (and nunneries) which were, and still are, an important feature of the Catholic Church.

Today, in the Catholic Church and the Eastern Orthodox Church, there are many orders for both men and women who take vows of poverty, chastity and obedience. Some teach or nurse the sick, others devote their lives to contemplation and prayer. Today, increased co-operation between all the Christian Churches and the search for common ground rather than differences is welcomed by all except those who have allowed dogma and doctrinal irrelevancies to blind them to the simple tolerance which Jesus preached.

Crucifixion was a method of execution the Romans learned from the Persians:

it was considered the most shameful, and reserved for slaves and those of no account. There can be few more painful ways to die. Reading the Gospel accounts of Jesus's agony on the cross it becomes clear that, like his birth, many of the details of his death are part of a ritual dramatization: the casting of lots for his clothes, the two thieves, the vinegar, are fulfilled Biblical prophecies. But Jesus did die at Golgotha, executed as a political criminal. And despite the over-laying of symbolism which appears in all four Gospels and later, often insensitive, interpretations, the human tragedy of his death is still real. Many details have the unmistakable ring of truth, such as the last anguished cry reported by both Matthew and Mark: 'My God, my God, why hast thou forsaken me?'

Christians believe that three days after his death on the cross, Jesus rose from the dead. Belief in the Resurrection marks the real beginning of Christianity and this dogma of hope even in death, together with the idea that Jesus, the Christ, died to redeem mankind, is largely the creation of Paul of Tarsus. It was Paul who believed in the universality of Jesus's teaching and who finally took the religion theologically beyond Judaism and geographically beyond Palestine. A Jew who had lived among pagans and knew the concept of a redeeming god who suffers, dies and rises again, Paul's powerful intellect welded together the many strands which made up early Christianity. His limitless energy took the new faith to Greece and Rome, laying the seeds which were to result in the adoption of Christianity by the Roman Empire. Paul of Tarsus created the Christian Church: in many ways he created Christianity.

Today the Churches of Christ are beginning to disentangle themselves from a compromising embrace with the State, and the cause of co-operation between the various Churches moves imperceptibly forward. And despite the persistence of dogmas which seem inexplicable and evil to many people, like the Catholic Church's prohibition of birth control, there is an increasing emphasis on programmes of social aid. Churches with falling attendances feel that a small and sincere congregation is preferable to one that is merely going through the motions of worship as a social necessity.

The future looks bright for Christianity, because despite the conscious and unconscious perversion of his doctrines, the re-writing and insensitive editing of the Gospels, the overlaying of myth through 2,000 years and the filtering through mediocre minds, the life and teachings of the man Jesus transcend it all. The Gospel of Matthew ends with the final prophecy: 'I am with you always, even unto the end of the world'. ☐

Religions of China

Europeans in China at the end of the 19th century sometimes expressed surprise that Chinese society had no formally organized, institutional religion. For answers to human problems inexplicable by contemporary knowledge or in moral terms—the supernatural side of religion—the Chinese people indulged in a vast number of practices and beliefs which, in Western eyes, amounted to nothing more than 'superstition'. The ethical functions of religion, on the other hand, were met by Confucianism, a secular orthodoxy in which China's scholar officials were indoctrinated.

These religious practices and beliefs were centred on temples, shrines, altars and places of worship all over China. They were devoted to the worship not of a single god but of many gods, each of whom had a different function, and the gods and their functions differed according to region, locality and the challenge of nature.

For the overwhelming majority of Chinese people this polytheistic tradition of functional gods was an essential part of a well-ordered religious system, encompassing Heaven, Earth and the underworld and constituting a supernatural hierarchy with the power to decide the fate of each and every man on the basis of his moral conduct.

The supernatural hierarchy was presided over by the monarch of Heaven, Yu Huang the Jade Emperor, to whom temples were dedicated in most parts of China. A heavenly court of gods including Taoist deities and deities of Buddhist origin formed the pantheon, beneath whom were the spirits of the earth such as mountains and rivers and the authorities of the underworld, such as Wu Tao Eskimo have learned to make stone East, West and Central).

This religious system, described by Max Weber as 'a chaotic mass of functional gods', ensured that religious life was both real and convincing for the Chinese. It was enhanced by the obvious correspondence between the hierarchy of supernatural beings on the one hand and the temporal hierarchy represented by the imperial government on the other—with the emperor presiding over his court of ministers and officials, the central administration, the provincial and local administrations. The Chinese people

Heaven and Earth are ruthless:
To them the Ten Thousand
  Things are but as straw dogs.
The Sage too is ruthless;
To him the people
      are but as straw dogs.
Yet Heaven and Earth
      and all that lies between
Is like a bellows
In that it is empty, but gives
      a supply that never fails.
Work it, and more comes out.
Whereas the force of words
      is soon spent.
Far better is it to keep
      what is in the heart.

Confucius, the great political philosopher, argued that harmony could be restored to the world only by the wisdom of exemplary rulers. His ethical and rational tradition endured for more than 2,000 years.

Mary Evans Picture Library

readily identified themselves with the inhabitants of the other world, and this increased the degree to which they were influenced by the political and religious systems.

The annual cycle of life was punctuated with festivals determined by common religious tradition and celebrated in the family. Yet they took place on a patterned, community-wide basis. The most important popular festivals in the cycle, based on the lunar calendar, were the New Year, Ch'ing Ming, Dragon Boat, Double Seventh, the Hungry Ghosts and the Double Ninth Festivals. These festivals are still celebrated in Taiwan province, Hong Kong and Macao and in overseas Chinese communities today.

The Dragon Boat festival was one of the few involving collective community action—inter-village dragon boat races were held in South China. One legend sees the race as a rain-making ceremony; another has it that the origin of the festival was to commemorate the death of the 4th century literary genius and political hero Ch'u Yuan, who killed himself by drowning, in protest against corrupt government. Rice dumplings were scattered on the water to feed the fish that would have eaten his body, while the splashing of the dragon boats' paddles was to scare off other fish, to symbolize attempts at Ch'u Yuan's rescue.

The Festival of the Hungry Ghosts occurred on the fifteenth day of the seventh moon when it was believed that malevolent spirits bereft of the consolation of ancestor worship are set free to wander for 24 hours, during which time they might claim living substitutes unless assuaged by money (specially printed and drawn on the Bank of Hell) and other offerings such as food. In Hong Kong it is still possible to see roadside fires where money, food and fruits are burnt to appease these hungry spirits and gain their gratitude.

Such festivals were mere punctuation marks in a calendar that determined days on which it was auspicious to travel, to ask the gods for blessings, to visit the barber, the tailor and so forth, covering all aspects of life and greatly influencing even the most well educated Chinese. But equally powerful an influence were the essentially rationalistic features of Con-

Claus Hansmann

fucianism, which played a role in China similar to that of Christianity in the West—the formulation and enforcement of moral values. But Confucianism set up no god as the premise of its teachings. At best it could be identified as a socio-political doctrine which touched upon ideas of heaven and fate in answer to certain human problems and developed a system dealing with the ultimate meaning of life; it was thus a doctrine with religious overtones.

On the eve of the present era, then, religious life was real for all Chinese. For the overwhelming majority the calendar or almanac guiding the activities of daily life was more influential than the august Confucian classics. And the Chinese were concerned much more with the functional efficacy of their gods than with any strict religious affiliation. Their preoccupation with the moral and magical function of cults had overlaid original theological contradictions and there was an almost complete disinterest in religious identity.

This was the result of a process of assimilation which had continued for centuries. Reconstructions of the early period before Shang (pre-1766 BC) suggest a clan-centred society in ancient China whose religious ideas included ancestor worship, animistic beliefs, concepts of heaven, grain and fertility gods and cosmological and calendrical theories. By the times of Shang itself, scapulimancy—divination from inscriptions on oracle bones—indicates sacrifices to nature deities and particular concern as to the link between ancestor and descendants.

After the Chou conquest in 1122 BC scapulimancy was supplemented by other forms of divination and religious activity became more systematized. The chief deity of the earlier dynasty had been

referred to as Shang Ti; it now became known as T'ien, or heaven. Chou kings were referred to as Sons of Heaven and assumed the role of mediators between Man and nature on the grounds that they enjoyed the 'mandate of heaven'. There was an ancestral temple of the kings where sacrifices were made to the supposed founder of the ruling house, an agricultural deity. Other sacrifices, made to heaven and earth, were probably the origin of the sacrifices continued up to the 20th century at the Altar of Earth and Temple of Heaven in Peking.

The middle and late Chou were periods of both political instability and great advance in Chinese thought. The decline of the established temporal and spiritual authority stimulated great philosophical activity, which coincided with the period of the Greek philosophers, the Hebraic prophets and Buddha in other centres of civilization. Significantly, however, Chinese philosophy was mainly humanistic—while still acknowledging Heaven, the spirits and supernatural beings, the emphasis shifted to focus on people as a social and political beings.

Philosophers became teachers and established schools of philosophy; it was against this background that Confucius emerged as the most influential philosopher of the period. He advocated a return from the anarchy of the present to the golden age of early Chou, stressing that government was an ethical problem to be solved by sound ethical conduct on the part of the ruler.

Confucius' thinking was conservative and therefore popular with the establishment, since it sought to consolidate the legitimacy of correctly exercised hereditary power. But it was also revolutionary, for it assumed the right to challenge the way hereditary power was exercised at

this time. This preoccupation with the improvement of government was responsible for the strong agnostic strain in the development of the Confucian tradition.

As it developed, however, the new tradition as expounded by those succeeding Confucius became something of a moral straitjacket, and this, together with the failure of Confucianism to curb despotic rulers, was responsible for the development of Taoism, a philosophy of protest and the next most important stream in Chinese thought at this time. Taoism was a reaction against conformity; the Tao or 'way' advocated in the texts was not Confucian, based on social and political patterns, but followed the pattern of nature.

Taoists stressed the mystical union of the individual with an impersonal natural order. The key to union with nature was the doctrine of *Wu Wei* or 'doing nothing', by which was meant not inaction but reliance on spontaneous achievement and avoiding activities that would upset the harmony of the universe. Thus, crime was a consequence of law and vice a consequence of virtue—Confucian moral precepts were deplored. Taoism was an excellent balance to the restricting social conformity of Confucianism and there is much evidence to show that neither was regarded as exclusive, since individuals and society frequently displayed attributes of both.

Before the advent of Buddhism, the third great literate tradition in China, both Confucianism and Taoism underwent changes. By Han times (206 BC–220 AD) Confucianism had become a synthesis of various schools of philosophy and popular religious ideas. At this point, the ideas of 'yin', 'yang' and the 'five elements', articulated much earlier by the Naturalist school of philosophy in an

(Left) A Wood-cut illustration of the 8 Immortals—the great teachers of Taoism. Stressing the human position in a vast natural order, Taoism urges its followers to preserve the harmony of the universe.

(Right) The Dragon Boat festival is still held annually in Hong Kong and other Chinese centres overseas. According to one legend, the boats imitated fighting dragons, to stimulate a real dragon fight in the heavens and so produce rain.

(Below) A New Year card shows the Door God, Yu-lei, in the guise of a general of the Tang period (618–907 AD). One of the major festivals in the Chinese calendar, New Year was a time for visiting relatives and worshipping the ancestors.

Marcus Brooke/Susan Griggs Agency

Claus Hansmann

attempt to explain nature's working, became popular.

According to such ideas, there was a basic dualism in nature comprising 'yang', being, for example, male, light, positive, and 'yin', being female, dark, negative. This constituted a complementary, interdependent and spontaneously balancing system. This school also claimed that nature was made up of combinations of five elements, wood, metal, fire, water and earth.

These principles led to the development of a pseudo-science including divination by earth, or 'fengshui', that has persisted throughout rural China to the 20th century. Taoism underwent similar change, and a major interest of Taoists became the search for immortality which led to alchemy.

The later Han period was dominated by the ethics of the founders of the Confucian school. In theory, this should have been advantageous to the system of centralized government, but with the emergence of great landed families its stress on ritual and scholarship proved of little use to a government struggling to maintain unity and economic viability. In practice its stress on family loyalties and filial piety contributed more to the challenge made by great landed estates to the central government. As the political and social order degenerated, Taoism, with its emphasis on the individual's relationship with nature, became the dominant stream of thought throughout China.

The political inadequacy of Confucianism also made the Chinese much more receptive to Buddhism, which first became influential in China during the first century AD. Soon Chinese converts who had visited India were propagating the religion and it spread from North to South China down through the rich and aristocratic circles to the peasantry, creating what is called the Buddhist age

The Temple of Heaven in Peking demonstrates the remarkable survival of different beliefs in China. T'ien, or heaven, became the chief deity after the Chou conquest in 1122 BC and Chou kings were known as 'Sons of Heaven'.

Emil Schulthes/Transworld Feature Syndicate

of Chinese history, from the mid-4th century to the end of the 8th century. Popular Buddhism and Taoism now amalgamated into a chaotic mass of religious practices and beliefs.

During this period, moreover, Buddhism itself was absorbed into the mainstream of Chinese culture. The method of absorption took two forms, intellectual and institutional. Intellectually, Indian schools of Buddhism were classified and those compatible with Chinese thinking flourished. One, better known as Zen, its Japanese name, was a development from primitive Buddhism and philosophical Taoism; this proved to be the most significant, outlasting all the others when Chinese Buddhism lost its identity.

Buddhism was absorbed institutionally because the fiscal menace of Buddhist monasteries increasingly removed large landholdings and considerable numbers of taxpayers from the tax register. Until taxation was related more closely to units of land Chinese administrations tried with only modest success to control the monasteries, even to the extent of incorporating them as a spiritual branch of government. But the difficulties of institutional control, coupled with the repugnance with which the Chinese viewed some Buddhist practices such as self-mutilation and cremation, were responsible for three major persecutions of institutional Buddhism, in 446, 574 and 841-845. The third persecution, in which 4,600 monasteries and 40,000 shrines were destroyed, dealt a mortal blow to organized Buddhism in China.

A Confucian revival occurred in China in late T'ang (618-906) and Sung (960-1297), coinciding with the Buddhist decline. This period saw a revival in the Chinese political state based on Confucian principles and, with the need for able administrators, a spread in Confucianism among the educated classes. It also saw the development of the philosophical synthesis known as neo-Confucianism. This marked the intellectual supremacy of Confucianism and brought developments in the application of Confucianism to social and political institutions that were to remain models until the revolution in the 20th century.

Despite the rigidity of neo-Confucian orthodoxy, which is often cited as the cause of China's subsequent slow economic progress and vulnerability in the 19th century, Chinese society was remarkably stable politically, socially and spiritually for a very long period. Even the

Mongol occupation (1279-1368), which exposed China to new religions like Islam and Christianity, failed to undermine this orthodoxy. In fact, when the Mongols were forced to leave China and a new dynasty, the Ming, was established, the Chinese turned back to the Sung, the T'ang and the Han for their inspiration.

The degree to which foreign religion could adapt itself to Chinese circumstances determined whether it would attract Chinese adherents and this yardstick may even be applied to the Chinese communist revolution. Significantly, it was only after Marxism-Leninism had been adapted to Chinese ways that it achieved lasting success. After four generations of predecessors had experimented with foreign ideas, Mao Tse-Tung succeeded in convincing intellectuals and peasants that the key to success in China's revolution lay in the 'creative application' of Marxism-Leninism to China. In the ensuing period,

the main threat to Maoism in China has not come from the political parties or institutionalized religion, but from Chinese tradition.

The main concern has been to ensure the security of Maoism by purging Chinese society of traditional beliefs and practices which might erode, and over a long period, absorb the new ideology. The available evidence suggests that in the struggle against theistic religions, particularly popular religions, there has been considerable success.

But the Chinese communists, being historically minded, are conscious of the fate of Buddhism, the only serious foreign ideological challenge to the Confucian tradition. They are therefore aware that the success of the new faith depends as much on maintaining satisfying social, political and economic conditions as it does on purging the Chinese society of the remnants of Chinese religious tradition. □

Islam

Perhaps the most haunting memory which the traveller brings back with him from the Middle East is that of the *muezzin* calling from the minaret of a mosque to bid the Faithful to their evening prayers. The long-drawn cry of '*Allahu Akbar*'—'Allah is Most Great'—introduces the basic statement of the Moslem faith, the *shahadah* or creed: 'There is no god but Allah: Mohammed is the Prophet of Allah'. The very name, Allah, emphasises the uncompromising monotheism of Islam. It means The God and thus by its grammatical form constantly reiterates His uniqueness.

The recitation of this 'word of witness' is the first of the five duties, the 'Pillars of the Faith', which Islam lays upon its adherents. In orthodox Sunni Islam, nobody who makes this statement may legally be excluded from the Moslem community. Like the other basic duties, its performance should be preceded by an inward or express statement of sincerity, the *niya*. Anyone therefore who makes this confession of faith intending to deceive, is not accepted. As the Moslem State expanded immediately after Mohammed's death to cover much of the civilized world, the definition of who was, and who was not, a Moslem, was important.

It is characteristic of the very personal nature of Islam, that the definition of a Moslem depends upon the individual's own action. He is not automatically born into the community, nor is he admitted on the promise of god-parents, for example, as in Christian Baptism, or by priestly intervention such as takes place in Confirmation. Becoming a Moslem is something a person does for himself.

Similarly with prayer, the second 'Pillar', the individual prays directly to Allah, without the intervention of a priest or the permission of a Church. The *Imam* who leads the worshippers assembled in a mosque is a leader only. He may have great influence as a leader, as a teacher and as an example of holiness, but he does not come between Man and God. The relationship between the individual and The One is direct: in the immortal words of the Koran, God 'knew a man before he was born and is closer to him than his jugular vein'.

Salat, prayer, is performed five times a day. There is a *hadith*, or tradition, that

In the name of Allah,
*   the Compassionate,*
*   the Merciful;*
Praise to Allah,
*   Lord of the two worlds,*
*   the Compassionate,*
*   the Merciful;*
Master of the
*   Day of Judgement;*
We worship Thee,
*   Thee do we ask for help;*
Guide us in the right path,
*   the path of those to whom*
*   Thou hast shown mercy;*
Not of those to whom
*   Thou hast shown anger,*
*   nor of those who go astray.*

elaborates on the occasion when the Prophet was said to have been carried to the seven heavens and there presented to the Lord by the angel Gabriel. The Lord at first made fifty prayers a day incumbent on the Prophet. But, on the advice of Moses, Mohammed returned several times and begged the Lord to reduce the number until only five remained. The Prophet was ashamed to return to ask for further reduction and so this became the prescribed number.

The basic 'unit' of prayer is a *rak'a*, or 'bowing', a series of recitations and movements which is repeated a different number of times at each of the five prayers. A worshipper commences by reciting the phrase '*Allahu Akbar*' with his hands raised and open on either side of the face. Then, standing, he recites the first verse of the Koran, the *Fatiha*, and other verses, holding his hands together at the waist. Next, he bows, placing his hands on his knees, and repeats the *Takbir*, *Allahu Akbar* and other praises of God. He then sinks gently to his knees, places his hands on the ground just in front of him and bends over to touch his nose and his forehead to the ground. After sitting back on his heels he repeats the prostration and then stands up again to begin the second *rak'a*. This is the same as the first but omits the initial *Takbir*. The whole set of

movements should be carried out in the same spot.

After each pair of *rak'as* he repeats more ritual salutations and ends by sitting to repeat his private prayers with the index finger of his right hand raised. After the last *rak'a* of each prayer the worshipper turns his head to the right and says 'Peace be upon you and Allah's mercy' and repeats this to his left. These greetings are perhaps addressed to the two guardian angels who look after each individual.

The whole process must be carried out as nearly as possible to the letter, and major deviations or mistakes mean beginning again. It is most improper, even sinful, to interrupt someone praying. After the prescribed prayers are over, the devout will continue to pray and recite texts, sitting. They will often tell the 99 beads of the rosary which remind them of the 99 names of Allah.

The Moslem day is reckoned from sunset, and so the sunset prayer, which requires three *rak'as*, is the first. The second, in the early evening, when it is dark, requires four. The dawn prayer is of two *rak'as*, and that of noon and mid-afternoon each have four. While it is considered good for all these prayers to be performed congregationally in the mosque, in practice most Moslems who say them do so privately at home or at work. Provided the ground or rug is clean, and the direction of prayer, the *qibla*, which is towards Mecca, is correct, this is acceptable.

The main prayers of the week take place on Friday at noon, when the faithful gather at the mosque. The Arabic words for mosque and for Friday both derive from the root meaning to assemble, and this idea is an important part of the Moslem sense of community. Developing as it did, in a society which is prone to division and faction, Islam is thus a powerful force in creating social cohesion. Social and religious teaching are inseparable in Islam, and the address given by the preacher *(khatib)* from the pulpit-like *mimbar* often contains elements of both just as the Koran does.

Mosques are usually provided with cisterns or fountains where there is a supply of running water, since a worshipper must wash in a prescribed manner before praying. At home a small copper vessel may be used, or a pottery jug called an *ibriq*. There are ritual salutations prescribed, too, for each stage of the ablution. This begins with a triple washing of the hands, and the right hand is then used to throw water three times into the mouth, and three times up the nostrils from which it is blown out while the nose is held with the left hand. Both hands are then used to wash the face three times. Then the right arm is triple-washed, next the left, and then the right hand is drawn once over the head and through the

The word of Allah, as revealed to the Prophet Mohammed by the angel Gabriel, is the basis of Islam. At the important crises of Mohammed's life Gabriel appeared to offer guidance or instruction.

Sonia Halliday

beard. The ears are attended to, then the neck, and finally the right foot and toes and then the left. This has obvious hygienic advantages in the dusty surroundings common in much of the Middle East.

Prayer thus plays an absolutely essential part in Islam. It is first of all an activity which the Moslem should perform often, and which serves therefore to remind him most constantly of the presence of God. The detailed prescription for the actions of praying aids concentration and emphasizes the equality of all in the sight of God. The bowing, particularly, emphasizes the basic meaning of the word 'Islam' which means 'surrender' to the will of God. It derives from the same s-l-m root as gives Arabic its words for peace (*salaam*), protection and greeting: all of these ideas are essential to

the relationship between people and Allah.

The third 'Pillar' of Islam is the giving of alms. strictly speaking *Zakat* is better called a tax, since it is prescribed at a fixed rate of one fortieth of a person's income. In early times it was regularly assessed, but it is now mostly left to the individual to pay. It is perhaps best seen as a prescribed gift to God via his earthly representatives, for the relief of poverty and suffering and for other religious purposes. A person may make additional, free-will, offerings, and can bequeath property to religious foundations, *waqf*. All such actions are considered meritorious and God will repay them many times over in Paradise.

The fourth 'Pillar' of the Faith is fasting. This takes the form of not eating or drinking during the daylight hours for the whole of *Ramadhan*, the ninth (lunar) month of the Moslem calendar. Since the lunar year and the solar year do not exactly match, *Ramadhan* progresses through the years, sometimes falling in winter, and sometimes in summer. When it falls in hot weather considerable strength of will is needed to maintain the fast. People who are engaged on a journey, or who are sick, during *Ramadhan* are excused fasting, but must make up an equivalent number of days later. Mohammed disapproved of anyone keeping the fast who could not do so without harming him- or herself. Nursing mothers, for example, are specifically excluded, as are young children.

Fasting encourage self-discipline and also reminds people of absolute duty of obedience to Allah. The small amount of suffering involved is held to be good for the soul and an antidote to pride. The many rules and safeguards which surround the practice also demonstrate the very pragmatic nature of Islam. It is meant to exalt, not to degrade, and takes careful account of what is possible in any given social and climatic conditions.

The fifth 'Pillar', *Hajj* or Pilgrimage, is in many ways the summary of the individual's whole duty to God. The essence of Islam is the 'giving' of oneself to Allah: in prayer one give time, in alms, wealth and in fasting, discomfort. In making the *Hajj* one give all three with the addition of the whole body, and even, perhaps, the family who may also be taken on the Pilgrimage. All are 'given' to God at His holy city, Mecca. Provided a person can afford it, should make the one Pilgrimage at least once.

For the performance of the ceremonies at Mecca a special white dress is worn. The Pilgrims visit the mosque in Mecca, run seven times round the *Ka'ba* and kiss the Black stone set into one corner of it. They also run between two small hillocks outside the sanctuary called Shafa and Marwa. On the 9th day of the month of the Pilgrimage (*Zul-Hajja*, the

Robert Harding/Robert Harding Associates

twelfth month of the Moselm year), the Pilgrims must attend a service and address at Mount 'Arafat, 20km (12 miles) to the east of Mecca. That evening the Pilgrims begin the journey back to Mecca and on the way, the next day, they offer sacrifices in the valley of Mina. Nearby there are stone pillars representing the Devil which the Pilgrims bombard with rocks. After the sacrifice at Mina the Pilgrims shave their heads, clip their nails and put on their normal dress: the essential ceremonies of the Pilgrimage are over. Many, however, will also visit the Prophet's Mosque at Medina to the north.

Many of the ceremonies performed are similar to those which existed before Islam, in the 'Time of Ignorance'. The Black Stone was preserved, for example, because of its association with another of God's prophets, Abraham (Ibrahim in Arabic). The Pilgrimage has always brought great profit to Mecca and fear of the loss of it was a major factor in the opposition of Mohammed's fellow-tribesmen, the Quraysh, to his preaching. It has been of incalculable value in bringing together Moslems from all over the world and has been of enormous importance in maintaining the Moslem and Arab sense of identity and community.

These five 'Pillars' represent the basic duties of a Moslem, but there are other social duties of a religious kind, enjoined by Islam. In fact, in all aspects of social,

Ritual washing precedes Moslem prayers and mosques, like this one at Meshed in Iran, have fountains for this purpose. Meshed is a centre of Pilgrimage for Shi'ites, who sometimes prefer it to Mecca.

The Muezzin, like this man from Morocco, calls the Faithful to prayer. His chant, 'Allah is Most Great. There is no god but Allah: Mohammed is the Prophet of Allah', is the basic Moslem belief.

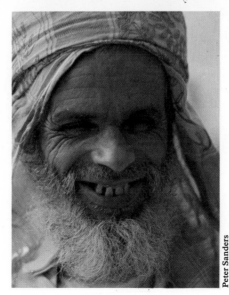

Peter Sanders

political, economic and legal matters Islam has developed a complex of attitudes based on Mohammed's teaching. One such duty, which is almost a sixth 'Pillar', is that of *Jihad* or Holy War.

In the early days of Islam, both in the initial period of Mohammed's preaching at Mecca, and after the flight, (the *Hijra* of 622 AD from which the Moslem era dates) to Medina, the intense opposition which Moslems faced from their countrymen made the duty of defence of the utmost importance to the survival of the community. In the years after the Prophet's death ten years later, the expansionist zeal of the Moslems carried them on a vast explosion of conquest. The *Jihad* took Islam across North Africa to the Atlantic in the west, and later across the Sahara to Sudanic Africa. The whole of the Middle East came under Arab domination, and the faith was carried far into central Asia. In the succeeding centuries it reached India and the Far East: it is still important in Malaya and Indonesia.

Even Europe did not escape. Crossing the Straits of Gibraltar, the 'Moors' swept up into Spain, which they ruled for many centuries, and even into France. Had they not been defeated at the Battle of Poitiers in 732 AD, the whole of Europe might have become Moslem. Much of the history of the Middle Ages is concerned with the Crusades, in which the

Christians fought the Moslems for control of the eastern Mediterranean and the Holy Places in Palestine.

In these circumstances, and in later reformist and revivalist movements, Holy War has meant war in a most literal sense. Such an interpretation was sympathetic and natural to the desert tribesmen of Arabia. Once the Moslems had established themselves, however, actual war became largely unnecessary and indeed an unsuitable activity for most of them. Within the community central government and the maintenance of the established hierarchy encouraged peaceful attitudes. One sect, the Kharijites, did maintain the idea of the 'internal' *Jihad* and asserted the duty of the community to depose the Caliph if he sinned, but their intransigence and violent methods brought them only limited support. The orthodox majority, the Sunnis, tended to play down the more uncompromising interpretations of *Jihad*, and the Kharijites, with their extremism, only survived in a moderated form in the Ibadi sect of Oman, Zanzibar and isolated peoples in the Maghreb.

The 'inner *Jihad*' was gradually reinterpreted as the Moslem's duty to strive

Islam was born amongst the desert Arabians and has remained and essentially simple and individualistic religion. It has always had an appeal to desert dwellers like the Tuareg of the western Sahara.

for the constant improvement of the community, to make it more truly Islamic, and to ensure that its social and political institutions kept to the correct paths of Islamic law and ethics. It became the duty of all Moslems to preserve and strengthen Islam in this way. Some found that the increasingly secular concerns which came to dominate the Caliphate were unsympathetic to this aim, and so began a more intensely and specifically religious search for a way to continue the 'inner *Jihad*'. In the Sufi movement which grew in part out of this desire, it found a degree of corporate expression.

A point worth noting, in this context, is the way Islamic institutions and practices constantly support and reinforce each other. It is no accident that the idea of 'war' should be reinterpreted in more peaceful circumstances. From the first the Prophet saw his teaching as a 'war' on ignorance and error. The idea carries through all spheres of Islamic social and political action and makes for coherence and integration between the various 'departments' of life. Islam is constantly adapting to new circumstances, and the separation between religion and the rest of life which has so reduced the effect, for example, of Christianity, has not gone as far in Islam. It is still quite hard to live in a Moslem country and not be a Moslem, because the effects of Islam on society are still all-pervasive. The signs are, in modern urban areas in the Middle East, that this integration is declining, and members of

The Moslem day begins at sunset, when the first of the five daily prayers are said. While some people go to the mosque, like this one at Kano, most will pray at home.

Every Moslem should make the Pilgrimage to Mecca once in his life if he can afford to do so. At the end of the main ceremonies the hair is shaved and the white Pilgrimage dress replaced by normal clothes.

Andrew Baring

Peter Sanders

the Moslem intelligentsia are devoting great efforts to finding ways of preserving it and to the continued adaptation of Islam.

In some ways Islam is particularly well equipped to undertake this process of continuous revision, because of the nature of 'authority' within it. There are in fact four sources of religious and social teaching which are acceptable as authoritative, in varying degrees, to the Moslem, and all find their basic roots in the teaching of Mohammed.

This teaching is mainly enshrined in the Koran, which was sent down by God from the highest heaven to the angel Gabriel in the lowest. Gabriel in turn revealed it, section by section, to the Prophet. Secondly, there is *hadith*, the collections of tradition in which Mohammed's immediate followers preserved his sayings and the manner of his life (*sunna*). This is an important source of additional material to the Koran, and offered a means of expanding and 'interpreting' the basic message. From these two sources it is possible to argue by analogy (*qivas*) and this gives the third source of doctrinal authority, while the fourth is *ijma*', the general consensus of opinion within the Moslem community. Thus equipped, it has always been possible for Islamic

theorists to innovate in practice while preserving the overall principle of a single source of authority, the word of God as revealed to and by the Prophet.

Mohammed was born in 570 AD to a respectable but relatively poor family of the Quraysh tribe of Mecca. His father, 'Abd Allāh died before his birth and he was brought up in his early years by his paternal grandfather. 'Abd al-Muttalib. He lost his mother at six years old and his grandfather died when he was eight; he then came under the care of his uncle, Abū Tālib. It was his uncle who first took him on trading journeys into Syria and on one of these journeys he was employed to transport the merchandise of a rich widow called Khadija. She was so impressed by Mohammed's honesty and integrity that she offered herself to him in marriage. He was about 25 years old at the time and she was 40. She bore him two sons, who died in infancy, and four daughters. One of these daughters, Fatima, became the wife of Mohammed's cousin Ali, the recognized divine successor of Mohammed by the Shi'ah branch of Islam.

When married to Khadija, Mohammed took no other wives and did not re-marry until after her death when he was fifty years old.

The Arabia of the 6th century AD was pagan, and a number of gods were worshipped. There were both Christians and Jews living there, however, and Mohammed may well have learnt more of these religions in the course of his travels. Many of their doctrines and many people mentioned in the Bible also feature in the Koran. Mohammed saw himself as part of the same prophetical tradition, and as the natural heir of Abraham, Moses (*Musa*) and Jesus (*Isa*). Opinion is divided as to whether Mohammed could read and write: he perhaps could not and it is unlikely that he had access to written accounts of Jewish or Christian doctrine. He contemplated making Jerusalem the focus of prayer (the *qibla*), and it is still considered by Moslems as a Holy City.

There was an enduring tradition in Arabia of individuals seeking religious inspiration through seclusion, meditation and often fasting. Such people were called *hanif*, and were respected by the Meccans. Mohammed's first revelation came to him when he was 40 at Hira outside Mecca, where he had withdrawn to pray. The angel Gabriel came to the Prophet with a cloth of brocade on which there was writing and commanded him to 'read', in the sense of to read out, or recite. The word used, '*iqr*, is the same as that in Isaiah where a voice said 'Cry!'.

Mohammed at first said he could not do so, but Gabriel pressed the cloth on him, and Mohammed, in terror, asked what he should read. Then was revealed *Sura* XCVI of the Koran:

Read!
In the name of thy Lord, thy Creator,
Who created Man from clots of blood,
Read, for thy Lord is most generous,
Who taught Man by means of the pen,
Who taught Man what he knew not.

The short, epigrammatic style is typical of the earlier *suras* of the Koran (which are the later ones in the present arrangement: the later chapters, revealed at Medina, having been placed first). The very great force and conviction which these Meccan *suras* carry helps to account for their acceptance by the initially small band of devoted followers of the Prophet.

Mohammed was terribly frightened by his experience and relied heavily on his wife Khadija's support and comfort. He also became depressed when further revelations did not come, until Gabriel appeared again and revealed *Sura* XCIII:

By the Bright of Day!
And the night when it is dark,
Thy Lord has not forsaken thee, nor
hated thee, and the next life will
be better for thee than the first . . .

The same *sura* continues with verses which sound very familiar:

Did (thy Lord) not find thee an orphan,
and give thee shelter?
And erring, and guide thee?
And poor, with a family to keep,
and feed thee?
Oppress not the orphan: drive
the beggar not away.
And of the goodness of the Lord,
Declare it!

Mohammed's preaching was at first secret and confined to his own immediate circle. Even some of his closest relatives opposed him and he and his followers suffered oppression and danger. Had it not been for the protection of his uncle Abu Talib, it is probable that he would have been killed: certainly he would have been prevented from teaching.

Eventually many of his followers fled from Mecca, and shortly afterwards the Prophet had to do so as well. They were received at the city, north of Mecca, called Yathrib, which thereafter bore the name *Medinat en Nabi*, City of the Prophet, the modern Medina. Even there life was not easy for the Prophet, his followers from Mecca and his Medina helpers, the *ansar*. Many who were secretly opposed to his preaching pretended to be converted: these are the Hypocrites so often reviled in the Koran.

The relationship between the Moslems and the Jews of Yathrib was also difficult. Some Jews accepted Mohammed, some

Islamic law and social customs influence all aspects of life. The position of women is carefully defined, and while under their husband's authority they have firm claims on his time and protection.

tolerated him, some opposed him. Eventually he felt compelled to fight them and killed many. But the main fighting of the Medina years was against the Prophet's own tribe of the Quraysh from Mecca and their allies. The Moslems sometimes acted provocatively: they once attacked a Meccan caravan during the sacred month of the Pilgrimage, and this led to the famous battle of Badr, where the Moslems were victorious.

In connection with this battle Mohammed had to lay down rules governing the distribution of spoils obtained in Holy War, and the *Sura* VIII, the Chapter of

the Spoils, is typical of the more extended, legislating *suras*, which characterise the Medina period of Koranic revelation. The influence of events on the content of the Koran is also seen very clearly.

Badr made total conflict with the Quraysh unavoidable: it had become clear that the whole spiritual and even temporal control of the Mecca region was at stake. Even in Medina matters were becoming difficult for the Moslems. Both Jews and Hypocrites were causing trouble and over the next few years Medina saw a number of murders and considerable unrest.

The next battle of consequence was at Uhud: it went badly for the Moslems and the Prophet himself was nearly killed. It took a little time to restore confidence and discipline: the dead of Uhud were honoured as martyrs. Two years later the Moslems were again victorious,

Gianni Tortoli/Colorific!

submit to him. Mohammed returned to Medina and from there sent envoys to advertise the Faith to the rulers of Rome, Abyssinia, Byzantium, Persia and many other places. He died shortly afterwards, in 632 AD and the Moslem community at Medina proclaimed Abu Bakr 'Caliph' or successor to the Prophet as the religious and political head of Islam. Abu Bakr was succeeded by 'Omar and he in turn by Uthman. It was under Uthman that the Koran was given its present form.

The overthrow of the fourth Caliph, Ali, the son-in-law of the Prophet, and the usurpation of the Caliphate by Mu'awiyya, led to the schism in Islam between the Shi'ites who supported the descendents of Ali, and the Sunni, or orthodox Moslems. The Sunni were in a majority and the main political centres of Islam thus became, successively, Damascus, Baghdad, Cairo and Constantinople (Istanbul). As a result of the steadily increasing Turkish pressure from the 13th century, Arab domination of the Moslem world declined. From the 16th century most of it came within the Turkish Empire and with the defeat of the Turks in the First World War, the political power of the Caliphate came to an end.

In the course of the 1,200 years which elapsed between the conquests of the 7th and 8th centuries, and the great changes of the 20th century, it is not surprising that Islam should itself have changed. New political responsibilities, the incorporation of many non-Arab peoples into the Islamic State, the development of large cities and of economic systems quite different to those which were familiar to the Arabians, have all meant that the social and legal prescriptions of the Koran have had to be developed to keep pace. What is remarkable is the way in which the essential bases of Koranic teaching have been preserved. Islam, as it is practised by most Moslems, is probably a great deal closer to its founder's original opinions than, for example, Christianity is. This is largely the result of the prohibition on altering the Koran and even, strictly speaking, on translating it, because it is seen as the actual word of God. The Koranic basis of education and literacy in the Moslem world also, incidentally, accounts for the way classical Arabic—the language of the Koran —has also changed so little.

The development of Islamic law has been a process of the greatest complexity. The process began with the Prophet himself sitting as a judge over the community at Medina. His decisions were absolute, but took existing usage into account. The custom of Jews and Christians was specifically protected, as they were peoples 'of the Book', that is, they had accepted God's revelation. They, had, however, to pay a special tax if they did not accept Islam when their lands had

helped by a ditch, the first time such fortification had been used, apparently, in Arabia. After this Mohammed was even strong enough to contemplate the conversion of foreign rulers: the Moslems were, however, not yet sufficiently strong to command victory against the Byzantine Emperor.

In 630 AD they did succeed in the final conquest of Mecca and the surrounding tribes who had resisted Islam. The Prophet threw down the idols of the *Ka'ba* and established himself as the supreme commander and law-giver of Arabia. Tribal delegates came from all round to

The Koran has formed the basis not only of religious instruction, but of most literacy and education in the Islamic world. This Moro girl in the Philippines is being taught to read with the Koran.

Ted Spiegel/John Hillelson Agency

From the 16th century the Ottoman Turkish Sultans ruled the Moslem world from Istanbul. As Caliphs, the successors to Mohammed, they claimed both religious and political authority which ended with their defeat in the First World War.

been incorporated into the area controlled by Moslems.

The recording of the Prophet's decisions doubtless began when he was alive, and immediately after his death the process of codification marched together with the recording of the definitive version of his revelation in the Koran. The example of the Prophet, in law as well as religion, is fundamental, for to the Moslem there is no real separation between the two. Thus *sunna* became the subject of *hadith* and is a basic source for Islamic law. As the Arab conquests proceeded, Roman Law and other existing systems came to be incorporated in Islamic Law as part of the process of adaptation to empire.

The Abbassid Caliphs of Baghdad encouraged legal studies, and it was during their reign that the four main schools of Islamic law grew up. These were the Hanafite school, the Malikite, the Shafi'ite and the Hanbalite, all named after their founders. The four bases of authority, the Koran, *hadith*, *qiyas* and *ijma*, were formulated by Shafi'i and accepted by the other schools, although some minor schools disagreed. The doctrines of the four schools have developed, but their basic positions have shown a great deal of consistency.

Islamic law distinguishes carefully the exact degree to which an action is in accord or at variance with basic tenets of faith. Forbidden actions are *haram* (—the same root as *harem*, thew area of the house forbidden to strangers), while some actions are obligatory (*fard, wajib*). Between these come categories which are recommended (*mandub, mustahabb*), or those which are discouraged, (*makrub*). Finally there are those which are neutral (*ja'iz, mubah*). In addition there is in each Moslem country a 'code' of customary practice (*'adat*) overlying this orthodox base.

There are, therefore, many areas of life which would be outside legal jurisdiction in most societies but which are legally controlled for the Moslem. Perhaps most important in this regard is the law of the family. A Moslem is permitted, as is well known, up to four wives. The husband must treat them all equally, and devote the same amount of attention to each. The law also lays down detailed rules as to inheritance, and the duty each child has of supporting his parents in old age. Rules concerning adultery, divorce, the proper conduct of the *harem*, all come within the sphere of Islamic law. It will deal with purely religious matters

on the one hand, like blasphemy, and on the other with matters called criminal in other systems, like murder and blood-compensation, theft and usury (which is forbidden to Moslems).

Even the calendar is part of Islamic law. It lays down when the months begin, especially where this is vital for religious practice, such as in fasting. The year is structured on religious events like the Pilgrimage and the Fast, and on the great festivals like the *'Id el Fitr* (Festival of Breaking the Fast) and the *Mulid* or Prophet's Birthday. The Shi'ites also celebrate the descendants of Ali, Hassan and Hussain in the *Mulid el Hassaneyn*.

Throughout the 1970s and early 1980s a revival of Fundamentalist Islamic precepts was seen in the Middle East, especially in Iran, whose people are predom-

inantly Shi'ite Moslem followers.

Some of the legal provisions with the most far-reaching effects are those concerning food and drink; e.g. a Moslem should not drink alcohol or eat pork.

Essentially, Islam, in all its aspects—religious, social and legal—is a system of balanced exchange. A woman gives herself to a man and is given support and protection. Parents give birth to children, support them when young, and are supported by them in return in their old age. Between the family and the tribe, between the section and the city, between ruler and ruled, the same system of balanced reciprocity pertrains. Above all the system governs the relationships between people and God. People perhaps get the better of the bargain; they give 'surrender', but gain peace. ☐

Communism

Communism seems to stir stronger feelings than any other ideological system. It has millions of ardent supporters, and many million more live in countries where the régime claims to follow the principles laid down by Karl Marx. Communism also has fanatical opponents, hysterically denouncing 'reds under the bed'.

But reality is obscured by the emotive images called up by partisans—of Chinese peasants happily chanting the praises of Mao Tse-tung, or of lost souls rotting in a Siberian labour camp. A more rational approach is to see Communism as one particular analysis of the world, with its own historical and social origins and producing its own ideas about how society should be organized.

Survival for human beings is not an individual process. Social organization and collective activity have always been an essential part of living. But different societies place different levels of emphasis on the individual's rights or duties. The industrial West puts a high premium on the principle of individual 'liberty'—in practice the individual's economic and intellectual freedom to advance himself. A consequence of this is an acceptance of inequality, leading to extremes of wealth and poverty.

Communism appeared in reaction to such extremes, and was developed as an ideology in the 19th century, when exploitation and social injustice were most clearly apparent. Since then, in a series of revolutions and acts of conquest, more than a dozen other countries have acquired 'Marxist' or 'revolutionary socialist' governments. The emphasis in these countries is on collective activity and the position of the individual is very different to that in the West.

The earliest indications of modern Communism appeared in England, which was more advanced economically than any other country in the 17th and 18th centuries. In the late 1640s and 1650s, the English Revolution or Civil War briefly established a 'Commonwealth' and per-

Communism has precedents in a long tradition of experiments in social equality. Robert Owen's establishments in England and Scotland provided workers and their families with exceptional conditions in the 19th century.

manently advanced the power of the gentry and merchants. In their struggle for power, these newly prosperous classes mobilized the support of the lower orders for their own ends.

The middle class sought to establish the right of property, to prevent arbitrary taxation and to enforce the sovereignty of a parliament with voting rights based on the ownership of property. As so often in history, however, the landless agricultural labourers, poverty-stricken farmers and workers of the towns had their own, far more radical, aspirations.

The most dangerous idea of the so-called Levellers was that leaders should be overthrown and all people exist as equals. In a remarkable parallel with events in the Russian army before the 1917 revolution, Cromwell's officers were challenged and even deposed by their own men, to be superseded by elected 'agitators'. In 1649 a still more radical development took place. A group of about 20 families, known as the Diggers or True Levellers, seized waste land on St George's Hill not far from London and began a programme of communal farming, owning all their goods in common.

The reaction was swift. The Leveller leaders were arrested and quickly put to death; and continual harassment finally drove the Diggers out of the St George's Hill commune. Yet it is clear that the Diggers were not an isolated phenomenon. In the upheaval and ferment of ideas thrown up by the middle class revolt, the

concept of private property was questioned by the lower orders at the very time it was being established.

A similar process took place during the French Revolution of 1789. The middle classes rose to throw off the yoke of the *Ancien Régime*, riddled with corruption and restrictive economic practices. By the winter of 1795–96 the Revolution had passed into a period of reaction, culminating in the rule of Napoleon. The government, which represented the interests of financiers and merchants, had abandoned the idealism of the Revolution and was allowing the working people of Paris to die of cold and hunger in the streets.

In this situation, The Society of Equals, led by Francois Babeuf, sprang into prominence, placarding the whole of Paris with demands for the abolition of private property. Babeuf, however, was arrested the day before his plan to seize power came into effect. Although he was never in a position to alter the course of events in any substantial way, Babeuf's ideas began a Communist tradition in France that still persists. His argument, in many ways anticipating Marx, was that the evils of society, from immorality to hunger, are the result of economic and political inequality.

Another early example was Robert Owen's attempt to lay the foundations of a more just and prosperous society based on industrial effort. Owen was a Welsh-born mill owner whose workshops in

England and Scotland were immensely successful in the early years of the 19th century. Moved by a deep humanitarianism, he was horrified by the ruthlessness of the new capitalist classes.

Like Charles Fourier in France, who had seen the population of Marseilles starving after his employers dumped a cargo of rice into the sea in order to force up the price of grain, Owen became convinced that the interest of one was the interest of all and put this principle into practice in his own factories, paying higher wages and ensuring better conditions than any of his competitors. He could even claim to be proved correct, for the output and discipline of his workers was extraordinarily high.

Unfortunately, Owen's system worked only when he was there to supervise it, and owed more to the benevolent strength of his personality than to any universal truth about paternal management. His failure was plainly demonstrated by his most ambitious project—the communal society at New Harmony, Indiana, set up after he abandoned corrupt Europe for the United States in 1826. Owen invited settlers to the community to escape from the three great oppressors of mankind: 'Private Property, Irrational Religion and Marriage'. The invitation apparently attracted swindlers and layabouts as well as honest workers, and Owen had to watch the project collapse in a little over three years.

Robert Owen reacted in a particularly high-minded way to the injustices created by the industrial revolution, which gave rise to extremes of degradation and poverty as landless workers flocked into newly founded slums in search of a living. By the middle of the century, however, these urban workers had found political leadership and the two main trends in socialist thought had emerged.

On one side, Marx and Engels proclaimed the theories of Communism, on which all modern Communist societies depend. On the other, the Anarchist ideal was born, and although this has not become the recognized system of any country, it has been the driving force in several revolutionary situations, providing a theoretical framework for activities as widely separated as communes and terrorism.

After their first meeting in 1842, Karl Marx (1818–83) and Friedrich Engels (1820–1895) spent their lives in exile from Germany, working towards the creation of an international workers' state. Their *Communist Manifesto* has been translated into literally hundreds of languages and few would dispute that their writings rank among the most influential literary works in history.

The basic theory of Marxism was thought through by Marx alone, and his phenomenal insight and singularity of purpose created an all-embracing philosophical system for revolutionary activity. Engels, on the other hand, was responsible for many of the more approachable writings and assisted Marx generally for nearly 40 years.

Marx's ideas grew out of the mechanical philosophical system put forward by Hegel, the German Idealist, at the beginning of the century. This saw history as a process in which a force (the *thesis*) gave rise to its own opposite (or *antithesis*), and the clash of the two produced a third, higher state (the *synthesis*). Hegel saw this process leading through thousands of years of human history to create the ideal form of human society in the Prussian monarchy.

Marx rejected this naive conclusion and applied the theory to contemporary society in quite a different way. He saw the economic and political domination of the *bourgeoisie* (the owners of industrial and financial capital) as the thesis and the *proletariat* (the exploited industrial workers) as the antithesis. The synthesis arising from this *dialectic* would be the establishment, through a process of revolution, of a classless society in which property ownership would be abolished.

In Marx's system, the revolutionary party would play a central role. After the inevitable seizure of power by the workers, a socialist state would be established with a strong centralized government (the 'dictatorship of the proletariat'). Leading this, the workers' party would direct the transformation from a system of private ownership and investment to one of nationalization and public investment.

The class-ridden nature of society would gradually be eroded and it would eventually be possible to abolish the state altogether, all men living as free individuals working in collective harmony for the common good. The maxim of this society would be 'from each according to his abilities, and to each according to his

Trotsky, Lenin and Stalin (below) dominated the development of Russian communism, setting trends which may still be seen today. (Above) Lenin addresses a crowd of factory workers, the backbone of the 1917 revolution which swept the final remnants of Czarism and capitalism from Russia (right). Stalin took control in the Soviet Union after Lenin's death in 1924; his emphasis on 'socialism in one country' was opposed to Trotsky's ideal of world revolution, which committed the Bolsheviks to support socialists elsewhere. Stalin hounded Trotsky out of Russia, eventually having him assassinated in 1940. Eastern Europe today is largely Stalin's creation—his policy of 'imposing revolution' (far right) went against Marxist thought.

needs'.

Marx and Engels were by far the most important revolutionaries in the 19th century, but their influence was not universal. Their leadership of the international revolutionary movement was soon challenged by the Anarchists, or 'Libertarian Communists'. Pierre-Joseph Proudhon (1809-65) had denounced the state as the principal enemy of the workers, to be totally abolished and replaced by a system of free association between individuals. According to Proudhon, 'property is theft'—so private ownership must be instantly abolished, not allowed to continue into the first years of the socialist society.

The major difference between the Anarchists and Marx, however, concerned the role of the state. To Anarchists, the idea of a 'revolutionary government' was an absurdity and the abolition of the state must be the immediate aim of the revolution. Mikhail Bakunin (1814–76) developed this concept, arguing that the revolution would contain the forms of the society it would go on to create. Marx's centralized party would thus lead to an authoritarian, centralized state, as bad as that which it replaced.

Converting the ideas and aspirations of revolutionary theory into reality proved difficult for Communists—Libertarians and Marxists alike. Marx saw revolutions occurring first in the most advanced capitalist countries, such as Britain, Germany or the United States. In fact, the first successful revolution took place in backward, semi-feudal Russia and had to wait until 1917.

Russia's susceptibility was the result of a number of factors, exacerbated by disastrous defeats in the First World War, and including the particularly effective organization of the Russian Bolshevik Party. The Revolution began in February with the overthrow of the Czar and the establishment of a Provisional Government headed by the liberal Kerensky. By October, however, the Bolsheviks had built up sufficient support in the 'Soviets' —councils of workers, peasants and soldiers that had sprung up throughout Russia—to carry out the coup led by Lenin and Trotsky.

Once in government, the Bolsheviks faced enormous problems. A counter-revolution began almost immediately, with sections of the army joining parties of the centre and the right in an attempt to smash the new government. The administration of the country began to collapse and a bitter civil war began.

The image of the Soviet Union in the modern world is of a huge and powerful centralized state, under repressive single-party rule with rigid control over social and political dissent. It is difficult to reconcile this with the high idealism of the Marxist tradition and of the original Bolshevik leaders in particular, to whom words such as 'democracy' and 'freedom' had great importance.

One explanation of Russia's failure to build the just an equal society promised by the Bolsheviks is to be found in the first years of its foundation. The Bolsheviks came to power largely as a result of their centralization and discipline, and when the civil war endangered their position this feature became even more necessary. In a situation of continuing emergency, the political opponents of the régime were silenced, one by one.

Even after the White armies, aided by the British, French and American expeditionary forces, had been defeated, imminent economic collapse led to further social unrest. Soon, opposition to the policies of the Party's central committee, the Politburo, was silenced within the Party itself. At the same time, huge state and Party bureaucracies grew up, administering the vast task of modernizing the Soviet economy. Very quickly, a figure of great administrative ability and political skill rose to the positions of greatest power within this complex machine—Joseph Stalin.

The Soviet Union today is very much Stalin's creation. When Lenin died in 1924, Bolshevik leaders were surprised to find so much power concentrated in the hands of this administrator. They, the heroes of the Revolution, had to bow to the inevitable and accept his supremacy. Stalin immediately began the task of ridding himself of his rivals. Trotsky, for example, was exiled and constantly hounded until Stalin's agents finally assassinated him in Mexico in 1940.

Stalin's absolute rule lasted until his

ТОВ. Ленин ОЧИЩАЕТ ЗОНТ ОТ НЕЧИСТИ.

DANSE CAUCASIENNI

POLOGNE TCHEC PAYS BALTES ROUMANIE BULGARIE HONGRIE CHINE ALLEMAGNE FRANCE

Garuba/Magnum

Moro, Roma

death in 1953, by which time the USSR was totally in the grip of extreme, unbending bureaucratic rule. Without exception, rivals to Stalin's power had been systematically exiled to Siberia or executed after show trials of ludicrously apparent injustice. No one is quite sure how many millions died at the hands of Stalin's repression. He accomplished the total centralization of power in Russia that still remains.

On the other hand, the material achievements of the Soviet Union should not be ignored. The Soviet people enjoy prosperity unthought of in Czarist times. Soviet technology rivals that of the West, as the success of the space programme shows. What appears to be lacking is any direct response to the desires of the people. Decision-making devolves from above through the descending committees of the Party. Trade unions and local govern-

Thousands of European communists joined the International Brigade to oppose Franco's Fascists in the Spanish Civil War. But the Communist Party's decision to suppress both Anarchists and Trotskyists caused considerable disillusionment.

ment bodies alike are mere agents of central policy.

Soviet citizens are well fed, clothed and generally comfortable, yet they have no say in how much of the wealth they produce is to be spent on the military machine and how much on goods for their own consumption. Dissident intellectuals are still persecuted and political opposition is consistently silenced. Lenin's original demand for 'all power to the Soviets', with its implications of direct and free democracy, seems to have gone by the board.

Yet there is substantial equality of opportunity, for education is freely available, though conditional on political orthodoxy. Production has been nationalized. Factories and farms are centrally controlled but often collectively operated. Different work is still rewarded at different rates of pay, although the differences are small compared with those in the West. In a survival from the past, some marginal lands are still farmed on a smallholding basis.

Another result of Stalin's rule was a change in the international aspect of Communism. Marxism involves a fundamental insistence on the links between

workers of different nationalities, behind the slogan 'workers of the world unite, you have nothing to lose but your chains'. Stalin instituted a new policy called 'Socialism in one country', which basically meant that the Soviet Union was no longer obliged to aid all revolutionary movements throughout the world.

Each country would have to pursue its own revolutionary course, with Soviet assistance at the Party's discretion, rather than of necessity. The Soviet Union would not be bound to antagonize Western countries where that was against her own interests. At the same time Stalin encouraged a policy of 'popular fronts' whereby Communist parties should try to co-operate with socialists and liberals in order to become 'respectable' in what Stalin felt was no longer a revolutionary situation.

The most extraordinary result of these policies, quite contrary to the teachings of Marx and Lenin, occurred in Spain during the Civil War of 1936 to 1939, in which Communists actively participated in suppressing manifestations of revolutionary zeal. Spain had a strong Anarchist tradition, going back to the time when Spanish members of the International had

Robert Capa/Magnum

Henri Cartier-Bresson/Magnum

In imperial times, China had little industry, and Mao's revolutionary strategy was based on the country-side rather than the cities. The legendary 'Long March' (below) marked the low-point in the Party's fortunes (1934–5); among the first tasks after victory in 1949 was the construction of dams for irrigation.

supported Bakunin against Marx. In the Republican areas of Spain during the Civil War, the Anarchists began their long-awaited process of collectivization with the help of Trotskyists and other Socialists. Restaurants, factories and farms were taken over and converted into workers' collectives under the democratic control of the workers themselves.

Literally hundreds of collective farms sprang up on lands seized from former landlords, ranging in size from about 100 to 5,000 persons. Governed by 'general assemblies', meeting perhaps weekly and consisting of all the members of the collective, many such farms could claim considerable success, raising the level of production substantially. On many collectives, the general assemblies also administered the justice and policing of the community, electing a committee to co-ordinate their activity, even to the extent of determining what wages should be paid.

All this was part of the Anarchist intention to establish a loose federation of independent collectives, freely trading with one another throughout Spain and requiring no central government. In Barcelona this meant, for example, that the cinema collective would arrange to issue a number of tickets to a local farming collective in exchange for food.

Meanwhile, the Spanish Communist Party consolidated its power in the Republican government and then turned on the Anarchists and Trotskyists, arresting their leaders and decollectivizing the farms. To observers such as George

Orwell, the English writer, this was a great betrayal and an intensely disillusioning experience. Communist Party supporters would argue that it was necessary for the successful conduct of the war.

Franco's Fascists eventually won the Spanish Civil War, destroying the Anarchist dream and leaving the Soviet-inspired Communist parties firmly in control of revolutionary activity elsewhere in the world. Since the Second World War, however, this picture has changed, for in 1949 the Chinese Communist Party established the Chinese Peoples' Republic, after prolonged wars against Japanese invaders and then American-backed Nationalists.

In the years since 1949, China has been transformed from a backward, poverty-stricken nation, torn by the interventions and exploitations of foreigners, into a major world power. At the same time, it is the country that the people in the West

find most difficult to understand, a mystery compounded by the bitter feud between China and the Soviet Union, and by Mao's 'Cultural Revolution' of the 1960s, which involved much publicized harassment of Western journalists and missionaries.

There is no doubt that Chinese society is very different from anything in the West, but it is important to realize that a great deal of what seems strange in Chinese Communism is more Chinese than Communist. Mao modified the doctrines of Marx and Lenin to suit Chinese conditions. Without a substantial proletariat, the major oppressed class in China was the peasantry, so Mao decided to base revolutionary activity in the countryside rather than the cities, establishing 'liberated areas' that could be defended against counter-revolutionary attack.

After the revolution, China embarked on a period of isolation during which foreign visitors were excluded. This was intensified by American policy, which denied China a seat in the United Nations or diplomatic contact with the West.

During this period, the process of making feudal China a modern Communist state was begun. The land was collectivized, the old landlords driven out or executed and their property expropriated, and a colossal programme of industrial development was set in motion. Much the greatest problem facing Mao and the Communist Party was the educational backwardness, illiteracy and traditional conservatism of the peasants.

A massive campaign of ideological struggle was launched, based around the personality cult of Mao and using his *Thoughts* in the form of 'The Little Red Book' as the central text for study. This campaign reached a climax with the Cultural Revolution in the mid-1960s when the party leadership felt that the economic and educational gains of the people were going stale.

As in Russia, the Party itself was taking too much of a lead, its committees making the decisions and its members enjoying the privilege and prestige of established bureaucrats. To combat this, the people were given a vigorous push to take control of the progress of the revolution themselves, behind the spearhead of the young Party members of the 'Red Guard'. Everyone was to be taught the peasant way of life. Since Mao's death in 1976, however, reports have shown that China was virtually under a reign of terror during this period. Anyone suspected of criticism or 'decadence' was liable to be rounded up by the Red Guards, paraded about in disgrace, beaten, tortured, or sent for near-slave labour. Nearly 35,000 innocent people were put to death, and 730,000 severely persecuted.

Several factors distinguish Chinese from Russian Communism. In China social control is exercised largely on the basis of encouragement rather than punishment. Minor offenders, for example, are tried by their co-workers with a Party official present to give advice. The process is most noticeable in schools, where constant reward is given to children for promising work or correct behaviour. On the other hand, there is no more liberty in a Western sense in China than in Russia. People in China have little freedom to move and are encouraged to stay in their localities rather than move to the towns.

At the same time, there is an attempt

Although the communist ideal is to create a society in which all men are equal and work for each other, expedience requires the creation of heroes. Mao Tse-tung, Fidel Castro and Ho Chi Minh have each been the subject of a personality cult.

(Below) Since the revolution, China's peasants have been organized in village communes and productivity has increased. The position of women has been much improved, but they still earn less than men for doing the same work.

(Below) Cuban students plant coffee on the Isle of Youth. As in China, the communists seek to develop an understanding of the value of physical labour in the educated sections of the community.

(Below) Refugees from Hue land at Da Nang during the last months of the Vietnam War. The fall of Saigon—now renamed Ho Chi Minh City—was a major victory for communism, especially in the area of South-East Asia.

'Workers of the world unite! You have nothing to lose but your chains.' A Chinese propaganda poster stresses the international aim of communism—a goal dismissed by capitalist opponents as imperialism, particularly in Africa.

to blur the distinctions between town and country, between technical and manual workers, and between men and women. Equality of education and very limited differentials in wages have already been established. Chairman Mao was on the upper of only two basic grades of pay, with another two slightly lower for women —an anomaly under attack in China as in the West.

The experience of other Communist countries tends to be based on the influence of either China or the USSR. Eastern Europe, liberated from German occupation at the end of the Second World War, tends to fall firmly under the Soviet thumb. Attempts to assert national independence in Hungary in 1956 and in Czechoslovakia in 1968 were ruthlessly crushed, but Tito's Yugoslavia fought a dogged battle with the Kremlin throughout the 1950s and established virtual autonomy. Yugoslavia has since made a series of compromises with capitalism, allowing small businesses to operate privately and following a pro-Western foreign policy. The odd-man-out is Albania, which consistently supports China against the Soviet Union and in 1981, Polish workers made an attempt to change their status within the system.

Cuba is perhaps the most interesting of the smaller Communist states, for it is firmly within the Russian political orbit and yet has spontaneously evolved social forms similar to those of China, including a personality cult—that of Castro. There is less emphasis on the development of revolutionary consciousness in the masses through propaganda, but there is a similar encouragement of the growth of local influence over production, housing and justice. Despite early setbacks, a similar enthusiasm for the revolution can be found in the countryside.

The Cuban approach to participation is summed up by a recent building scheme in Havana. New apartment blocks are being built at government expense to be available at low rents, but priority on the application list is given to workers who help the building programme in their spare time. Disputes about the allocation of the flats are decided by committees of the workers involved. In ways such as this, it is hoped that the bureaucratic aspects of Russian life will be avoided.

Many revolutionary movements are active in the non-Communist countries of the Third World. With the exception of those in South-East Asia, however, few have grown to a position where they can

seriously challenge for state power. In the West, countries like Italy and France have influential Communist parties, dominated by the popular front ideas of the 1930s. These parties seem from time to time to have a chance of being elected to government and are no longer revolutionary organizations, but legal, parliamentary parties.

To the left, a myriad of Trotskyist and Maoist groups operate in all Western countries. With largely student memberships, they maintain the revolutionary fervour of the Bolsheviks but are without the substantial base in the working class

In Western Europe, the revolutionary left has failed to win any substantial following since the war. The 1968 uprising in France saw a rare but shortlived alliance between students and trade unions.

they seek. A smaller number of Anarchists and Libertarian Communists also operate in constantly interchanging groups, waiting for a situation to arise more propitious for revolution. Very rarely, a group of this type—such as the Angry Brigade in Britain or the Baader-Meinhoff Group in West Germany—takes up Bakunin's call for revolutionary terror with an isolated bombing campaign.

Occasionally, the revolutionary left is capable of more concerted and broadly based action, as in the Paris student revolt of 1968. The rising only partially supported by workers, yet committed and organized Maoist and Anarchist groups were able to confront the power of the state, controlling parts of the city for some days.

Through Western eyes, the anti-liberal aspects of Marxist ideology demonstrated in Communist societies often seem little short of barbarous. In Marxist terms, however, such coercive acts are both necessary and correct. For Communists, anti-revolutionary activity is as criminal as theft in the West. Until 'bourgeois individualism' finally disappears, restrictions on freedom are considered necessary.

Nonetheless, Communist societies have made enormous material progress. Both the Soviet Union and China were economically backward, and both are now wealthy and powerful, demonstrating the effectiveness of centralized economic planning. Attempts to do away with exploitation and social injustice have also been largely successful.

These countries may have gone only a short way towards creating the Communist society envisaged by Marx, but they have certainly done much to create the material conditions by which he set great store. The problem remaining for Communists is the establishment of realistic dialogue between centralized government and the people. □

Giancarlo Botti/Camera Press

Giancarlo Botti/Camera Press